MYTHS AND LEGENDS OF FLOWERS, TREES, FRUITS, AND PLANTS

Third Edition 1911
Charles Skinner

New Edition 2020
Edited by Tarl Warwick

MYTHS AND LEGENDS OF FLOWERS

COPYRIGHT AND DISCLAIMER

The first edition of this work is in the public domain having been written prior to 1926. This edition, with its cover art and format, is all rights reserved.

In no way may this text be construed as encouraging or condoning any harmful or illegal act. In no way may this text be construed as able to diagnose, treat, cure, or prevent any disease, injury, symptom, or condition.

MYTHS AND LEGENDS OF FLOWERS

FOREWORD

This fine work is one of the foremost botanical guides I have ever personally had the pleasure of reading. Crafted in the sweet spot of occultism (roughly from the 1880s through the 1920s) between the pre-rational and philosophically "modern", it is mainly a compilation of three types of lore: Ancient legend, Christian legend, and then-modern folk tales.

The ancient legends tend towards the Norse and Greco-Roman Many of those tales are fairly well known (particularly tales such as that of Narcissus and Echo, the latter pining away for the former, the former eventually staring into his own reflection until he too succumbs, unable to sleep or eat because of his own egotistical regard for his physical form.) Others are a bit more obscure.

The Christian legends are mainly from tales of the high middle ages told after that era had actually ended; much of that lore is religious in nature and has to do with some permutation of Jesus, Satan, or the Virgin Mary. It is most lopsidedly catholic in origin. We may regard the tale of Saint Patrick converting the Irish to Catholicism by assuaging their confusion over the idea of a trinity by pointing to the leaves of the shamrock (at once a single leaf in three lobed portions.)

It is most amusing to see the folklore of the era in which this work was actually made, since it was modern then but is now over a century old. We have tales even today about botanical things. Some of them are semi-true; such as the modern folk tale about morning glory heaven (that you can go there if you eat morning glory seeds.) The seeds are psychoactive and contain chemicals similar structurally (but less potent than) LSD.

MYTHS AND LEGENDS OF FLOWERS

It is perhaps interesting to note that some species are considerably more noteworthy than others- a dozen pages are dedicated to the rose, and long passages to species such as the willow and oak, while some species are worthy of only a minor inclusion- a few sentences, or a paragraph. Were a second edition made today, there would surely be more entries since just in the last twenty years, the advent of the internet has vastly expanded botanical folklore and its availability in a manner not seen since perhaps the same era in which this work was itself penned.

This edition of "Myths and Legends of Flowers" has been carefully edited for format and content. Care has been taken to retain all original intent and meaning.

MYTHS AND LEGENDS OF FLOWERS, TREES, FRUITS, AND PLANTS

PLANT LORE

When the legends and fables of simpler times pertain to trees and flowers, they are especially luminative of the mental processes of unschooled men; for the vegetable world has changed little in three thousand years, and the marks and colors that explain some beliefs are still impressed on the leaves and petals. The symbolism adopted therefrom is wide in meaning, and to this day is in common use. It is poetic, hence it appeals to every intelligence; for while we affect to prize poetry for its beauty, to the savage it was native speech, inasmuch as his vocabulary was allegoric- a humanization of the skies, the sunsets, the storms, the flowers. We sometimes hear that ours is a material, dull age, yet we perpetuate terms and usages which ally us to the childhood of the race, and which stand for imagination and sheer loveliness. We still speak of laureled brows, palms of victory, the rose of beauty, the lily of purity, the oak of strength, willowy grace, fig-trees of shelter, and corn of abundance; we extend the olive branch of peace, we put our legs under our host's mahogany, we indicate poison by nightshade and toadstools, and health by flowers and fruits. Though Bacchus is no longer with us, we emblemize him in our reference to the vine. Moreover, states and nations choose their flowers, and certain Scottish Highlanders still wear them as badges of their clans. The liking for these things, their service to the eye, antedates history, and although Shakespeare lived when there was no botany, and only an enjoyment of nature in place of the study of it, his chance mention of one hundred and fifty trees and plants hints at the regard such matters enjoyed in those days.

MYTHS AND LEGENDS OF FLOWERS

The very religions of all lands have fruits and trees in their cosmogonies, and plant-lore opens a quaint human document in its disclosure of that self-complacency which assumed the earth to be a strictly human property, in which all was for the service of man, and nothing existed of its own right. Out of this notion came the doctrine of signatures- "a system for discovering the medicinal uses of a plant from something in its external appearance that resembled the disease it would cure." For instance, the leaves of aspen shook, hence it must be good for shaking palsy; gromwell had a stony seed, so it was prescribed for gravel; saxifrage grew in cracks in the rocks, therefore it would crack the deposits known as stone in the bladder; knots of scrophularia were prescribed for scrofulous swellings, the pappus of scabiosa for leprosy, the spotted leaves of pulmonaria for consumption (notice how these beliefs and uses have named certain species), nettle tea was for nettle rash, blood-root for dysentery, turmeric for jaundice, because it was the color of a jaundiced skin; wood sorrel, having a heart-shaped leaf, was a cordial, or heart restorative; liverwort corrected an inactive liver; dracontium, or herb dragon, was a cure for snake poison; briony cured dropsy, because its root suggested a swollen foot. The estimate of plants is denoted not merely in their common use as food and ornament, but in the adoption of their names by people, civilized and other. Until the goddess Carna was invented, Italy's soil produced no vegetables without men's help, excepting spelt and beans; hence in her particular feasts the usual offering was beans. In the Roman courts or in public bodies where questions were put to vote, the ancient ballot was a bean, a white one representing innocence; a black one, guilt. Such, then, was the importance of the bean that we need feel no surprise that one of the foremost families in Rome, the Fabians, to wit, should have taken the name of it. The Coepiones of that day were merely the Messrs. Onion; the Pisones were the Peas; Cicero was Mr. Chick-pea; the Lentucini were the Lettuce family. To this day we have in like wise, among our friends, the Pease, Beans, Pears, Cherrysy Berrys, Olives, Coffeys, Nutts,

MYTHS AND LEGENDS OF FLOWERS

Chestnuts, Oakes, Pines, Birches, Roses, Lillies, and Asters, while our Indians, excelling us in variety and fitness of names, give such to their daughters as Wild Rose, Budding Poppy, and Bending Lily. And as it was honorable to employ the name of a plant, a tree, a flower, in naming a dignified family of a dignified race, it came about easily that such plant or tree or flower was in place about the homes, the tombs and temples, of that family, and that in time it was borne upon the family coat-of-arms.

Names do not always mark resemblances, for they are sometimes freaks of accident or have gone astray through wrong spellings. For instance, our "butter and eggs" was originally bubonium, because it cured buboes- then; but a slip in a letter made it bufonium, and as bufo is toad, we have the name of toad-flax, which means nothing. In like manner, Jerusalem artichoke was twisted into girasole artichoke; tansy is alleged to be a corruption of athanasia, or immortality, though what the two have in common no man can guess; while borage is a mispronunciation of courage, for that (cor-ago: I bring heart) was supposed to be heightened by drinking decoctions of the herb. When the doctrine of signatures began to transcend the visible signs written on the flower or leaf, it widened the possibilities of medical practice wonderfully. Thus, the holy or blessed thistle (carduus benedictus), at first a cure for itch, became by force of its blessed state a sovereign remedy for sores, vertigo, jaundice, bad blood, red face, red nose, tetter, ring-worm, plague, boils, mad-dog bite, snake poison, deafness, defective memory, and other ailments. Another variety of the plant, the "melancholy thistle," was a cure for the blues if taken in wine. But the thistle was not the only blessed plant, by any means. One species after another developed saintly associations, and by virtue of them became a cure for more than its "signature" would indicate.

All flowers that bear the name of lady were dedicated to Our Lady the Virgin. Such are the lady's slipper, lady's hand, lady's tresses, lady's smock, lady's mantle, lady's bedstraw, lady's

MYTHS AND LEGENDS OF FLOWERS

bower, lady's comb, lady's cushion, lady's finger, lady's garters, lady's hair, lady's laces, lady's looking-glass, lady's seal, lady's thimble, and lady's thumb. Beneficent influences exerted by plants thus fortunately named or associated were instanced in a wider crop of superstitions than had grown from the mystic or significant markings, but the sanctifying of plants through their association with saints and angels was no new thing in Christian times. The heathen gods had their floral favorites, and the first garland was culled from the trees of heaven by the Indian Venus, Cri, who put it on the head of Indra's elephant.

The animal, intoxicated with the perfume, flung the wreath to the ground, thereby so angering Siva that he cursed Indra for permitting the sacrilege and threw him to the earth also, thus condemning him to lose his vigor, and all the plants on earth to lose eternal life. The Greeks and Romans planted sacred flowers in their gardens, those especially loved by the Greeks including the rose, lily, violet, anemone, thyme, melilot, crocus, chamomile, smilax, hyacinth, narcissus, chrysanthemum, laurel, myrtle, and mint. Laurel, narcissus, hyacinth, myrtle, cypress, and pine were nymphs or youths transformed from human shape; the mint was a woman whom Pluto loved; the mulberry was stained with the blood of lovers; it was Lycurgus's tears that begot the cabbage. The plane sprang from Diomede's tomb. The rose-tinted lotus arose from the blood of a lion slain by Hadrian. The vine sprang, by miracle, near Olympia, and sports and ceremonies incident to its festivals in early Hellas are perpetuated as faint memories in the use of the eucharist and loving-cup. It took some of the early investigators a long time to overcome their repugnance to making practical use of plants associated with legendary harm and violence; indeed, accurate observation of the remedial effects of plant juices and decoctions is a matter of recent days, although we find tokens of therapeutic study in other centuries. The rosemary had no "signature," but we discover reason in its use, whether the effects agreed with the allegation or not, in that it was prescribed for carrying by mourners and attendants at funerals two hundred years ago, the odor being hostile to the "morbid effluvias" of the corpse. It was also burned in the chambers of fever patients. So, in time, this rose-of-Mary (it is really *ros marinum*) because a token to wear in remembrance of the dead, and later it was prized as a stimulant to all memories.

Poisons appear to have been studied almost as early as simples. Forbidden things of the dark were used in incantations, and the mysteries of diabolism and magic could not have been practiced without vegetable material. Monkshood was used to breed fever; deadly nightshade caused the eater of it to see ghosts; henbane threw its victim into convulsions; bittersweet caused skin eruptions; meadow saffron and black hellebore racked the nerves and caused their victim to swell to unsightly proportions; briony set the nose a-bleeding; eyebright sowed seeds of rheumatism in the bones. Larger and finer meanings are read into the older legends of the plants, and the universality of certain myths is expressed in the concurrence of ideas in the beginnings of the great religions. One of the first figures in the leading cosmogonies is a tree of life guarded by a serpent. In the Judaic faith this was the tree in the garden of Eden; the Scandinavians made it an ash, Yggdrasil; Christians usually specify the tree as an apple, Hindus as a soma, Persians as a homa, Cambodians as a talok; this early tree is the vine of Bacchus, the snake-entwined caduceus of Mercury, the twining creeper of the Eddas, the bohidruma of Buddha, the fig of Isaiah, the tree of Aesculapius with the serpent about its trunk. These trees of the early cosmogonies are not all actualities, by any means. There is no botanical class for the tree of Siberian legend, which sprang up without branches. God caused nine limbs to shoot from it, and nine men were born at its foot; fathers of the nine races. Five of the branches, that turned toward the east, furnished fruit for men and beasts, but the fruits that grew on the four western branches God forbade to men, and he sent a dog and a snake to guard them. While the snake slept, Erlik, the

MYTHS AND LEGENDS OF FLOWERS

tempter, climbed into the western branches and persuaded Edji, the woman, to eat the forbidden fruit.

This she shared with her husband, Torongoi, and the pair, realizing their guilt, covered themselves with skins and hid under the tree. These relations between the human and the vegetable world are also indicated in legends of curses and blessings, wherein faiths have grown from incidents, and in not a few of these instances the fortunes of men, towns, and even dynasties are related to trees. The old pear of the Unsterberg, for instance, would signify the end of imperial power by withering, and when the German empire was dissolved in 1806 it ceased to blossom; but in 1871 it suddenly woke to life and bore fruit. To primitive people who thus symbolized natural phenomena, vegetable life was, in a manner, glorified, because it sustained all other life. The tree supplied lumber, fuel, house, thatch, cordage, weapons, boats, shields, and tools, as well as fruit and medicine.

Everywhere the flowers are a calendar of the seasons, and in early moral codes and proverbs the tree is a likeness of strength and graciousness. The Brahmins have fitting metaphors for the kindness of the oak in shading the woodman who hacks its trunk, and of the sandalwood that responds to the blow of the ax with perfume, the meaning of these symbols being that the perfect one will love his enemies. The mystic is added to the symbolic through the ages, in that the leaves have been speaking to those who listened. The palm, stirring in the wind, spoke to Abraham in language that he translated as the words of deity, and Mahomet commands its worship as the tree of paradise, the date being chief of the fruits of the world, for it came out of heaven with wheat, chief of foods, and myrtle, chief of perfumes.

MYTHS AND LEGENDS OF FLOWERS

EARLY CHRISTIAN LEGENDS

A throng of legends bring to mind Christ's agony and crucifixion, and some of them are betokened in usages of the present day. For example, it is believed in Austria that hawthorn and blackthorn were the materials from which the wreath of torture was fashioned; hence on Good Friday there is a sport of retaliation in which Christian hoodlums put "thorn apples" into the hair of little Jews.

The veritable crown was reported by the faithful to have passed into the hands of Baldwin, who gave it to Saint Louis. That king received it as a penitent, barefooted and clad in a hair shirt, bore it to Paris in splendor and solemnity, and built that perfect piece of Gothic architecture, the Sainte Chapelle, as a casket for the relic, though some of the thorns have been given to other churches, and they have as miraculously multiplied as have fragments of the true cross. The hawthorn is so covered by white blossoms in the spring that its long spikes are hardly seen, but they are capable of inflicting a painful wound. On the way to Calvary a bird fluttered down to the head of the Victim and pulled out a thorn that was rankling in his brow. The sacred blood tinged the feathers of the little creature, who has worn the mark since that day, and we call him robin red-breast. Hawthorn often flowers in a mild English winter, and the famous one of Glastonbury habitually puts forth blossoms at Christmas; at least, it is known to have been in bloom on Christmas day so recently as 1881. This holy thorn is- or, shall we say in our doubting time, was- believed to have been carried into England in the year '31 by Joseph of Arimathea, when he went to teach Christianity to the Britons. On reaching Wearyall Hill, near the present town of Glastonbury, he struck his walking staff into the earth to indicate his intention to abide there; and leaving it thus, with its end in the soil, the sap stirred to fresh life, put forth leaves, and flourished for centuries, a noble specimen.

MYTHS AND LEGENDS OF FLOWERS

Some declared that it bloomed at the moment when the rod was forced into the frozen ground. The sale of its flowers, twigs, and cuttings brought large revenues to the monastery that was built near the scene of the miracle. It was finally destroyed by the Puritans as a reproof of the superstitions charged upon the followers of the Roman church. Another famous hawthorn is that of Cawdor Castle, scene of the "Macbeth" tragedy. The first thane of Cawdor was told in a dream to load an ass with gold, allow it to wander free, and build a castle where it stopped to rest. This the dreamer did, and the donkey lay down under a hawthorn.

The heavenly injunction was so implicitly obeyed that the architect built the first tower with the hawthorn in the center, and its aged trunk is still seen in the dungeon, its branches penetrating the breaches in the wall, and its root extending far under the flagging. Once a year Lord Cawdor assembles his guests about the trunk, and they drink health to the hawthorn, thereby signifying health to the house. Some maintain that Christ's crown came from the acacia, or shittim wood, while others say that the holly was the bush from which the crown of thorns was torn. Indeed, the name of the latter means "holy," and it was only through a careless shortening of the vowel that it came to be as we know it. The use of this plant for Christmas decoration still further proves this association with Scriptural incident. The purple of the jack-in-the-pulpit and the red stain of the Belgian rood selken mark where the blood of the crucified fell in the hour of agony, as the color of the red bud, or Judas tree, tells how the tree burned with shame when Judas hanged himself upon it. Speedwell, or germander speedwell, is in the botanies disguised as *veronica chamoedrys*, yet in that name is a token of its history, for on the way to Calvary Christ paused for a moment while Saint Veronica wiped the blood and sweat from his face. The cloth she used in this ministration was stained thereafter with a miraculous portrait of the Savior a *vera ikonika*, or true image; whence, Veronica. Where the blood dropped on

MYTHS AND LEGENDS OF FLOWERS

the flowers she was wearing, they shared in the sacred impress, and so they took her name, because they are thought to show a human countenance like that upon her napkin.

Cyclamen- "cock of the mountain," the Arab calls it- strange flower with bent back, curved petals, and crimson eye looking down, as if expectant of the earth to yield treasure to it, abounds in Holy Land, where it was dedicated to the Virgin because the sword of sorrow that pierced her heart is symbolized in the blood drop at the heart of this flower. For the like reason it was also known as the bleeding nun. Other legends respecting the crucifixion are indicated in the name of "blood drops of Christ," as applied in Palestine to the scarlet anemone; in the selection of the flowering almond as a symbol of the Virgin; in the repute of the bulrush, or cat-tail, that it was the scepter that the Jews put into the hands of Christ when they mocked him as their king; in the monkish declaration that the red poppy contains a divine revelation, since it bears the cross in its center; in the Canary Islands the custom of cutting bananas lengthwise because when cut across they show the symbol of the crucifixion; and in the story that the figs of the Cistercian convent in Rome, when cut through, show a green cross inlaid on a white pulp, with five seeds at its angles representing the five wounds. The Rose of Sharon is also held to be a symbol of the resurrection, for when its blossoms fall they are borne by the wind to a distant place there to root and bloom anew. Vervain (*verbena hastata*), once used for garlanding the poor brutes led to the sacrifice in Rome, has long been known as the holy herb. The Greeks so called it; the Druids and Romans employed it in magical and mystic ceremonies, and as a drug; hence it was easily adapted into the Christian legends, and it became one of the crucifixion flowers. Because the spurge yields a milky juice, it is called Virgin's nipple, though we lack a tradition that connects the plant with any word or act of the Virgin. The white lily as well as the hierochloa, or holy grass, is sacred to her. "Madonna lilies" burst into bloom on Easter dawn; they put forth from the rod of St.

MYTHS AND LEGENDS OF FLOWERS

Joseph, and were borne by the angel of the annunciation. Walking in the garden of Zacharias, whither she often repaired to meditate on the burden laid upon her as the bride of God, the Virgin touched a flower which till then had exhaled no fragrance, but at that contact gave forth a delightful perfume. This was doubtless the lily. A careless use of the name by older writers leaves us in doubt as to the plant referred to in the sermon on the mount.

The little flower we call Star of Bethlehem, whose bulb is roasted and eaten by orientals, is part of that very light which shone in the heavens at the birth of Christ; for after it had led the wise men and shepherds to the manger it burst, like a meteor, scattering acres of flowers about the fields. It was as if it had been drawn from the glorious company of the skies by the great glory of the Babe. Joseph, going out at dawn, gathered handfuls of these blossoms from the wintry earth, and, pouring them into the lap of Mary, said, "See, the star in the east has fallen and borne fruit in kind." Then, there is hellebore, otherwise black hellebore, Christmas rose, or Christmas flower. This was held in estimation from early times, though it was believed to absorb its ill odor from the sick. The Greeks regarded it as a remedy for madness, and in sending the insane to Anticyra, where it abounds, they afforded one of the few instances of anything like attention to the needs of the suffering and unfortunate in a land and age that were without almshouses, hospitals, and asylums. Down to the time of Queen Elizabeth it was the hellebore cured melancholy, and the Germans, who connected it with Huldah, the marriage goddess, later gave to it the name of Christmas rose. The story of its birth is this: On the night when heaven sang to the shepherds of Bethlehem, a little girl followed her brothers, the keepers of the flocks, under guidance of the light. When she saw the wise men gathered at the inn, offering vessels of gold and fabrics of silk to the child and its mother, she hung timidly back on the edge of the crowd, and was sad because her hands were empty; because the look in the face of the babe had filled

MYTHS AND LEGENDS OF FLOWERS

her with admiration and wonder, and she wished to testify her love. She had no goods, no money to buy them, so after a little she turned away toward the silent hills. But when she had gone back to her flocks, at the border of the desert, under the lonely stars, a light suddenly shone about her, and behold, one of the announcing angels- a glorious creature whose robe was like molten silver, whose locks were as the sun. "Little one, why do you carry sorrow in your heart?" he asked. "Because I could carry no joy to the child of Bethlehem," she answered. With a smile the spirit waved a lily that he carried, and suddenly the ground was white with Christmas roses. The girl knelt with a joyous cry, filled her arms with the flowers, and hastened to the village, where the people made way for her, looking with wonder on the burden she bore that winter night. As she reached the manger the holy one, turning from the gems and gold of the magi, reached forth his tiny hands for the blossoms, and smiled as the shepherdess heaped them at his feet.

The chrysanthemum, which was born at the same time as the babe of Bethlehem, was the token to the wise men that they had reached the spot whither the star had bidden them; for, searching along the narrow ways of the village toward the fall of night, these rulers of tribes and expounders of doctrine wondered greatly what should be disclosed to them. There was no excitement among the people, to denote a strange event; there were no welcoming sounds of music, dancing, or the feast; all was silent and gloomy, when at a word from King Malcher, the caravan stood still. "It is the place," he cried, "for look! Here is a flower, rayed like the star that has guided us, and which is even now hanging above our heads." As Malcher bent and picked it, the stable door opened of itself and the pilgrims entered in. Malcher placed the chrysanthemum in the hand extended to receive it- the hand of a little, new-born babe- and all went to their knees before the shining presence, bearing as a scepter the winter flower, white likeness of the guide star.

MYTHS AND LEGENDS OF FLOWERS

Cacti are of power over witches, and that queer specimen of the race, the "'old man," with its long gray spines like hair, is to the Mexican the soul of a baptized Christian, hence not to be touched by unclean hands.

FAIRY FLOWERS

Flowers were as naturally associated with fairies as with sunshine, moonbeams, and other bright, beautiful, or tricky things. The "little people" hid in flowers, made their cloaks of petals, their crowns of stamens, their darts of thorns, their cradles of lilies, their seats of fungi. As the burly gods of the Norsemen and the majestic deities of Greece represented nature as force, so the fairies impersonated nature's gentler, daintier attributes. They were the souls of the flowers, mischievous when the flowers exhaled a poison; beneficent when the flowers were wholesome.

The mottlings of the cowslip and the foxglove, like the spots on butterfly wings and on the tails of pheasants and peacocks, mark where elves have placed their fingers. On the foxglove these marks are dull and threatening, denoting of the baneful juices that the plant secretes, and which as digitalis (digitus: a finger) we turn to account in our pharmacopoeia. This evil quality gives to it the name of dead-man's thimbles in Ireland, and its patches are held to resemble those on the skins of venomous snakes. In Wales, the plant is known as the fairy glove, but it is Virgin's glove or "gloves of our Lady" in France, while in old English herbals it is witch's glove, fairy thimble, fairy's cap, folk's glove; yet in Norway Reynard claims it again, for there it is fox bell. A legend of the North is that bad fairies gave these blossoms to the fox, that he might put them on his toes to soften his tread when he prowled among the roosts. The anemone is a fairy shelter, curling up as night or storm approaches, and thus protecting its occupant, but the wee creatures sit oftener in the cowslip cups, and those human and undoubting souls that can listen at such a time with the ear of

MYTHS AND LEGENDS OF FLOWERS

childhood hear a fine, high music, like a harmonized hum of bees. This oftenest comes from the flowers when the sun is shining on them. In England the cowslip used to be the key flower, or key wort, or St. Peter's wort, because the umbel is supposed to resemble the bunch of keys carried by St. Peter; indeed, the Germans still call it the key of heaven.

Fairies protect the stitchwort, and it must not be gathered, or the offender will be "fairy led" into swamps and thickets at night. One of the oddest of beliefs is that St. Johnswort and ragwort are a day disguise of fairy horses. If you tread them down after sunset a horse will arise from the root of each injured plant and that night will gallop about with you, leaving you at dawn either at home or far abroad, as it may happen. They have a kinder plant in China, although it bears the name of sin; for, being eaten, it changes a man to a fairy and gives him a long lease of youth. England has a fungus known as fairy butter, and our country has fairy rings of toadstools and coarse grass that spring in the footsteps of the sprites as they dance. The fruit of the mallow is fairy cheese, toadstools are fairy tables, and the tiny cup fungi, like nests with eggs, are fairy purses. Our elm is elven, or elf tree, and fayberry is a name still extant for gooseberry. In Denmark a fairy is an elle, and elle-campane and elle-tree, or alder, are favorites with the "little people." Should you stand beneath an alder at midnight on midsummer eve, you may see the king of the elles, or elves, go by with all his court. The alder has understanding, too, and will weep blood if it hears talk of cutting it down. Originally the alder and the willow were two fishermen who refused to spare time from their labors to join in the worship of Pales, whereupon the goddess turned them into those two trees, and to this day they haunt the banks of streams, leaning over them as if watching for fish, and the willow letting down its lines into the water.

MYTHS AND LEGENDS OF FLOWERS

NARCOTICS AND STIMULANTS

We who eat and wear and smoke the plants and drink their sap and juices find in them not only sustenance and shelter, but dreams, medicine, and death; the sharpening and dulling of our nerves; support for the weak and refreshment for the fainting. We find, moreover, oblivion and inspiration, so frail an instrument is this whereby we move and think, and so obedient to suggestions from without. There are persons so sensitive that a breath of air blowing from poison ivy will cause them to break out in an unseemly manner, though we are told that Indians make themselves immune to its outward poison by the occasional eating of its leaf. Out of the visions created by the action of drugs on the brain or nervous centers have come not merely the consecration of plants themselves, but the growth of religious practices and beliefs. We find in nearly all cosmogonies a recognition of the tree, and at this day among savage tribes vegetable life is exalted, as is that of humanity and the animals, in rites, observances, and faiths. The use of plants among priests and medicine men indicates their remedial value in disease, and whatever confers health or happiness is by implication heavenly in its origin. It is an article of savage faith that certain of these plants are universal in their power, though we may doubt if serpents eat fennel to sharpen their sight, or hawks eat hawkweed for the same purpose. It is a fact, however, that cats, dogs, and other carnivorae resort to herbs as medicines and stimulants.

The mescal (*anhalonium Lewini*) is a variety of cactus that grows in the desert all the way from Oklahoma to Mexico, and from it the aborigines gather the bean or button which, in Moqui phrase, enables man to commune with God. The plant is revered in the same manner as is the rattlesnake who bears away the prayer for rain after the snake dance. Mescal produces on the optic nerve something of the same effect as rubbing the eyes. In spite of governmental and scientific objection, it continues to be used, and apparently causes a local inflammation or congestion which reflects itself in a sense of bright colors in kaleidoscopic patterns and shifting clouds. To obtain these consolations, the bean is swallowed, and the colors sometimes take on fantastic shapes wherein one reads prophecy. Few, if any, races have escaped the influence of narcotics and stimulants, and, inconsistent though it seem, those who do with the least of them are not the most progressive peoples. The Chinese smoke opium, it is true, and the Indians tobacco, but civilized man has accustomed himself to opium, tobacco, wine, tea, coffee, and cocaine. The use of plants that estranged the senses from their sane functioning accounts for not a few religious practices.

The Druids made their altars under the oak because that tree inspired to prophecy. Brahmins drink soma, the juice of *asclepias acida*, to obtain second sight, for it is "the essence of all nourishment." The Delphic oracle ate laurel leaves, sacred to Apollo, to hasten the toxic effect of the volcanic gases which ascended the cleft where the sacred tripod was placed. Prophets slept on beds of laurel, also, as certain dream interpreters among the Russian peasantry sleep on beds of "dream herb," or *pulsatilla pateus*, for a like purpose. Among stimulants or irritants, not many of us would include the pretty yarrow, or milfoil, of our waysides, with its delicately fragrant and finely divided leaf, yet its other name of field hop points to its former use in beer, and the drink made from it is said to be more devastating than the ordinary kind. In the Orkneys it is both a tea and a cure for melancholy, while in Scotland it is a salve. In Switzerland it sharpens vinegar, and in some other countries it is "old man's pepper" and cures toothache. Its botanical name of achillea records its use by Achilles in healing the wounds of his soldiers.

Tobacco was known to our Indians before white men ever heard of it, and they smoked it both for pleasure and as a ratification of contracts for centuries before the landing of Columbus. The first pipe was a tobago, or double roll of bark, placed at the nostrils and held over a bunch of the burning leaf, but the men of the north have had their stone pipes for a thousand years, no doubt, and they were shaped from the sacred rock at the command of the Great Spirit, who ordained the ceremonial of smoking in confirmation of brotherhood, the pipe passing from mouth to mouth as the loving cup passes at our tables. Smoking suggests coffee, without which it is hardly worth while. Coffee grew in Arabia for ages before it was the good fortune of the dervish Hadji Omar to discover it. This happened in 1285. He had been driven into exile from Mocha because of his attempts to establish the strange custom of honesty among its governors, and in the extremity of his hunger he ravened upon coffee berries that were growing wild in the environs. They were pretty bad, so in the hope of softening their acerbity he tried the experiment of roasting them. This made them more tolerable, and they yielded a pleasant savor and an entrancing smell, but they were viciously hard. Hadji then boiled them in water, and they became more nearly edible, but the water was the best part of them. By eating and drinking of the coffee, he did not satisfy his appetite, yet he so effectually suppressed it that it was the next thing to having dined. Here, then, was a discovery! He hurried back to inform the public of it, trusting to be forgiven for his reforms. And he was not only forgiven, but was promoted to be a saint. It took centuries to introduce the berry to a wider circle of admirers, for even in the middle of the sixteenth century it was disapproved by the priesthood of Constantinople, who said that the habit of idling over the coffee cups was taking worshipers from the mosques, and that the coals on which the beans were roasted were the coals of hell. An enemy of coffee declares that its introduction to the world of men was made when an Arab herder in the fifth century discovered that his goats, having ignorantly eaten it, were cutting capers like those possessed of devils.

MYTHS AND LEGENDS OF FLOWERS

He tried the berries himself, found they were a slow poison, introduced them delightedly to his "system," and so died, beloved and endorsed by millions. Tea has left its record on American history, for who knows if the Revolution would have revolved without the Boston tea party? In the want of the herb the Yankee housewife solaced herself with substitutes derived from catnip, nettles, tansy, and other doubtful plants, and although she sternly refused to accept an article unjustly taxed, there is no doubt that she sighed for the better fortunes of her English sisters and brothers. In an old commendation, tea "easeth the brain of heavy damps; prevents the dropsie; consumes rawnesse; vanquishes superfluous sleep; purifieth humors and hot liver; strengthens the use of due benevolence."

In Okakura Kakuzo's '"Book of Tea" we discover that the brewings of the herb are more than a stomachic comfort: they have spiritual importance, and there is even a "teaism," "founded on adoration of the beautiful among the sordid facts of every-day existence." The leaves were formerly powdered before being placed in the water, and some heavy-handed cooks crushed them in a mortar, worked them into cakes, boiled them with spices, ginger, salt, orange peel, milk, rice, and onions! In the Cha-king, or holy scripture of tea, a book of three volumes, we learn that the best leaves must be wrinkled like a Tartar's boots, curled like a bull's dewlap, must unfold like mist from a valley, shine like a lake in the breeze, and in dampness and softness suggest the earth refreshed by rain. Another poet describes the effect of his various drafts: the first cup moistens his throat; the second relieves his loneliness; the third revives memories of books and stimulates him to write them; the fourth causes a sweat in which all that is wrong in life passes out at the pores; the fifth completes the purification; the sixth summons him to the gods, and the seventh wafts him into their presence. The Japanese tea-room is kept bare and simple, that the fancy, liberated by the draft, may not be arrested from its flights by the intrusion of unimportant objects.

MYTHS AND LEGENDS OF FLOWERS

PLANTS OF ILL RENOWN

There was once in the middle of Java a certain tree that dripped and breathed poison, destroying animal and vegetable life for miles around. Even the birds fell dead when flying past. It stood alone in a valley which it filled with vapors, and all about it the earth was covered with the skeletons of men and animals that had strayed into the neighborhood. This famous upas tree (upas is Malay for poison) was the only one in existence, but the name is still applied to a tree of the same order as the breadfruit and mulberry. Its juices, mixed with pepper and ginger, are smeared upon arrows to make them irritating, and its bark yields a fiber used in native cloth which will cause itching unless it is soundly washed before wearing. On so slight a basis was the legend of the upas reared. Allied to the dreadful tree of Java is the rattlesnake bush of Mexico, with its venomous thorns. From this arose a story of a tree of serpents that wound its arms about men and animals that tried to pass, and stung and strangled them to death. Nearly as vexatious is the kerzra flower, of Persia, for if you so much as breathe the air that has passed over it you must die. Nor is the manchineel an object of fond regard, inasmuch as death comes to any that shall rest beneath its branches and suffer themselves to sink into the sleep that its exhalations will induce.

Trees usually bring luck to their owners, but the walnut is an exception. It is thought to kill vegetation near it, and to bear especial enmity to the oak. Paschal II hewed down a walnut in Rome because he discovered that the evil soul of Nero was living in its branches, and after the destruction of the tree the Church of the People was built upon its site as a security against the demon. Thus it appears that the wakiut is hospitable to wicked spirits. By some similar token, the yew was long thought to be dangerous to life and health, although thousands of men made bows from its wood and carried them without hurt except

MYTHS AND LEGENDS OF FLOWERS

to other people. While the powers of good control various of the plants, others are under spell of evil creatures who work their will by poisons, but who also show themselves to those they would afflict. Belladonna is so beloved of the Devil that he goes about trimming and tending it in his not abundant leisure. He can be diverted from its care on only one night in the year, and that is Walpurgis, when he is preparing for the witches' sabbat. If on that night a farmer looses a black hen the Devil will chase it, and the watchful farmer, suddenly darting on the plant, may pluck and put the weed to its rightful use; for by rubbing his horse with it the animal gains strength, provided the herb is gained in the way here indicated. The apples of Sodom are held to be related to this plant, and the name belladonna, or beautiful lady, records an old superstition that at certain times it takes the form of an enchantress of exceeding loveliness, whom it is dangerous to look upon.

We may dismiss as mythical the traveled tale of a Venus fly-trap which was magnified into quite another matter before Captain Arkright was through with it, for such tales grow larger the farther they go from their beginning. It was in 1581 that the valiant explorer learned of an atoll in the South Pacific that one might not visit, save on peril of his life, for this coral ring enclosed a group of islets on one of which the Death Flower grew; hence it was named El Banoor, or Island of Death. This flower was so large that a man might enter it- a cave of color and perfume- but if he did so it was the last of him, for, lulled by its strange fragrance, he reclined on its lower petals and fell into the sleep from which there is no waking. Then, as if to guard his slumber, the flower slowly folded its petals about him. The fragrance increased and burning acid was distilled from its calyx, but of all hurt the victim was unconscious, and so passing into death through splendid dreams, he gave his body to the plant for food. Dreads such as are recorded in this narrative extended to the humblest forms of vegetation, and our uncanny fungi have not escaped the ascription of many evils. True, their reputation for poisoning is in part deserved, though there are more beneficent mushrooms than mischievous, and, as Hamilton Gibson proved, hundreds of tons of wholesome food go to daily waste in our fields for lack of knowledge among the people to recognize the edible varieties or to know when to gather and how to cook them. The common puffball is ripe for the kitchen while it is in its white state, for instance, but is past eating when it has turned leathery and throws out its gust of "smoke" or spores when trodden. A giant puff-ball is reported which held food for at least one family, inasmuch as it weighed forty-seven pounds and was three feet thick! It is the threads of old puff-balls that supplied our grandfathers with tinder in the days when fire was started with flint and steel, and their dust was also used to stop blood flow, as some use cobwebs in emergencies today. Punk, in use on our Fourth of July, is also made from fungus. In parts of England the puff-ball is Puck's stool and Puck's fists, and some etymologists identify Puck with pogge, or toad.

Why are toadstools so named? Surely none ever saw a toad seated on one of them. The stools are apt to be kicked to pieces by the peasantry, especially if they are found growing in pixie rings, for then they surely shelter elves; and if an elf peers at you then quinine should be taken, for you are "due to come down with fever." If it is a cow that is looked at by the elf, she is thenceforth bewitched, and will give sour milk, or discover a disposition to dance and turn somersaults. These pixie rings are merely growths spreading centrifugally and sometimes overlapping. As grass inside the rings is shadowed by the fungi and loses a measure of its sustenance to them, the country folk ascribe the bare appearance of the sod to the dancing of the elves. The rings disappear in three or four years, and then it is said that the fairies have taken offense and gone elsewhere. The spores dropping from the parent plant exhaust the soil as they take root, and for that reason the growth is outward, not inward, the circles constantly widening toward new feeding grounds. The low form of life known as lichen spreads in a similar manner. It

MYTHS AND LEGENDS OF FLOWERS

is the purple streaks on its stem rather than the scathe in its juice that gives a bad name to water hemlock- the plant that put Socrates to death- for these streaks are copies of the brand put on Cain's brow when he had committed murder. The plant bears the names of spotted cowbane, musquash root and beaver poison, in America, and is related to carrot, parsnip, parsley, fennel, caraway, celery, coriander, and sweet cicely, the latter also unwholesome. Jack-in-the-pulpit, or Indian turnip, known in England as lords-and-ladies, is another plant from which it was wise to keep a distance. Its name, *ariscema triphyllum*, signifies bloody arum, because its spathe is purple where Christ's blood fell upon it at the crucifixion.

In our own country the laurel or kalmia was regarded with such dislike that people were warned against eating the flesh of birds that had fed on its berries. Even worse than laurel is the savin, called likewise magician's cypress and devil's tree, because it was used by wizards in some of their most sinful ceremonies. Our common milkwort, *polygala vulgaris*, is beneficent, and increases the milk of mothers who carry it in procession or wear it as a garland in Rogation week; but the Javanese variety, *polygala venanta*, is a dreadful herb, inasmuch as the native who touches it must sneeze himself to death. Another plant of fell property is the garget or poke, although its young shoots are boiled and eaten like asparagus, and its tincture is administered for rheumatism by granny doctors.

The catalog of roadside mischiefs would be incomplete without the henbane- bane of hens- or hog's bean, whose scientific mask is hyoscyamus, and which is held to be of so evil an aspect, with its woolly leaves and unsanctified-looking flowers, that one hardly needs to be warned from it. Witches use this in their midnight stews, and the dead in hades are crowned with it as they wander hopelessly beside the Styx.

MYTHS AND LEGENDS OF FLOWERS

FLOWERS, TREES, FRUITS AND PLANTS

ACACIA

Our locust tree, the blossoms of which exhale ravishing odors in the spring, is the American variety of acacia, the "incorruptible wood" of which was made the ark of the covenant and the altar of the tabernacle. It also provided thorns for the crown of Christ. The Buddhist, to whom it is sacred, burns its wood on his altars; and a species of it, known as the sami, is used by Hindus in the ceremonial begetting of fire for sacrifices. A folk-tale of the nineteenth Egyptian dynasty is almost identical with a legend of our Arapaho Indians, except that in the American story a blue feather replaces the acacia.

The Egyptian narrative is as follows: Bata, a predecessor of Joseph, is loved by the wife of his elder brother, but he will none of her, so, enraged, she tells her husband, Anpu, that Bata has attempted violence toward her. Bata proves his innocence, but he can no longer find comfort in his old home, so he mutilates himself and departs, leaving Anpu to mourn his loss and kill the deceitful woman. Reaching the valley of the acacia, Bata removes his soul and places it in the topmost flower of that plant for safekeeping. The gods pity the young exile, and the Sun orders that a mate be made for him, "more beautiful in her limbs than any other woman in the land." Bata is comforted in her society, but tells her that while he is hunting she must keep to the house. She does not obey, but in his absence walks by the shore. The Sea reaches after her, roaring to the acacia to detain her; but the most the tree can do is to lower a branch and tear out a lock of her hair, which it drops into the sea. This floats to the Egyptian shore, where they are washing Pharaoh's linen. The perfume of acacia blossoms, clinging to the hair, so sweetens the Nile waters that it is imparted to the garments, and the King asks its origin. A priest tells him that the fragrance comes from the

MYTHS AND LEGENDS OF FLOWERS

hair of a daughter of the gods. In his eagerness to know her, Pharaoh sends to all parts of the world. Bata slays all but one of the invaders of the acacia valley, but this one brings a larger force and abducts the woman. She is willing, and asks Pharaoh to destroy the tree on which her husband's soul is concealed. The king sends another troop into Bata's land, and the tree is cut down. Bata falls dead. Far away, Anpu, sitting at his meat, calls for a pot of beer. It foams and boils. He calls for wine, but that is foul. By these signs he knows that his brother is dead, and he sets off for the acacia valley, to recover his soul, if possible. The body is there, but the tree that guarded the soul is gone. After a three-years' search, he discovers the seed-pod of an acacia, and in the hope that it may contain his brother's spirit, he puts it into a cup of water. The thirsty soul drinks until no drop is left. Then Anpu fills the cup again and puts it to the lips of his dead brother, whose limbs had shaken as the seed-pod absorbed the water.

The corpse drinks eagerly, then stands erect again- a man. He goes to Pharaoh, sends away his wife, and on the king's death reigns for thirty years, being succeeded by Anpu.

ACANTHUS

The acanthus has been immortalized in architecture by the Corinthian column, the capital of which is a free copy of its leaves. Its use was suggested in this manner: A little girl of Corinth died and was buried in a spot where the acanthus grew. Her old nurse, carrying to the tomb a basket of the dead child's toys and ornaments, placed it upon one of these plants. When the young leaves came up they were bent by the burden into a curve and prettily framed the basket; and the sculptor Callimachus, chancing by, was so charmed by the grace of their lines that he perpetuated them in stone.

MYTHS AND LEGENDS OF FLOWERS

ACHYRANTHES

This plant is indigenous to India, and in one of the religious ceremonies of the Hindus a flour of its seed is offered at daybreak to the god Indra. Many demons had this hero-deity slain, but the monster Namuchi finally overpowered him, and Indra was glad to make peace with him by promising that he would never again slay any creature with either a liquid or a solid, by day or by night. This appeared to Namuchi to embrace all possible contingencies, but Indra plucked a plant, which is neither solid nor liquid- at least, in his reasoning- and, falling upon Namuchi in the dawn, when it is neither day nor night, he slew that astonished creature. As soon as the demon was dead, the achyranthes sprang from his skull, and with this plant Indra flogged all the other demons out of existence.

ACONITE

We call this plant "monkshood" in America, because of its upper petal. Its caplike form gives it the name of "troll 's hat" in Denmark, and "iron hat" and "storm hat" in Germany, where it is also "the devil's herb," for it is associated with the spells whereby witches invoke the devil. In Norway it is "Odin's helmet," there recalling the tarnhelm, or cap of darkness, which made its wearer invisible. The plant's power for mischief has been recognized since the earliest recorded times, and even appears in the age of myth, as shall forthwith be disclosed: When Theseus returned from his wanderings he did not at once reveal himself to his father, Aegeus, but resolved to learn first how he might be affected toward him. "I have delivered the land from many monsters," he told the old king, "and I ask for payment." Then entered Medea, the beautiful witch, and, standing close to Theseus, so that the subtle perfume of her garments soothed and enticed him, she poured a flashing liquid into a golden goblet. "Welcome to the hero, the destroyer of evil," she said. "Drink

MYTHS AND LEGENDS OF FLOWERS

from this cup the wine which gives rest and life and closes every wound. It is the cup that gods might drink." Taking the vessel into his hand, Theseus held it toward her, seeming about to drink to her eyes. Then he stood transfixed, for while Medea's face was lovely, and the cloud of hair about it shone like the sunset, the eyes into which he had looked were glittering and reminded him of a snake's. "The wine is nectar from Olympus, and its odor enraptures the sense, but she who brings it is fair beyond all other mortals," he said. "It will give a finer flavor to the cup if she will taste it first, that the perfume of her lips may linger in the wine." Medea faltered and grew white. "I am unwell," she answered. "Drink, or, by the gods, you die at my hands!" cried Theseus, for he read the meaning of her hesitancy. The king and court looked on speechless with astonishment and fear. With a swift movement, Medea dashed the goblet to the floor, and ere the prince could strike had fled in her dragon chariot, never to be seen again. As the spilt liquor spattered over the floor, it caused the marble to crack and dissolve to powder, seething as it gathered into pools. Then the prince disclosed himself, and the palace was filled with rejoicing.

While from its action on the marble we should assume Medea's poison to have been a violent acid, tradition says that it contained aconite. It was with the juice of this plant that ancient armies anointed their spears and arrows, that a scratch might cause death, and it is said to be still used by some savage tribes. Chiron, the centaur, discovered the mischief in it by accidentally dropping an arrow thus poisoned on his hoof, dying in the discovery. By reason of its maleficence it was dedicated to Hecate, queen of hell, in whose garden it was sown by Cerberus, the three-headed monster who guards the place of shadows.

ALLIGATOR TAIL

In the old days alligators believed that life offered nothing more profitable than napping, eating, and lying in a shady swamp. But finally men penetrated the jungle, to the astonishment of the saurians, and as these men's rude speech resembled the universal tongue of the jungle, some of the alligators understood. The men said such reptiles occupied the water on the other side of the mountains, and one stranger declared, "Our people over there believe alligators to be gods, so they feed them and care for them." Here was a prospect to rouse wild hopes among the listeners. After the strangers had departed, several young alligators scrambled up the banks and awoke a veteran of their family. The veteran was unmoved. "Those strange animals that have been talking here are called men," he told them. "Once they were monkeys, and lived in trees. They had to come down and walk on the earth because they cut off their tails, and ever since they have been so vain, because they are different from the rest, that there is no believing anything they say. They do not worship alligators, you may be sure. On the contrary, they worship only themselves." The young alligators ascribed the veteran's *blase* air to an indisposition to move. So hundreds of them set off for the promised land. At night they were tired with their unusual exertions, and, crawling into the marshes of the river known as the Winding Snake, they fell asleep. As they lay there the water gods discovered them. Now, these gods, having bidden the saurians keep to the hot lands, resented this curiosity and intrusion on the secret places. So they seized every alligator and thrust his head into the earth, leaving his tail gyrating in the air. As alligators they ceased to be, but as plants they continue to this day, and explorers in the wilderness have, among other obstacles, to buffet their way through plantations of the tree known as the *rabo de lagarto,* or alligator's tail. These trees stand as a warning to all the alligator tribes never to leave the lowlands.

ALMOND

The Princess Phyllis, and the youth, Demophoon, whose ships had been wrecked on the Thracian coast, fell in love with

MYTHS AND LEGENDS OF FLOWERS

each other, and it was agreed that they should wed. But first Demophoon, his ships being repaired at the cost of his host, the Thracian king, set sail, with the promise that he would return as soon as he could put his affairs in order. Alas for the frailty of his sex, he was met at home by a maid so much fairer, in his eyes, that he forgot his promise. Phyllis watched at the shore, her heart leaping whenever a sail appeared on the horizon. In time she grew ill, and at last faded away in grief. But she was not carried to the grave, for the gods betokened their admiration for her constancy by turning her into an almond tree, and in that form she kept her watch, her arms still beckoning the unfaithful one.

So she stood when Demophoon returned, whether repentant or in quest of some advantage does not matter now; at all events, he learned what had happened, and, conscience-smitten, he sought the tree, fell at its feet, and embraced its trunk, watering its roots with tears, whereupon it burst into bloom for gladness. And in the Greek tongue the name of the almond became phylla. In Tuscany branches of almond are used to find hidden treasure, as the hazel is used elsewhere. Catholics assign the tree to the Virgin; Mahometans see in it the hope of heaven; and in Hebraic lore it was an almond that budded and fruited in the Tabernacle in a day, when Aaron had held it as his rod. Now, this rod of Aaron, being preserved with reverence, reached Rome and became the staff of the Pope, whereof another story. Wagner has familiarized the world with the Tannhauser legend, though it long had currency in other than its musical form. The hero of the tale was a minnesinger, and while on the way to take part in a singing contest, he came to a cave in the hillside, at the entrance of which stood a woman of surpassing loveliness. Obeying her invitation, the minstrel followed her far into the mountain, where the cave broadened into a splendid chamber. It was Venus, queen of love, who had summoned him.

Thought of time, duty, and memory of his fellow creatures slept in his mind for years; but there came a day when the perpetual revel palled, and he hungered for the coarser fruits of the earth. In vain he begged his captor to lead him to the outer world again. At last he fell on his knees and implored the Holy Virgin to rescue him. At the end of a long prayer, with closed eyes, he felt a cool breath touch his cheek, and, looking up, he discovered that he was on the Horselberg, back in the world, the sun shining overhead. He wept for joy. A priest to whom he confessed declared that no other man had so offended, and that absolution could come only from the Pope. Tannhauser plodded wearily to Rome and appealed to the holy father. The recital of his experience filled Pope Urban with horror. "Guilt like yours," he cried, "can never be forgiven! Before God Himself could pardon you, this staff that I hold would grow green and bloom!" The doomed one went his way, and in course of time found himself at the Horselberg once more. In sudden desperation, he called aloud to Venus to take him back. The goddess did so, and three days after the mountain had closed upon them, the Pope's staff suddenly put forth almond flowers and leaves. A great horror and a great sorrow filled the holy father, for he understood that God's judgments are gentler than ours. He sent messengers in pursuit of Tannhauser, but to no purpose. He was lost to the world.

Another legend concerns the novice in a monastery, who, in order that he might learn patience and obedience, was commanded to water a branch of styrax daily for two years, although he had to carry the water from the Nile, two miles away. Patience was rewarded when the branch, seemingly dead, burst into flower. Indeed, these legends of blossoming staffs and branches go back to the Romans, at least, for Virgil tells of the miracle in his Aeneid. Turpin's history of Charlemagne also relates an occurrence of this sort, but more unusual and startling, for the spears of the emperor's troops, which had been thrust into the earth when he made camp, became a forest during the night and shaded the tents. In Jewish lore the terebinth grew from a staff carried by one of the angels who visited Abraham. It is also said that the staff carried by Joseph, when he sought the hand of Mary, broke into leaf in token of heaven's sanction of the compact.

AMARANTH

In the faith of the ancients, amaranth, "The neverfading," gemmed the fields of paradise. Though the asphodel was the flower of death, the amaranth, as the flower of immortality in the symbology of the Greeks, was used for funerary purposes. The Swedes have a national recognition of the flower in their Order of the Amaranth. That variety of the plant which we call "love-lies-bleeding," because of its bloody crimson, and that in France is "the nun's scourge," sirse to the Gallic mind it suggests the flagellations endured by penitents, is almost the only form of it familiar in our gardens. In countries that confess the Roman faith, the amaranth is one of the flowers chosen to decorate the churches on Ascension Day, thus showing the persistence of its Greek association with the life hereafter. Globe amaranth, prince's feathers, cock's comb, flower gentle, velvet flower, flower velure, and floramor are recent and ancient names for the plant.

ANEMONE

When Adonis had fallen, pierced by the fangs of the boar in whose pursuit he was more eager than in his response to the proffered love of Venus, that goddess bedewed the earth with tears, and as too precious to evaporate back into air, the earth, with heaven's alchemy, translated them into anemones. Their English name of wind-flowers commemorates the belief that they opened at command of the first mild breezes of the spring. To the Chinese, they are flowers of death, hence there is a wide association of them with grief and suffering, and they are often regarded as dangerous- a recent notion, for the Romans gathered them as a cure for the malarial fevers that the mosquitoes carried into the city from the Campagna.

In another legend, the "'little wind rose," as the Germans name it, was a maid attached to the court of Chloris, where she was seen and loved by Zephyrus, the god who caused flowers and fruits to spring from the earth by breathing on it. Chloris fancied that the wind god was about to sue for her hand; hence, on discovering his passion for Anemone, she drove that nymph from her presence in anger. Finding her broken hearted, and hence dismal company, and having also to make his peace with Chloris, Zephyrus abandoned the poor creature, but in taking his leave changed her into the flower that bears her name. The ancients gathered the anemone to decorate the altars of Venus, since they were the tokens of her love, and also to wreathe the faces of the dead. The idea of immortality seems to have long pertained to it, and it is still known in parts of Europe as the Easter flower, or flower of the resurrection. As "the cow bell," it garlanded the cow in the Easter festivals of the Germans. In the holy land it is "the blood-drops-of-Christ" (a name oddly given to the wall-flower, also), for the sacred blood fell upon the anemones that were springing on Calvary on the evening of the crucifixion, and they became red from that hour. As the fathers employed the triple leaf of this plant to symbolize the three personalities of the godhood, it also took the name of "herb trinity."

APPLE

There is much symbolic use of the apple, and it appears in folk-lore as well as in Scripture; for it is grown in all lands where the sun is not too weak or too hot. We connect it with the oldest legend in the world- though there is really nothing in Scripture to show that the fruit with which Satan tempted Eve was not a pomegranate or a pear. The apple was also related to Venus, and praised by Solomon. It was eaten by Swiss lake-dwellers, and prized by the Greeks and Romans, who tell how

MYTHS AND LEGENDS OF FLOWERS

Atlanta lost her race by stooping to pick up the golden apples dropped by her competitor, whose life was forfeit if he failed to reach the goal ahead of her. It is the apple that unhappy Tantalus strives to reach, that he may ease hell's torments, but its boughs are ever tossing upward as he has them almost in his grasp, just as the stream flows away from him when he stoops to drink. The apple of discord, and the apple of the Hesperides, are familiar figures in poetry.

In the Norse legend Iduna kept a store of apples which the gods ate, thereby keeping themselves young. Loki, the fire-god, stole the fruit, and affairs went badly till the other deities had recovered it. A golden bird that seeks the golden apples of a king's garden figures in northern fairy tales. The Poles tell how an adventurous youth, by fixing a lynx's claws to his feet and hands, climbs to the summit of a glass mountain where grow golden apples, and there frees a princess from enchantment. In a German folk-tale, a girl who consents to act as godmother to a babe of the dwarfs is rewarded with an apronful of apples that turn to gold as she emerges from their underworld. The apple-tree supplanted the May-pole as a phallic symbol in England, and young people danced about it, singing their hopes for a year of plenty after sprinkling it with, cider. In various lands the fruit or seed or blossom is used in divination, and I have seen Yankee cooks toss a paring over the shoulder, when they were peeling the fruit for sauce or pies, that they might learn the initial of their future husband, the paring as it fell being expected to shape itself to those letters. In England a girl will name a number of seeds for her prospective sweethearts, and the seed that stays longest when moistened and placed on her forehead indicates the man who will marry her.

The legend of St. Dorothea has two versions, one of which (see under head of roses) represents her as returning from heaven with flowers for the gibing Theophilus, while in the other she sends fruit. This latter recounts that the lawyer cried tauntingly to the saint, when she was led to death for heresy, "Send me some fruit from heaven." "As you wish, Theophilus," she answered; then asked the guard to halt a moment while she prayed. Suddenly a beautiful boy was discovered standing near, whom no one had seen to approach. In his hands was a basket of flowers, and, lying upon them, three great apples, streaked with emerald green and ruby red, vied in color and perfume with the blossoms. The saint said, "Give these to Theophilus, and tell him there are more in paradise, where I hope to meet him." A little later her head was struck off. Theophilus, smelling and tasting the fruit, was filled with wonder at the miracle, and presently embraced the faith he had despised, thereby winning martyrdom for himself, and with that heaven.

In Persia, the apple is the fruit of immortality, as we learn from the tale of Anasindhu, a holy man who lived in a wood with Parvati, his wife, speaking only thrice a year, and giving all his waking hours to meditations on virtue. The reputation he gained for wisdom and goodness made him tho admiration of his country; but he had his heavenly reward also, for Gauri gave him an apple as a token that the gods wished him to live such a life forever. He placed it at his lips, but before tasting it his wife came into his mind- his overlooked and discontented wife. She had shared the hardships of his secluded life; why not its blessings, now that they had come? But to his astonishment she refused the fruit. "Why should I wish immortality?" she asked. "I could never be happy here in the forest, seeing no other faces, sharing no happiness with others, and begging from every passing pilgrim."

Anasindhu was indignant. "If the gods wish me to live thus, is it for you to protest?" he cried. And she, being a woman, was silent. But after a little she asked, "Can you not be as useful to the gods and more useful to men in town? Are you always to live in this wretched place? What harm to see our fellow creatures, to hear music, to eat better food, to see the palaces and temples and splendor of the capital? Oh, I would have servants and a golden carriage and a palanquin of perfumed wood, and you should be the king's minister, and all should hold you in awe and obey you. And you should build great temples and be admired."

"I can not do these things, woman- I who beg and am poor." "But you can sell the fruit of immortality for a price." The holy one was shocked, yet the woman artfully showed how the money could be put, not merely to his advantage, but to the welfare of the race and the glory of the gods. "In the first place," she said, "you have nothing to prove that it is an apple of life, and if a spirit has merely made you a subject of pleasantry, you will be none the better for eating, and none the worse for losing it. If it is really a gift of heaven, you will never be happy on earth if you continue this joyless life, whereas you may glorify the gods if you sell it, and be happy in good works so long as you may live, even if you are not chosen the more surely for immortality for this service." Anasindhu was struck by this pleading, and the end of it was that he went to the city and sold the apple to the king. But the king also aspired to holiness. He thought how selfish it would be in him to monopolize the gifts of the gods; he reflected on the charities that the pious hermit would doubtless give with the money received for the fruit; he thought of the gain in heaven that would come of renunciation. "No," he cried; "I am not worthy to be immortal." In the garden, where he went to meditate, he saw his queen. "Eat," he exclaimed, "for this is the apple of immortality. There is none in the world so worthy to live as you, none so beautiful, none of such a bird-like voice, none of such gentleness. Eat, and delight the world with your beauty forever."

The queen smiled brilliantly and took the fruit with thanks, while the king, after kissing her feet, returned to the palace. But when it was dark, and he was asleep, the queen crept forth into a shaded place whence presently came the sound of kisses. And in the morning the captain of the guards walked proudly about the garden with the apple in his hand. Yet he was not happy. He looked at the fruit with longing, for it was a queen's gift, but he remembered also a little serving-maid whom he loved more dearly than his queen. "I will make her a goddess," he murmured. "She shall have the apple, and her beauty and goodness shall never fade." But, lo! on the next day a girl in humble dress fell at the king's feet and offered to him a withering apple. He started when he saw it. "Great ruler," she said, "I am only a servant, but there has come into my hands this apple which, being eaten, confers immortality. I am not worthy to touch so great a gift. I pray you eat it and become as the gods, doing great deeds and worshiped by all mankind."

The king grasped the apple and demanded, "Who gave you this?" "My betrothed, sire; the captain of your guard." The captain was sent for. When he saw what his sweetheart had done he was much afraid, but confessed at last that the queen had given the fruit to him. At this the king, in a blaze of anger, ordered him to instant execution, and commanded that the queen be burned in the square. "And this is human grandeur!" he reflected bitterly. "Yesterday I was happy; today I am the most miserable of men." Then, calling his chief priest, he commanded him to give all his riches to the poor, dressed himself in his oldest garb, and left his kingdom forever, to sleep at the roadside and beg his way through the land. As he left the palace, Anashindu came by dressed in silks, and riding in a golden litter attended by many servants. The king extended the apple to him. "Take it," he cried, "for there is none other in this kingdom worthy to receive it. Be immortal, and, if you can, be happy." Anashindu gladly took the fruit and put it at his lips. "There is no doubt," said he, "that the gods wish me to live forever." But as he opened his mouth a jolt of the litter caused him to drop the apple, and a dog that was running by gulped it at a mouthful. So immortality is denied to men, but in the East a dog is wandering from hamlet to hamlet, unable to die, and taking little happiness.

MYTHS AND LEGENDS OF FLOWERS

A somber tradition concerns the Micah Rood apples, or bloody hearts, that made their appearance in Franklin, Connecticut, but are now widely cultivated in other towns and States. They are sweet of flavor, fragrant, handsomely red outside, and while most of the flesh is white, there is at the core a red spot that represents human blood. Near the end of the seventeenth century there lived in Franklin a farmer named Micah Rood, who was regarded by his neighbors as of rather a worthless sort, fond of leisure yet fond of money. In the early days of the colony trading was done mostly by roving peddlers, and while these gentry gained modestly in their dealings with people who were of the narrowest means, they sometimes carried sums that would excite the cupidity of men less moral than the New Englanders. One day a peddler, making the rounds of the settlements, was found dead on the Rood farm, with a gash in his head and his pack empty. Rood was suspected, and either knowledge of this suspicion or the proddings of his conscience forced him into strict seclusion.

If he had robbed the man, he had small good of his plunder, for he spent money no more freely than before. Indeed, he became neglectful of his farm, and his house fell into disrepair. That year the tree beneath which the peddler had died did a strange thing; it put forth red apples instead of yellow, each with a blood stain at its heart, as if in witness against the murderer; and the gossips would have it that the decay of the farm and the air of misfortune that clouded the life of Micah Rood in his last days were the results of his victim's curse. Rood died without revealing his secret, if he had any, but his tree lived, and its fruit has been grafted on hundreds of other orchards. Although there is plenty to prove that St. Dunstan pulled the devil's nose with hot tongs, and so freed himself from temptation for all time, the farmers of the south of England will have it that the saint, who was brewer as well as blacksmith, sold his soul to the fiend on condition that his beer would have a better sale than his neighbor's cider.

MYTHS AND LEGENDS OF FLOWERS

As part of the bargain, all apple-trees were to be frosted or blighted on the 17th, 18th, and 19th of May, so these dates are watched anxiously by farmers. The 19th is not only St. Dunstan's Day, but brings Frankum's Night, when one Frankum compacted with witches for a specially good crop of apples, and got a frost instead, as he deserved. The apples of the south of England are famous for the quality of cider that they make. The monks of Tavistock Abbey had a fine orchard, and the drink they brewed from it would turn almost any man into a monk; yet at times it was edgy or sharp, and as mixing it with wine was expensive, to say nothing of the effect of the blend on heads that should be filled with pious thoughts, the abbot offered a prize for some process that should make rough cider smooth. Ere many days a little old man with a limp applied for work, saying that he knew all about orchards and cider-presses, and would be satisfied not to lodge in the monastery- an empty cask would do. The appearance and conduct of the man roused the curiosity of Father John, who had the making of the cider, and, peeping into the barrel when the ancient was napping, he was not half astonished to discover that the stranger had one foot shaped like a hoof, while a yard of snaky tail was hanging out at the bung-hole. As quickly as the good friar could pipe new cider into that sleeping apartment he did so, and with a vast spluttering and cursing the hired man leaped out of the cask, shot into the air, and disappeared; incidentally giving off such quantities of hot and sulfurous breath that the cider was almost boiling. Father John gave a grunt of satisfaction that he had rid the monastery of so dangerous a guest, and when the drink was cool he had the hardihood to taste it. His eyebrows went up, and his heart, too, for the cider was sweet and rich and smooth. So he took his lesson from the devil, and thereafter poured the harsher kinds on burning sulfur, making it the best of all cider. Devon men call fine cider "matched," because it has been treated with brimstone. And that is how it happened.

MYTHS AND LEGENDS OF FLOWERS

ARBUTUS

Old Peboan sat alone in his ragged tepee. His locks were white, scant, lank as the icicles that festooned the pines above his lodge. He was wrapped to the nose in furs, yet he was cold, as well as weak with hunger, for he had found no game for three days. "Help, Great Spirit!" he cried, at last. "It is I, Peboan, the winter manitou, who calls. I am old, and my feet are heavy. There is no food. Must I go into the north to find the white bear?" He breathed on the morsel of fire; it flared for a moment, and it was as if a warm wind stirred the deerskin cover of his lodge. Peboan crouched over the little flame and waited. He knew that the Great Spirit would hear him. Presently, the tepee door was lifted and there appeared a handsome girl with fawn eyes full of liquid light. Her cheeks were rose; her hair, of deepest black, fell over her like a garment; her dress was of sweet grass and young leaves. In her arms were willow twigs with velvet buds upon them. "I am Segun," she said. "Come, Segun, and sit by my fire. I have called for help from the Great Spirit. What can you do?" "Tell me what you can do, yourself," answered Segun. "I am the winter manitou. I was strong when I was young. I had only to breathe and the streams would stand still, the leaves would fall and the flowers die." "I am the summer manitou," the maiden replied. "Where I breathe the flowers spring. Where I walk, the waters follow."

"I shake my hair, and snow falls like the feathers of the swan. It spreads as a death-cloth over the earth.", "I shake my hair, and rain comes, warm and gentle. When I call the birds answer. The grass grows thick under my feet. My tepee is not close and dark like this. The blue lodge is mine- the summer sky. Ah, Peboan, you can stay no longer. The Great Spirit has sent me to say that your time has come." The old man looked up and drew his furs yet tighter about him, but his strength went out in the effort. His head fell upon his shoulder, and he sank at length upon the earth. The patter of melting snow began to sound. Segun waved her hands over the prostrate manitou, and he grew less and less till at last no trace of him was left. His furs turned to leaves, his tepee to a tree. Some of the leaves were hard with ice, but Segun, stooping, placed them in her hair; then, as they changed color, she put them into the ground and breathed on them. At the touch of the warmth they freshened and flushed and gave out a delicate perfume. "The children shall find these," she said, "and they will know that Segun has been here, and that Peboan has gone away. This flower is my token that I possess the earth, even though there is snow about it. When the rivers run the air shall be sweet." And this was the planting of the trailing arbutus.

ARUM

The arum vies with the skunk cabbage in its eagerness to take the air after the long confinement of winter; hence it is out of the earth almost before the snow has cleared, though it shows less haste in blossoming, for its flowers are often delayed till June. When these flowers convert to red berries, and the hood that covered them disappears, we see why the plant gained the name of "bloody men's fingers." It has many other names, however, such as snake's food (which of course it isn't), adder's meat, poison berries, Aaron, Aaron's root, Aaron's rod, cuckoo pint, cuckoo pintle, priest's pintle, parson in the pulpit, parson and clerk, devil's men and women, cows and calves, calf's foot, starchwort, karup, friar's cowl, wake robin, wake pintle, lords and ladies, passion flower, and Gethsemane. Because of the poison in its root, and its curious faculty of increasing in temperature while its sheath is expanding, the arum was long regarded as a plant to be avoided, although it is significant that the evil being who invented starch, for the torture of his fellow creatures, extracted that malefic substance not merely from corn and potatoes, but from the arum, thereby deepening its disgrace. Two thousand years ago, it was believed that there was food in

MYTHS AND LEGENDS OF FLOWERS

the arum, and that when bears awoke from hibernating they were restored to vigor by eating it. When the spies of Israel went into the promised land, it was said that they carried Aaron's rod, as a part of their belongings, and used it in transporting the bunch of grapes they picked at Eschol, since the fruit was so heavy that two men could lift it only by attaching it to the staff. When they arrived with the grapes they mechanically struck the rod into the ground, and the arum grew upon that spot to symbolize the abundance they had proved. To this day the plant is held to indicate a season's fertility, and farmers in some parts of the world gauge the size of their crops in advance, by the size of the spadix of the arum.

ASH

The name "ash" was derived from the Norse aska, meaning man, for it was from a twig of this tree, crooked like an arm, that Odin fashioned the first of our race. Achilles used an ashen spear, and Cupid made his arrows of the wood. The clubs of early warfare were often of ash, for its wood is tough and lasting. Its names of "husbandman's tree" and "martial ash" indicate its importance in the industries and arts of battle. Pliny, in his unnatural natural history, assures us that evil creatures have a dread of it, and that a serpent will cross fire rather than pass over its leaves. English mothers would rig little hammocks to ash trees where their children might sleep while field work was going on, believing the wood and leaves to be a protection against dangerous animals and more dangerous spirits. A bunch of the leaves guarded any bed from harm, and that house which was surrounded by an ash grove was secure indeed. "May your footfall be by an ash's root," is an old English form of wishing luck. The Germans gave honey from the ash to the new-born babe, just as the Scottish Highlanders give a drop of its sap to the infant as his first food. During Yule-tide festivals the ashen log was burned, and the ashen fagot carried the sacred fire from the old year to the new. In England the burning of ashen logs and

MYTHS AND LEGENDS OF FLOWERS

fagots at Christmas was the gladdest occasion of the year, and the first withe that broke in the fire indicated the early marriage of the girl who had chosen it.

In Scandish legend, the foundation of the world was the sacred ash Yggdrasil, which sprang from the void, ran through the earth (a disk with a heavenly mountain in the center), and threw its branches into the higher heavens. Its leaves were clouds, its fruits the stars. Its three roots delved into hell, or Hela's realm, where, before the creation, was no light, no life. At each root gushed a spring- the spring of force, the spring of memory, the spring of life. Beside the main stem were the wells, that of Mimir in the north, from which the ocean flows; and that in the cheery south, where the waters of Urdar spread, with swimming swans that symbolize the sun and moon. Says the Voluspa: "An ash I know called Yggdrasil, high and refreshed by purest water that comes back in dew, it stands ever green over Urdar." Midgard, or the world, was attached half way up the trunk and supported by the branches. Outside of the habitable land stretched the ocean, and on the earth's extreme rim, lying on the surface of the sea, lay the serpent, its tail in its mouth as it encircles the world, symbolizing continuity and eternity. Still outside the ocean were mountains forming a barrier to any adventurous foot that might wander so far. On the fruit of the tree, which Iduna, goddess of life, threw down to them, the gods lived and increased in strength, though other forms of the legend say that the fruit was not ash-berries, but apples. Three sisters, or norns, representing the past, present, and future, kept the tree flourishing with melted snow from the northern hills.

Other Norse legends are associated with Yggdrasil:

Odin's leaving his eye to Mimir as a pledge means only that the light of his eye was darkened when the sun sank every evening in the sea- when he descended to learn wisdom of the dwarf. The life-giving mead that Mimir drank every morning

MYTHS AND LEGENDS OF FLOWERS

was the daybreak. The fourth day of the fourth week was Ash Odinsday, or Wodensday. And every year the people were taught of Yggdrasil by the priests; how its life pervaded all lesser things, making of men who shared it the relatives of beasts and even of the trees; how beneath the tree is hid the gjallarhorn that shall sound over the world when comes the twilight of the gods, or day of judgment; how on that day Yggdrasil will bow, the sea rush foaming over the land, heaven open, and the fire spirits leap from below, spreading ruin everywhere. Yet after the destruction Yggdrasil shall grow again, larger and more beautiful than before, the gods will reassemble, men shall live, and the chain of being will be carried higher than it has yet reached.

There is a little tree known as the sorb, roan, rowan, or mountain ash, that saved the life of Thor when he was swept away by a flood in the Vimur. Feeling himself lifted from his feet in the current, he laid hold on the tree, and so came into vogue the saying, "The sorb is Thor's salvation." For a long time after the North was nominally converted, it was still the custom for ship-builders to put at least one plank of sorb into the hull of every ship, in the belief that Thor would look after his own. The Scottish Highlanders put a cross of rowan over their doors in order to keep their cows in milk, for no witch would enter where this cross was placed. To make the cattle doubly safe, hoops of rowan were fashioned that the cows might be driven through them on the way to stable. Good fairies are kind to children who carry rowan berries in their pockets, for these berries may at one time have been prayer beads, the occurrence of the ash near Druid monuments giving rise to a belief that it was sacred in more than one faith. In Iceland, the tree springs from the graves of innocent persons who have been put to death, and lights will shine among its branches; yet it is a mischievous thing, for whereas Thor's plank will save a Norwegian ship, it will sink one made in Iceland; it will destroy a house, moreover, and if buried on the hearth will estrange the friends who sit around it.

MYTHS AND LEGENDS OF FLOWERS

The variety of ash called the service tree, which is related to the shad bush of this country, has edible berries, and yields an intoxicating beverage. As the spirit of this tree watches cattle, a Finnish shepherd will sometimes plant a stick of it in his pasture, when offering prayers for the protection of his stock.

AVOCADO PEAR

The avocado, or alligator pear, a soft and rather salve-like fruit, used pleasantly in salad, was a favorite food of Seriokai when he inhabited the wilds of Guiana, and he often rambled about the forests of the Orinoco gathering store of it. During one of these excursions the tapir saw the woman, fell in love with her, and at last won her heart. When the unsuspecting Seriokai went to gather fruit, as usual, his wife followed close with a stone ax, for cutting fuel. As the man was descending an avocado tree she struck at him so vehemently that his right leg fell from his body, and he lay helpless.

Gathering up the fruit, the woman hurried to the tapir's hiding-place, and the wicked couple went away together. Seriokai was found by a neighbor, who stanched his wound and took him home, where he was nursed back to health. So soon as he could, he mended his leg with a wooden stump; then, armed with bow and arrows, he started after the runaways. Although their path had long been obliterated, the Indian traced them through the wilderness by the avocado trees that had sprung from the seed scattered by the faithless wife. It was a long and weary following. He climbed mountains and forded rivers, but always there were avocado trees stretching away and away, and leading him nearer to his revenge. The trees grew smaller, showing that they were young. They shrank to saplings. They became mere sprouts. At last there were no trees, but only seeds, and then footprints. And so, at last, he overtook them. The outraged husband sent an arrow through the body of the tapir just as the beast bounded off from the edge of the world, and, seeing her

MYTHS AND LEGENDS OF FLOWERS

companion so transfixed, the woman leaped also. Hot in his thirst for vengeance, Seriokai followed, and he still hunts the unrepentant ones through space. He is Orion, the woman is the Pleiades, and the tapir is the Hyades, with bloody eye.

BALM

Garden balm, or melissa, cured hypos and heart troubles. Paracelsus saw in it the elixir of life. Taken in wine, it cured the poison of snakes and of rabid animals. Of faith in its medicinal virtue we have a tale from Staffordshire:

It was the Wandering Jew who was crossing the moors on a Whitsun night, suffering from thirst. He knocked at a cotter's door and craved a cup of beer. This the cotter gave to him, and the Jew, refreshed, commented on the pallor and weakness of the man. "You are ill?" he asked. "Yes, past help. It is a consumption will end me presently.", "Friend, do as I bid you, and by God's help you shall be whole. In the morning put three balm leaves in a pot of thy beer and drink as often as you will. On every fourth day put fresh leaves into the cup, and in twelve days you will be whole."

The sick man pressed the stranger to stay and break bread with him, but the Jew's doom of unease was upon him, and he rushed away into the night. The peasant culled the balm, and in twelve days was sound in health again; wherefore the memory of the man who has been wandering about the earth since the crucifixion is not wholly evil.

BALM OF GILEAD

It is said that not an ounce of true balm of Gilead leaves the Turkish empire, although it was long an article of commerce. Joseph's brothers were trading in it when an excess of the business spirit prompted them to sell him into slavery. The tree amyris yields it in three forms: xylobalsamum, which is obtained by steeping the new twigs; carpobalsamum, expressed from the fruit; and opobalsamum which is extracted from the kernel. The best, however, is the balm, or sap, obtained from incisions in the bark. It was believed that, so powerful was this substance, if one would coat his finger with it he could pass it through fire or even set fire to it without suffering. Hence we continue to use the phrase, "There is balm in Gilead," when we would signify that there is healing and comfort for the ill and afflicted. In the East the balm sweetened the bath, for it was deemed that when the pores of the skin were open, they would absorb the perfume and return it to the air. It was also a safeguard against plague.

BASIL

Basil, or sweet basil (ocymum), bears the name of king (from the Greek, basileus), for reasons unknown, unless it be that it was once a king over pain. It was a subject of almost fantastic differences of opinion between medicine men in the old days, some declaring that it was a poison, and others a cure. Some hold that the name basil is shortened from basilisk, a fabulous creature that could kill with a look. In India, where the basil is native, it is a holy herb, dedicated to Vishnu, whose wife, Lakshmi, it is in disguise. To break a sprig of the plant fills him with pain, and he commonly denies the prayers of such as trespass against it; yet it is permitted to wear the seeds as a rosary and to remove a leaf, for every good Hindu goes to his rest with a basil leaf on his breast, which he has only to show at the gate of heaven to be admitted. In Persia and Malaysia basil is planted on graves while in Egypt women scatter the flowers on the resting places of their dead. These faiths and observances are out of keeping with the Greek idea that it represented hate and misfortune, and they painted poverty, in apotheosis, as a ragged woman with a basil at her side.

In Romania, the maid who has set her cap for a young

MYTHS AND LEGENDS OF FLOWERS

man will surely win his affection if she can get him to accept a sprig of basil from her hand. In Moldavia, too, if he so accept it, his wanderings cease from that hour, and he is hopelessly hers. In Crete, where it is cultivated as a house plant, it symbolizes "love washed with tears" but in parts of Italy it is a love-token, and goes by the name of little-love and kiss-me-Nicholas, a name that of course invites the swain when he discovers it in the hand or in the hair of his mistress. Voigtlanders hold it to be a test for purity, as it withers at the touch of the unchaste. Isabella, whose story has been told by Boccaccio, Keats, and Hunt, in tale, poem, and picture, was a maid of Messina who, left to her own resources by her brothers- they being rich and absorbed in business- found solace in the company of Lorenzo, the comely manager of their enterprises. The brothers noted the meetings, but, wishing to avoid a scandal, they pretended to have seen nothing. Finally they bade Lorenzo to a festival outside of the city, and there slew him. They told their sister that Lorenzo had been sent on a long journey, but when days, weeks, even months, had passed, she could no longer restrain her uneasiness, and asked when he would return. "What do you mean?" demanded one of the brothers. "What have you in common with such as Lorenzo? Ask for him farther, and you shall be answered as you deserve."

Isabella kept her chamber for that day, a victim to fears and doubts; but in her solitude she called on her lover, making piteous moan that he would return. And he did so; for when she had fallen asleep, Lorenzo's ghost appeared, pale, blood-drabbled, with garments rent and moldy, and addressed her: "Isabella, I can never return to you, for on the day we saw each other last your brothers slew me." After telling where she might find his body, the speaker melted into air, and in fright she awoke. Unable to shake off the impression of the scene, she fled to the scene of the tragedy, and there, in a space of ground recently disturbed, she came upon Lorenzo, lying as in sleep, for there was a preserving virtue in the soil. She was first for moving corpse to holy ground, but this would invite discovery, so with a knife she removed the head, and, borrowing "a great and goodly pot," laid it therein, folded in a fair linen cloth, and covered it with earth. Some basil of Salerno she then planted, and it was her comfort to guard the growing plant sprung from her lover's flesh, and water it with essences and orange water, but oftener with tears. Tended so with love and care, the plant grew strong and filled the room with sweetness. Her home-staying and the pallor of weeping led the brothers to wonder, and, thinking to cure her of a mental malady, they took away the flower. She cried unceasingly for its return, and the men, still marveling, spilt it from its tub to find if she had hidden anything beneath its root; and in truth she had, for there they found the moldering head which, by its fair and curling hair, they recognized as Lorenzo's. Realizing that the murder had been discovered, they buried the relic anew, and fled to Naples. Isabella died of heart-emptiness, still lamenting her pot of basil.

BEAN

By what mad inversion of reasoning, defiance of observation, or perversion of use came the bean into its ancient disrepute? If one reads the records truly, it begat insanity; it caused nightmare; to dream of it meant trouble; even ghosts fled shuddering from the smell of beans. The goddess Ceres, in doing good to men, set apart the bean as unworthy to be included in her gifts. The oracles would not eat it lest their vision be clouded. Hippocrates was that kind of physician who taught avoidance of it, lest it injure sight. Cicero would none of it, because it corrupted the blood and inflamed the passions. The Roman priests would not even name it, as a thing unholy.

The only tradition concerning the bean relates it to the philosopher Pythagoras, who spread among the Egyptians the belief that on leaving their bodies certain souls became beans. Believing, then, that the bean was half-human, he refused to eat it. Being pursued by enemies who required his life, because he was reputed to be a magician, he came to a bean-field, and, recognizing in the vines only fellow souls that he could not trample, he stood still and permitted himself to be killed.

BEECH

In Tusculum the hill of Corne was covered with beeches, curiously round like evergreens in a topiarian's garden, and dedicated to Diana, to worship whom the people came from miles around; and one of these trees was a favorite of the orator Passenius Crispus, who read and meditated in its shade, embraced it familiarly, and often testified to his regard by pouring wine on its roots. It was of beech that Jason built the Argo, too- all but its speaking prow- and Bacchus quaffed his wine from beechen bowls, possibly cut from the purple beech, which shows wine stains in its leaves.

Our Indians occasionally buried their dead in trees and under them, that no wild animals might reach the bones, and it was to save the body of chief Polan that it was hidden under a beech after the battle of Sebago Lake in 1756. His brothers pried the tree out of the earth till a hollow was left below the roots in which they placed the dead in panoply of war, his silver cross on his breast, and bow and arrows in his hand; then the sapling was straightened, and it grew to a fine height, feeding on the corpse and marking the resting place of the brave with a noble monument. One of the marriage ceremonies in India is an exchange between bride and groom of a betel for an areca nut. The betel is esteemed for no less than thirty virtues, which possibly become implanted in those who chew its leaves industriously. Indeed, there should be compensations for this employment, and one of them is that it dulls appetite. It is said that among the wretchedly poor of India and other eastern lands the betel is chewed less to sweeten the breath than to allay the bite of hunger. In the belief of the Hindus the plant was brought from heaven by Arjoon, who stole it from a tree he found there. In memory of this performance, the Hindu who desires to plant a betel steals the shoot.

BIRCH

The birch, praised as lodge and canoe, used as plate, pail, basket, and cloak, was also the paper for the books of Numa Pompilius, written seven hundred years before Christ, and the sybilline leaves bought by Tarquin were of its bark. And it must have been highly useful in the past, for it was variously a safeguard against lightning, wounds, barrenness, gout, the evil eye, and caterpillars. The fasces of the Roman lictors- bundles of rods with battle axes in the center- were of birch wood, and its expression of authority lingers with us, though the schoolboy, smarting from it, found surcease from sorrow in nibbling at the black birches spicy bark. It is a graceful tree, the birch, though its dwarf variety has never regained the stature it enjoyed before Christ was beaten by rods of it, for it was stunted, then, with shame.

The Russian still believes the tree a symbol of health, because its "wine," or sap, is a "cure" for consumption, its oil a lubricant, its bark a torch, and it is a cleanser, for in the sweat baths the defendant is flogged into a perspiration with birch. In the top of a birch the Virgin disclosed herself to the faithful of Buian- a disclosure that folklore associates with that of the Wild Woman of the Wood, who shows herself to a German shepherdess, asking her to stop her spinning, and dance. The shepherdess, dazzled by the shining white of the stranger's raiment, and admiring the beauty which is heightened by a crown of wild flowers, complies, and the twain dance together gleefully for three days, the Wild Woman stepping so lightly that she does not bend the grass. Then she fills the girl's pockets with birch leaves that turn to gold as soon as she has reached home. In Russia, however, the genius of the forest is masculine, and is

MYTHS AND LEGENDS OF FLOWERS

invoked by cutting down young birches, placing them with points inward, in a circle, then standing in the enclosure and calling him. When he appears he is conducted respectfully to a seat on a stump, facing the east; his hand is kissed, and he is implored to grant various favors, which he does willingly enough if the petitioner will give his soul in return.

BLACKBERRY

Blackberries are luxuriant in Cornwall, where John Wesley, preaching to the poor people of that county, had to subsist largely on the fruit he picked along the roadsides. "We ought to be thankful that there are plenty of blackberries," he remarked to a brother in the church, "for this is the best county I ever saw for getting a stomach, and the worst I ever saw for getting food." It is in that quarter one hears the story of the Princess Olwen, fair daughter of a dark, sour man, and twin of a dark and bitter woman who in nature was her father over again. Between the two girls there was no quarrel till the king's son stopped at their door to beg a cup of milk; for it was Olwen, the fair, who gave it, while it was dark and jealous Gertha who had hoped to ensnare him. In order to leave the field to Gertha, the father sent Olwen away to be cared for by a witch. Of course, the prince went back in a day or so for another cup of milk, and was so visibly sad when Gertha poured it for him that she hated her good sister more than ever. The prince soon learned where Olwen had been sent, and went to see her, but was told that she had died and that a blackberry, blooming out of season across the way, marked her grave. The witch had turned the girl into a bush, but released her back to her human form when the prince had gone, not realizing that a wizard's wit is as good as a witch's, and that the prince had an adviser at his court who was skilled in white magic. This man of science put the prince into the form of a chough, that he might fly to the witch's hut and see what would be happening; and the young man was delighted to meet his adored Olwen, released from her bush, and willing, when he was a man again, to go with him to the ends of the earth. They were making desperate love when they were discovered by the witch, who ended the meeting by changing the girl to a vine, while the prince, as a bird, flew to his palace. "Put the form of a bramble on Olwen forever," shouted the wicked old parent, when he learned how the prince had outwitted him, "and make her fruit green and black by turns, and sour, and the stems thorny." But the court wizard, as he disguised his lord for another flight, cautioned him, "To your love, and kiss the bloom, and when the berry is sweetest, bring it." And when the berry was black and shining and full of honey the prince carried it to the wizard, who undid the spell of the witch and restored Olwen to her own fair form.

Perhaps because of this brief association with virtue the devil hates blackberries, and, having nothing better to do when St. Michael had defeated him, he specially cursed the plant, so that it never bears fruit till St. Michael's day has passed. A better reason for the devil's hatred is that it furnished the crown of thorns that pressed the brow of Christ, and it was also the burning bush in which the Lord appeared to Moses. On St. Simon's day, October 28, the fiend stamps around the blackberry patches, and not a berry appears after. As if his other feats of villainy were not enough, the devil throws his cloak over the bushes and withers them whenever and wherever he can, though in Ireland it is not the arch-rascal, but Phooka, one of his imps, that does the mischief. If you have loose teeth, snake bites, rheumatism, pop eyes "that hang out," and a few other ailments, eat the leaves as a salad, and you may feel better; and if you burn or scald yourself apply the leaves, wet with spring water, saying, "There came three angels out of the East. One brought fire and two brought frost. Out fire and in frost. In the name of the Father, Son, and Holy Ghost. Amen."

MYTHS AND LEGENDS OF FLOWERS

BLOOD TREE

The tree with whose juice the Aztecs dyed their cotton of a fine dark red, and which their descendants tap today, has its blood legend: In Amatlan lived a prince whose delight it was to deck himself in gold and precious stones. He had a corps of bandits in his employ, and whenever a merchant went from one town to another, his spies informed him, and, doffing the raiment of a prince, he rode with his company to a defile in the hills or the depth of the woods and there awaited his victim, who went on with empty saddle-bags and an aching heart.

When the prince had shared with his troopers, reserving the lion's share for himself, he dismissed his band, all but a single slave, with whose help he buried his treasure. As the slave bent to place the plunder in the pit, the prince slew him, tumbling the corpse into the hollow and covering it, with his own hands, for the ghost of a person buried with treasure would guard it forever. For years the prince pursued his evil course, but the reckoning came. After a successful foray he withdrew to bury the loot, after his fashion, but this time the slave who was to dig the pit turned suddenly upon his master and with a blow of a spade clove his skull. He flung the body into the cavity, covered it, and carried away the treasure. And presently blood trees grew above every pit where dishonest money had been hidden, but the sap of the tree that sprang from the grave of the robber prince was the deepest red of all.

BOX

Box, trimmed in grandfather's garden to hedges and borders, and in older pleasances tortured into shapes of animals, decanters, and rolling-pins, has become so rare in this country that stout plants which have taken a hundred years to grow are valued at a hundred dollars or more. As it resembles myrtle or bay, the box was regarded with apprehension by the ancients, for they feared that if it were used by mistake for that other tree in the rites of Venus, that goddess would revenge herself by destroying their virility. Boxwood was a precious stuff, to be carved and inlaid with ivory for jewel caskets. Its branches were convenient for the Jews, also, when they would celebrate the Feast of Tabernacles; and to this practice of symbolizing or conventionalizing the lodges in the wilderness with a green bough may be due that of masking English fireplaces at Whitsuntide with foliage. The Turks plant the tree in cemeteries, and in rural England it was till lately the custom to cast sprigs of it into the grave at burials.

BRIONY

In medieval Atri, Italy, stood an old tower with briony striving for a hold on its wall. And this vine tells a story that has lived through several centuries. We have Longfellow's version in his "Bell of Atri." It was the king's order, proclaimed through the region by heralds, that if any citizen suffered wrong he was to ring the bell in the tower and demand justice, and it would be given to him. It was not often that the bell rang, for the people were disposed to honesty and peace; hence the bell-rope frayed with age, and some one tore off a branch of the briony and braided it upon the end, leaving it fresh and green and covered with leaves. There lived in Atri a knight who, from a joyous and adventurous youth, had lapsed into a mean and saving age.

Of the relics of his active days he held to only one- a poor old horse outworn in his service. But his daily thought was how to save, and at last he said, "This horse is useless. The pennies I squander for hay could as easily go into my cash-box. There is plenty of grass. He shall go into the roads and live for himself." So the equine wreck was whipped into the highway, and the stable locked against him. The poor beast shambled on till he came to the bell-tower, and there was the rope, new

MYTHS AND LEGENDS OF FLOWERS

mended with briony, the first green, inviting thing he had seen in weeks. He laid hold of it in earnest, and his tugging caused the bell to rock on its trunnions. The people, always curious as to trouble, came pouring out of their houses to learn of the matter. Great was their astonishment when they recognized in the lean old hack, ringing for justice, the horse of the miser knight. The magistrate of the town, reading a lesson in the incident, commented on the pride that went forth on horseback and came back afoot, adding that greatness was not in wealth or titles, but in deeds, and deeds of kindness most. On being told what his horse had done, the knight was not much disturbed, and affected to treat the matter lightly, saying that he could do as he liked with his own; yet for shame's sake he made no resistance when the multitude marched back with the animal and saw him safely installed in the stable of his owner. The people exacted an assurance that he would be treated with better humanity in future.

BROOM

Planta genista, or broom, has lent its name to the Plantagenets since the day when Geoffrey of Anjou thrust it into his helmet, as he was going into battle, that his troops might see and follow him. As he plucked the badge from a steep bank, which its roots had knit together, he cried, "This golden plant shall be my cognizance, rooted firmly amid rocks, yet upholding what is ready to fall. I will maintain it on the field, in the tourney, and in the court of justice." Another origin is claimed for the heraldic use of this yellow flower in Brittany, of which province it is the badge. There a prince of the house of Anjou assassinated his brother and seized his kingdom, but derived no comfort from the power and riches that crime had won, so that he was fain to leave his castle and make a pilgrimage of repentance to Holy Land. Every night on the journey he scourged himself soundly with a brush of "genets," or genista. Louis XII of France continued the use of this token, and his bodyguard of a

MYTHS AND LEGENDS OF FLOWERS

hundred nobles wore the broom-flower on their coats, with the motto, "God exalteth the humble." When Christ was praying in Gethsemane on the night before the tragedy he was disturbed by the sawing and crackling of a broom plant. It continued its noise till those who sought him approached, with Judas at their head, when, seeing the array of swords and spears, he said to the broom, "May you always burn with as much noise as you are making now." It was the broom and chick-pea, also, that by their rustling and snapping so nearly disclosed the hiding-place of Mary and Jesus when they had taken refuge among them from the soldiers of Herod. Hence the plant has reason for the humility which its employment for sweeping continues to enforce, and it has additional disgrace in that it was a choice of witches who chose to ride abroad on it at night.

BUGLOSS

Among the plants that thrive in the unlikeliest of places is the bugloss, with its furry stems and juiceless-seeming leaves. The flowers issue as magenta, but fade to a blue of quality that suggests red litmus paper after it has been dipped into alkali. It was anciently held to be a plant of lies, because the root of one variety, anchusa tinctoria, was used to falsify the complexions of fayre ladyes. It provided a rouge before carmine had been discovered. In common speech the plant is viper's bugloss, rather than bugloss, because its seeds are thought to resemble snake heads, that likeness under the doctrine of signatures specifying it as a cure for the bites of serpents.

CABBAGE

It has become generally forgotten that the man in the moon was sent there because of his predilection for cabbage. His hankerings for this fragrant vegetable had become so keen that one evening he could resist them no longer, and, having no cabbages of his own, he filched one from his neighbor. Such conduct is not uncommon, but this particular evening happened to be the 24th of December, and he who would steal cabbages on Christmas eve is worthy to be translated. He was. Comes a child in white, riding, who says, "'Since you will rob on this holy night, let you and your basket go to the moon!" Whisk! He was lifted beyond all temptation, and where all who see may offer him as on object lesson to youth. But there is another legend concerning the cabbage:

Lycurgus, prince of Thrace, having destroyed the vines in Dionysius's vineyard, was bound to a vine as punishment, and he lamented his lost liberty so earnestly that his tears had substance and took root as cabbages, in which is symbolized the old belief that the cabbage is an enemy of the grape and will cure intoxication. Indeed, the cabbage has been held as an enemy of all other plants, because it draws to itself the fatness of the earth and starves its neighbors. It was so sacred a plant, despite its stupefying properties and its smell when cooking or decaying, that the Ionians swore their oaths upon it; and fairies travel on the stalks, as witches do on broomsticks.

CACTUS

The arms of Mexico are an eagle with a serpent in its beak, resting on a cactus. When the Aztecs set off on their pilgrimage, seeking the land of plenty and security, their wise men told them to build where they should find an eagle, a snake, and a cactus. Reaching what is called by the people of the present Mexico City the plaza of Santo Domingo, in 1312, they beheld that for which they were seeking, and there they rested, and built, laying the foundation for a finer and greater state than they had dreamed.

Sorcerers in Peru are said to use the thorns of the cactus to accomplish the death or injury of people at a distance, after the manner known to Voodooists. An image of the person to be afflicted is made of rags or clay, and this the Peruvian wonder-worker jabs with cactus thorns, muttering spells the while. The cactus stores water in regions almost waterless, hence it is precious to those who are lost in the desert; and it also exhibits a glory of bloom that is little appreciated by those who live in countries where the wild flowers are of gentler aspect. Of the six hundred species, we make use of the nopal as a food for cochineal, while others yield fruit, fodder, and cordage. It is believed in some parts of the South that if a horse rubs against a cactus and is pricked by its spines, his white spots will be poisoned, whereas if he has no white spots he will not suffer.

CAMELIA

This flower is named for Kamel, a Moravian Jesuit, who, returning to Spain from the Philippines in 1639, had audience with the queen, Maria Theresa, and gave into her hands a glossy shrub bearing two flowers of intense white. The queen accepted the gift, and immediately dismantled it of its blooms, for her husband, Ferdinand, was pacing the next room in a fit of melancholy, and she wished to divert his thoughts. Fortunately, that celebrity was in a mood to be pleased, and he ordered the plant to the royal greenhouses.

The camelia is a type of purity, since it is not only of the whiteness of snow, but is devoid of odor. Yet the younger Dumas has bestowed a sinister meaning on it by naming the erring heroine of his famous play Camille, or, "the lady of the camelias."

CAMPANULA

Campanula speculum, also known as bell flower, is held to resemble an ancient mirror; hence its name of Venus' looking-glass. Venus, it seems, owned a mirror which had the power of adding to the beauty of what was reflected in it. She mislaid this

MYTHS AND LEGENDS OF FLOWERS

treasure, on one occasion, and it was found by a shepherd, who, suddenly enraptured of his own perfections, stood as a fixture, gloating. Cupid, who was seeking the glass, came upon him, and, half in amusement, half in vexation that his mother's treasure should be thus handled by a yokel, struck it out of his fingers and left him wailing. But the object, being divine, left its impress on the sod in a host of flowers- the campanula. There is a variety of this flower known as Canterbury bells, which takes its name from a resemblance to the bells rung by pilgrims while wending toward Canterbury to pray at the tomb of Thomas a Becket.

CAMPHOR

As disclosed in one Japanese legend, the spirit of the camphor tree has power over the elements. One of these trees, a big and gnarly specimen, stands in the temple grove at Atami. Here once lived a pious hermit, who from his place of meditation could look over the water and warn the sailors of coming storms, or of those rufflings of the surface that indicated the incoming of a school of herring. In one of the seasons of scarcity the priest, weary with praying and advising, fell asleep and dreamed that the shore was heaped with fish. He was about to go to the water and give thanks to the sea spirits, when he awoke, terrified by a roaring and hissing and the uproll of vast clouds out of the sea. A volcano had exploded under the ocean, vapor darkened with dust was rushing for miles into the air, and the steam had killed the fish, which lay in heaps along the beach. The ground shook, and the people, half-choked with steam and gas, were running inland in alarm. There was a great lurch in the ground in which the camphor tree split from crown to root, and a beautiful figure stepped from the trunk, and, holding toward the hermit a branch which the earthquake had shaken down, bade him take it, wave it three times above the boiling ocean, and in the final turn cast it into the water in the name of the goddess Kwanon, the lady of mercy.

MYTHS AND LEGENDS OF FLOWERS

The hermit hurried to the shore and in a loud voice called on the sea to be calm, whereupon the eruption ceased, the fish swam safely once more, excepting such as had left their bodies to feed the villagers, and there was peace. The priests say that the goddess who emerged from the camphor tree, as if she were the soul of it, was the goddess Kwanon herself.

CANNA

Our canna, with its pompous banners of red, is dear to the oriental in that its seeds are the beads of the Indian rosary. According to the Burman, the canna sprang from sacred blood. The diabolic Dewadat, jealous of Buddha's influence and fame, and hearing that he was to undertake a journey, climbed upon a hill and awaited the saint's coming. He had poised a monstrous boulder at the brink of a slope, and when the object of his hate was passing the fiend pushed the mass over. The boulder plunged to Buddha's very feet, where it burst into a thousand pieces. A single fragment, striking the good man's toe, drew blood, which, as it soaked into the earth, arose again- the canna; while the earth, with equal sensibility, opened just under the feet of the wretched Dewadat and swallowed him.

CARNATION

In our grandparents' day the carnation was known as the pink, because the more popular varieties were pink in color. In that very fact some essayed to read the occasion for its later name, for pink is the hue of carne, or flesh; but we are also told that carnation is no more than coronation, because the spicy-smelling blossom was used for crowns and garlands with which the ancients decked themselves. The flower was held in affection, too, because cooks had learned to use it as a seasoning for dishes, and experts in drinking also found that it gave tang to beer and wine. The flowers were candied, like rose-leaves, and these conserves "wonderfully above measure do comfort the

MYTHS AND LEGENDS OF FLOWERS

heart."

There is a popular belief that the plant springs from the graves of lovers, hence it has come to be used as a funeral ornament; but it should also be a flower of rejoicing, inasmuch as it is one of those that appeared on earth for the first time when Christ was born. The Italian house of Ronsecco displays the carnation in its armorial bearings for the reason that it was a parting gift of the countess Margharita Ronsecco to her lover, Orlando, when he was hurried from her side on the eve of their bridal, to rescue Christ's tomb from the Saracens. A year later a soldier brought her news that Orlando had fallen in battle, and he returned the lock of her shining hair that Orlando had carried as his talisman, together with the withered carnation, which his blood had changed from white to red. Margharita discovered that the flower had begun to set its seed, and these she planted in memory of her beloved. The plant budded, and there was revealed a white flower, such as she had given to her knight, but with a red center like none ever before seen in a carnation.

CAROB

There is a Talmudie legend that finds its counterpart in the folk-lore of half the world, the version we best know being "Rip Van Winkle." The Hebraic narrative sets forth that the Rabbi Chomi, wandering abroad, came upon an old man who was planting a carob by the wayside. Chomi laughed at him for his foolishness.

"Do you expect to gather fruit from it- you, with your hair of white? It takes thirty years for the carob to ripen, and before that time you will be gathered to your fathers."

"It is true, master," replied the old man humbly. "I am not planting for myself. I have eaten carobs that other men have planted, so why may not I do the like for other men? The sons of my sons will eat of this and thank me."

Chomi wandered till he was overcome by weariness and dropped upon the earth to rest. When he awoke the sun was rising, and, grieving for the anxiety he had caused to his family by sleeping in the field all night, he arose and began to retrace his steps. But his limbs had suddenly grown weak and shrunken, his joints were stiff, his head was heavy, and his thoughts were slow. After a time he came to the spot where he had met the old man, and he started in wonder, for instead of a sapling there was a great carob, filled with ripened pods. A boy was looking up at it with longing, and to him Chomi put the question, "Who planted this tree?" "My grandfather. He put it here the day before he died." Chomi turned away and resumed his journey, doubting the truth of his senses. Passing his hand over his face, in the way people have who have freshly waked, he was startled by discovering a long white beard. Arriving at his town, he did not know a single face. Yet he knew the house of his son when he had reached it, and entered there with joy. But the woman nursing an infant in the corner was a stranger to him, and the bearded man who turned to question him he had never seen before. "I ask pardon for my mistake," the rabbi faltered. "I took this for my- for the house of Chomi's son." "Chomi's son was my father, and both he and Chomi have been dead these many years."

"Dead! My son! Is he, then, dead?"

"Perhaps you knew my father," said the bearded man.

"If so, you are welcome."

"Yes, I knew Chomi."

"How could that be?"

MYTHS AND LEGENDS OF FLOWERS

"I am Chomi."

"Chomi? Impossible! It is seventy years since he died. He wandered away, and somewhere in the wilderness he fell prey to beasts." "No, no! I tell you, I am Chomi. I am not dead."

He grew so weak that he could no longer stand, and his grandson- for the bearded man was the son of Chomi's son- supported him to a couch. He lingered there for some days, but his heart was heavy and his soul eager for the beyond. And so, as the pods were opening on the carob tree that had been planted under his eye, he blessed his survivors, and passed into the everlasting sleep.

CEDAR

When the fragrant cedar was cut for Solomon's temple and cunningly carved by artisans, the trees grew plentifully on Lebanon, but they are now disappearing there and everywhere because of the ruthlessness of men. As it was a tree of good fortune, much of its wood was demanded for figures of saints and gods- idols, in common term. The name, "life from the dead," that it bore two thousand years ago, betokens it an emblem of eternity, but this name may have signified no more than that its oil drove insects from the tombs. Because of its preservative qualities, the Egyptians used it for mummy-cases, and it has proven wonderfully lasting, for carved figures of a supposed age of three thousand years have been taken from the burial places and may be seen in our museums. In a Chinese tradition, the king of a country set his evil eyes on the wife of a faithful subject, whom he threw into prison on a baseless charge, to have him out of the way, and there the husband died of grief, while the unhappy woman flung herself from a height to escape the hateful attentions of the monarch. Even in death the twain were divided, by the king's order, but a cedar sprang from each of the graves, as if to reprove and lament his wickedness, and,

MYTHS AND LEGENDS OF FLOWERS

rising to a vast height, interlaced their roots and branches. They were known as "the trees of the faithful loves."

CHAMOMILE

This humble and rather rank-smelling wayside plant, with its innocent, daisy-like flower and finely-cut leaf, is an ingredient in a tea wherewith "granny doctors" used to afflict the youth of the country, in the attempt to "break up colds" and exercise like mercies. It is hardy, doing its best on the cold and foggy shores of New Brunswick, where its blossoms vie in size and seemliness with those of our own whiteweed or daisy. It has a wide range, however, and was esteemed in Egypt to the degree of reverence, for it was sanctified to the gods. Incidentally, it cured the ague, and among the Romans it was one of the innumerable remedies for snake bites.

CHERRY AND PLUM

It surprises the stern citizen of the west to learn that years are given by the Japanese to such a matter as flower arrangement. The art originated in Japan with Buddhism. In the fifteenth century Yoshimara disclosed his system, which he had developed that he might present his floral offerings in a way that would be acceptable to the gods. So the Japanese are pilgrims to cherry groves and iris gardens, they decorate their houses, they devise special flower arrangements for feasts and seasons, and they show the stems and leaves as integral in beauty and importance with the blossoms. Combinations they seldom use, for they believe that the single flower should show its beauties to the full. They avoid symmetry, and never crowd flowers into masses. But it is the orchards in which the Japanese most delight. April, their cherry month, installs the simple pleasures of the year. The cherry is small and crooked in its native hills, but skillful nurserymen have evolved from that type the large and gorgeous bouquets on stalks that are the gathering-places of

MYTHS AND LEGENDS OF FLOWERS

festive companies. The newspapers announce the probable date of the buds' opening as gravely as an American newspaper announces the opening of a social season. On Sunday, when labor leaves its tools, and the housewife her home industries, the Japanese throng to the parks where the trees are flowering, and there is much eating and drinking, much singing and jollity. It is the unfolding of the plum blossoms that really marks the spring in Japan, and this is a great occasion in "the silver world," as the plum grove near Tokyo is called. After the plum, "eldest brother of the hundred flowers," and used with pine and bamboo as an emblem of long happiness, sheds its petals, and its fragrance becomes a memory, the brighter cherry makes the wood's edge gay and the nightingale sings among its branches in the moon.

As the Japanese cherry has no food value, its fruit being small, acid, and not abundant, and its bark alone having uses in the arts, its perpetuation is due to the islanders' keen sense of color. It was an emperor of the fifth century who, sailing on a lake beneath the cherries, held forth his saki cup to drink, and some of the pink petals fluttered into the wine, crowning his cup as the Romans crowned their goblets with roses. So pretty were these silken flakes as they swam on the saki, that the emperor kept the practice of taking his wine beneath the trees at every season of bloom; hence wine-drinking is now a part of the celebration. A later emperor, who praised the cherry in verse, caused it to be planted abundantly about his palace and so established it in common favor. And that the regard for its beauty is genuine may be inferred from that tablet at the Sumadera monastery which bears the warning, "Whoever cuts a branch from this tree shall lose a finger." The gods of the woods resent an injury to their favorite cherries, pines, and cedars, and the maid who has been disappointed in love seeks her redress by presuming on that fact. If she has resigned hope of winning back the recreant lover she dresses as if for a conquest, and in the middle of the night attaches three lighted candles to her head dress, and a mirror to her neck. In her left hand she carries a straw image which represents the deceiver, in her right a hammer and nails; then, in the temple grove she nails the doll to a tree and prays the gods to take the traitor's life, promising that as soon as this is done she will draw the nails and trouble the tree and the gods no more. For several nights she goes to the sacred grove and repeats her prayers, adding a nail at each visit, confident that the gods will sacrifice a life in a land where lives are so many, to keep their trees, that are so few.

It was to support the cherry at Iyo that one Japanese gave his life. He was a soldier who in youth had played under its branches, and yearly, when not on service, sat in its rain of April blossoms. Time passed, and he attained great age; his wife, his children, and all his other relatives were dead. All that linked him to the past was the cherry tree. One summer it died. In this he seemed to read the command of nature to himself. The people planted a young and handsome tree close by, and he pretended to be glad, but his heart was sore. When winter came, he bowed himself under the dry branches and said, "Honorable tree, consent to bloom once more, for I am about to give my life for you." Then, spreading a white cloth on the ground, he committed hari-kari, and as his blood soaked into the roots and his spirit passed into the sap, his tree burst into bloom. And every year it blossoms on his death day, even though the ground is white and all other trees are leafless. We have no legends of the cherry, except that one was cut by the youthful Washington, but the Reverend Mr. Weems, who gives this touching and ennobling instance, has been, to put it rudely, discounted by the historians. We have, however, one historic fact concerning the cherry that is worth record, because it affects the comings and goings of millions in the American metropolis. Broadway should not only have been broad, as it is not, but straight, and in the original plan it was so; but where Grace Church stands was a cherry tree beneath which Hendrick Brevoort, tavern-keeper, loved to smoke his pipe on warm evenings. When map-makers arrived with a street plan which contemplated the extension of Broadway, and

MYTHS AND LEGENDS OF FLOWERS

the Herr Brevoort found that it ran straight across the roots of his cherry tree, he went to the officials and swore it was not to be thought of; so they, realizing that the city would never grow so far as his tavern, obligingly diverted the street, and he peacefully smoked his pipe beneath his tree for some years longer. The site of the peaceful inn where he sold his flip and mulled his ale is one of the busiest spots in Gotham today, and the multitudes who follow the crook of the street westward as they go uptown do not know that they are turned out of a straight path by a cherry tree that died long, long ago.

The plum is held by our Pawnees to symbolize plenty, but in parts of Europe it is held to be unlucky, because its stone is said to enclose the damned soul of a suicide. The myrobalan plum, too harsh for food, but used as medicine, was no such matter to the Hindu, for the wife of Somacarman struck it thrice with her wand, whereupon she ascended as an eagle and alighted on a golden hill in a city of gold. Like all stone fruits, the cherry and plum contain a trifle of prussic acid, most virulent of poisons; hence their reputation and effect may be related.

CHESTNUT

We in America have done little to keep our chestnut in favor by trying to improve its size and quality, but in Europe the tree is so well esteemed that venerable specimens receive all the care that is given to famous oaks and elms. One in the grounds of Tortworth Castle is a thousand years old, and was noted for its size in the eleventh century. A group of five chestnuts on Aetna, that grew into a single tree a hundred years ago, making a trunk seventy feet thick, was known as the Tree of a Hundred Horsemen. It has been suffered to fall into ruin, but is perpetuated in old accounts and engravings. It was on the chestnut that Xenophon's army lived during the retreat, and indications of a sacred significance are found in the solemn eating of it on St. Simon's day, and distribution to the poor on

MYTHS AND LEGENDS OF FLOWERS

the feast of St. Martin.

What we know as the horse-chestnut is thought to have obtained its name from the likeness to a horse's hoof in the leaf cicatrix; indeed, it may have been in accord with the doctrine of signatures that the nuts, crushed as a meal, were given to horses for various diseases. The horse chestnut originated, however, in Turkey, where it was created by a Mahometan saint- Akyazli. This anchorite, desiring to roast his meat, thrust a stick into the earth to support it over the fire, and such was his sanctity that heaven caused the wood to strike into the earth and increase to the tree we know.

CHICORY

In the meadows about our New England towns, there is in summer a pretty show of pink and blue blossoms, shaped like those of the dandelion, but growing from scraggy plants: the chicory, or succory. Its leaves, when young and tender, are pleasant as a salad, but it is somewhat out of estimation because it has become a common adulterant for coffee. The plentiful rays of the flower make it almost inevitable that it should have become the subject of a sun legend, and we find it in Romania, where Florilor, "the lady of the flowers"- a name she enjoyed in virtue of her gentleness and surpassing beauty- attracted, first the notice, then the admiration of the sun god, who descended from the skies to make love to her. Realizing the disparity in their positions, and doubting if he meant marriage, Florilor repelled him, to his indignation and astonishment. In retaliation for the slight, he commanded her to become a flower. She took the form of chicory, in which shape she is compelled not only to observe the sun from dawn to dark, but, as in mockery, to wear his likeness. So its old names are sunfollower and bride of the sun, and the Germans name it the way-light.

For centuries the plant has been prized as a love potion,

MYTHS AND LEGENDS OF FLOWERS

the seed being secretly administered by the lover to his mistress to secure her affection. In a German story, a girl whose lover had gone away on a voyage devoted her life thereafter to sitting at the wayside and looking for him. She kept her watch so constantly that she finally took root and became the pale blue flower known as the watcher of the road. One version of the story attributes the woman's desertion to good cause, and where that idea prevails the plant is known as the accursed maid.

CHRYSANTHEMUM

In 246 B.C. the throne of China was occupied by a cruel monarch, who learned that in the islands off his coast was a rare plant that would yield an elixir of life. But only the pure in heart could touch it without causing it to lose its virtues. Evidently the emperor himself could not do the errand, nor could he rely on his court; but a young doctor in his employ suggested that three hundred young men and three hundred girls should undertake to cross the narrow seas and search for the flower. The emperor approved the plan, and ere many days the expedition was on its way to what is now Japan. Whether they ever found the flower we do not know, but the junks never reappeared, and the emperor died. But there is a notion that, having landed on the pleasant islands out of his majesty's reach, the physician concerned himself a great deal more with furthering flirtations than he did with even so glorious a bloom as the chrysanthemum- if he found it. He may have selfishly extracted its juices for his own advantage. It is a part of the legend that he knew when he was well off, and that he remained king of the new country, which his followers replenished with a stock more moral, able, and vigorous than they had left in China.

But the chrysanthemum is of Chinese origin, and was introduced into Japan only a couple of thousand years ago. It became the national flower in the fourteenth century after a "war of the chrysanthemums" that may be likened to the war of the roses, save that, owing to the lack of quick-killing devices, it lasted for fifty-six years. The kiku, as it is called, symbolizes the sun, and in the orderly unfolding of its petals marks perfection, a like symbolism being denoted in the crystal balls which the Japanese cut so skillfully, as they stand for the orb of the sun, betokened on Japan's flag. The flower is less varied in the Mikado's country than in ours, where new strains are sold for extraordinary sums, but it grows in beauty and abundance and is admired by all classes, the commonalty cheerfully paying their two and a half cents a head to see the annual show in the Dango-Zaka, or florists' quarter of Tokyo, where figures shaped of withes and plaster are clothed entirely in chrysanthemums, which likewise become figures of animals and boats, and are even placed on floral waves as foam. This is topiary at its most grotesque, though the flowers are not cut, but rooted in the straw with which the figures are stuffed. Every night the exhibits are drenched with water, and in this way the flowers are kept for weeks. Flowers are sold cheaply at this great bazaar and in the gardens whole acres blaze with red, white, and yellow. The Japanese have two hundred and fifty varieties of chrysanthemum, but other florists are creating new strains with bewildering frequency, by the crossing of forms and colors, symmetrical and ragged, prim and flamboyant, streaked, spotted, and single-hued, straight and curled, a foot wide or an inch. Our catalogs show more than five hundred varieties, one of which is green and one lavender, the nearest that the flower can approach to blue. Extreme oddities are so far removed from nature's intent with the flower that they seldom produce seed; yet many thrifty forms of today did not exist twenty-five years ago. It is said that blossoms are made to show color on one-half the disk and white on the other by covering up the latter half so that the sun shall not strike it. The plant has been urged into bushes twelve feet high, and it has been encouraged to hide close to the earth and put out stars no bigger than buttercups. Coming at the ripeness of the year, it symbolizes human perfection. Its lasting qualities give to it a meaning of longevity which is taken literally in Kai,

MYTHS AND LEGENDS OF FLOWERS

where a certain stream is bordered with these flowers. As the petals fall into the water, the people drink of it, believing that it will increase their days on earth, and to the same end they sometimes place chrysanthemum petals in their wine cups.

Chrysanthemums grow all over the Mikado's empire, save in Himaji, where it is ill luck to raise them, for this reason: In a castle of thirty towers in that city lived a lord who employed a servant named Okiku (kiku, chrysanthemum,) to look after his bronzes, figures of brass, jewels, shrines, carvings, crystals, porcelains, and other works of art. Among these objects were ten dishes of gold. In counting the dishes one morning she discovered that one was missing, and, though innocent of its loss, she so dreaded her employer's anger that she cast herself into a well. Her ghost returns nightly to count the golden dishes, and cries loudly when it has counted nine, so distressing the populace that Okiku's flower- the specter plant- is no longer grown there.

CINCHONA

Quinine- known also as Jesuits' bark, Peruvian bark, and cinchona- has been a popular medicine for nearly a century. Its virtues were discovered in a singular manner, according to the legend: A high wind had thrown some cinchona trees into a pool which had been used by certain people as a reservoir. They noted the unusual harshness of the water, and sought a supply elsewhere.

One man who had fallen ill of a fever, being consumed with thirst and wandering near the tarn where the trees were steeping, went face downward at the shore and drank greedily. He began to mend of his illness directly, and went about telling of the bark that had imparted its virtues to the water. Its curative powers being thus made known to the Countess of Cinchon, vice-queen of Peru, she caused the bark to be powdered and experimented with by the faculty, the drug being therefore known originally as "countess' powder," and so introduced to Europe.

CINNAMON

The spice which is known as cinnamon is the inner bark of the *laurus cinnamonum* whose leaves, woven into wreaths, decked the temples of Rome, while an oil extracted from the wood was used to anoint the sacred vessels and the persons of the priests themselves in the Hebrew tabernacles. So greatly was the bark esteemed in Arabia that only priests were allowed to collect it, and they were required to give the first bundle to the sun god, placing it on his altar, where he was expected to light it with a ray of fire. As cinnamon most abounded in valleys where poisonous serpents were, the men who gathered it were forced to wear bandages on their hands and feet to protect them against stings, and this fashion of reserving it from the touch of naked flesh may have had its part in sustaining its aristocratic reputation.

CITRON

Such popularity as the citron has, among those who use it as an addition to their dietary, is due to the Jews, who carry it to the synagogue, in the left hand, during the Feast of Tabernacles, and eat it as a conserve during that observance. It was regarded almost with reverence in the Middle Ages, for it was so powerful an antidote for poisons that criminals, condemned to die by snake bite, often ate freely of citrons and returned from the ordeal in health and gaiety of spirits, leaving the authorities in sad plight as to what to do with them, since, having been bitten by law, they were legally dead. In India the citron was carried by widows going to immolation in the suttee, and probably in that case it symbolized life turned bitter because of the death of the mate.

MYTHS AND LEGENDS OF FLOWERS

CLEMATIS

Our clematis, once called love, for its clinging habit, was also traveler's joy, because it afforded shade for inn porches and at roadsides where the wayfarer might refresh himself. Wild vine, smoking cane, tombacca, devil's cut, devil's twine, Bohemian plant, ladies' bower, virgin's bower, old man's beard, and beggar's plant are other and puzzling names. Tombacca and smoking cane indicate the use of its stems as filling for pipes and substitutes for cigars, as boys occasionally smoke rattan. The gray, insubstantial down that floats the seeds to new anchorage justifies the comparison with an old man's beard, and the apparently insulting name of beggar's plant came from the practice of professional mendicants abroad, who rub its leaves on cuts made for the purpose till they have created ulcers of hideous aspect. The plant secretes an irritating juice that causes a superficial sore, and where pauperism is encouraged by miscellaneous giving, an invented affliction of this nature appeals to the charitable as strongly as do pretended lameness and assumed blindness.

CLOVER AND SHAMROCK

The considerable family of which clover is the type is widely distributed and highly useful. Honey is made from the clover of our fields, and the deliciously fragrant wild clover, that forms bushes six feet high, is a common haunt of bumble-bees. The long-headed crimson variety lately introduced into the Eastern States makes a field of color as brilliant as a flower garden. The leaves, too, are as oddly marked as are those of ornamental plants. At the quaint cemetery of St. Roch, in New Orleans, you are sometimes accosted by children who ask if you will buy clovers with Jesus' blood on them. You pay your nickel only to discover, shortly after, that patches of the plant with a red, heart-shaped spot on the upper side of the leaf are to be found all over the cemetery. Although this is called the mark of Jesus' blood, there is no local or other warrant for such a tradition. On the contrary, the old people of the French quarter recall the tale they had of their parents, to the effect that a girl who died on the eve of her marriage was buried here, in old St. Roch, and in despair her lover shot himself beside her tomb. His blood flowed over the sod, and all the clover that grew there afterward had the spot of red on its leaves. Clover has long been esteemed a flower of good luck when it has four leaves instead of three, and we still use the phrase "in clover" to denote good fortune and plenty, although that symbol expresses rather the joy of grazing animals on being turned loose in a field of it than any superstition as to luck. Those wise in visions tell us that even to dream of clover is fortunate.

The clover which we call wood sorrel was anciently a charm against snakes and other poison-dealing creatures; and witches, too, would none of it. On going into fights soldiers would tie a sprig about their sword-arms, or to the handles of their blades, that they might be secure from the foul strokes of enemies who had black and secret ways of killing. The Arabic word for the trefoil is shamrak, and Persia makes it sacred as "emblematic of the Persian Triads." Our wood sorrel is white with faint ruddy or purple streaks in the petals. A pink variety appears in England earlier than the white, but, as in other flowers, the farther north we go, the more of white appears in the flower, bluebells being white in Russia, and red campion emulating the snow in Arctic lands. Wood sorrel is "the hallelujah" in Spain and Italy, because of its blossoming when the Hallelujah is sung, after Easter; the Welsh name it fairy bells; the Scots call it hearts and gowk's meat. Cuckoo sorrel is a common name for it in the British islands, where it appears when the cuckoo begins to sing.

Among the plants one no longer eats is this same wood sorrel, once used as a salad. Sheep or field sorrel, which is of a

MYTHS AND LEGENDS OF FLOWERS

different botanical family, is still used as greens, though it is sharp to the untrained palate. The acid of wood sorrel (oxalic, from the botanical name of the plant, oxalis) is extracted as "salt of lemons," a chemical in some demand for commercial purposes, but a rank poison. Its leaves yield five per cent, of acid. Because of their heart shape, the doctrine of signatures prescribed them as a remedy for heart troubles. The variety cultivated in Bolivia as oca has a tuberous root as well prized as the artichoke; another four-leaved variety is used on Mexican tables; the Peruvian species, arracha, is also eaten, both root and leaf stalk. Wood sorrel is held by many to be the original shamrock, as its Persian name implies, although the plant commonly worn as such on the 17th of March, when all the world bows to St. Patrick, is Dutch clover. It is a little disconcerting that the authorities are not a unit as to what shamrock is. The Erse word seamrog is from seamar, three-leaved, and og, meaning small. It occurs variously as seamrog, seamsog, seamroge, shamrote, shamrocke, shamrug, seamar-oge, and chambroch. The plant actually used by St. Patrick may have been Dutch clover, or trifolium repens, or trifolium minus, or wood sorrel. Early references to it in Irish literature represent it as a food plant. Campion, in his history of the island, printed in 1571, speaking of "shamrotes, water cresses, and other herbes they feed upon." Matthias Lobel, a Flemish botanist, tells of the purple and white trefoil, and says of the white variety that it is good for fattening cattle, but that it is also ground into meal for consumption by the peasantry. Spenser, the poet, also relates how, during the wars of Munster, the people escaped starvation by feeding on cress and "shamrokes"; and Fjoies Moryson describes them as devouring this herb of sharp taste, the acrid wood sorrel, one may fancy, "which as they run and are chased to and fro, they snatch like beasts out of the ditches." If, however, the ditches contained water, the plant was probably cress, which we still use as a garnish to our meat. The religious association of the shamrock, and its adoption as the emblem of Ireland, is due to an inspiration of the pioneer of Christianity in that country: After his landing St. Patrick found his pagan subjects in deep trouble over the Trinity. Preach and argue as he might, he could not prevail on them to accept its possibility till, looking down on the earth, in the course of one of his homilies, he chanced to spy the little divided leaf of the shamrock. It exemplified his point to a nicety. Stooping, he plucked it and showed how, though a leaf, it was yet three leaves in one. After the Irish accepted Christianity, they used the shamrock as their sign, the three leaves typing, in their formulary, the national virtues of love, heroism, and wit.

The leaf was already in general use as a defense against witchcraft in St. Patrick's time, and many a peasant plucked a trefoil before he ventured across the moors and bogs where banshees cried and fairies stole the souls of wayfarers. It was the power of the shamrock, indeed, over poisonous and maleficent things, that enabled St. Patrick to drive the snakes from Ireland, for he had only to hold it toward them to see them go scuttling into the sea.

COLUMBINE

The pretty flowers of scarlet, red, purple, and white that grow on our rocky hillsides and also make a handsome show in our gardens, take their name of columbine from the Latin columba, a dove. The scientific name of aquilegia shows that it suggests quite another sort of bird from the dove to some observers, for that is derived from aquila, an eagle. Its old name of lion's herb points to a belief that it was "a favorite plant of lions." An association has been formed to make this the national flower of the United States, as the rose is the flower of England and the lily of France, for its common name suggests Columbus and Columbia, its botanical name associates it with the bird of freedom, it can be raised from seed in almost any of our gardens, and it is native to nearly all of our States.

MYTHS AND LEGENDS OF FLOWERS

CORNEL

The Rome of centuries-to-be having visioned itself in splendor before the imagination of Romulus, that founder of empire began to set bounds and sites for its defenses, and, wishing to advance the walls to the Palatine, he hurled his spear from a distance and saw it plunge into the earth upon that hill. The handle of the weapon was cornel wood, and where it struck the earth it put forth roots and branches and so became a great and thrifty thing, foreshadowing in its growth the spread and strength of the Roman state. It came to be so vehemently regarded by the populace that if any one observed it in a drooping condition, as would happen now and then in a hot and droughty season, he set up a shout of alarm that brought the citizens hurrying to its rescue with pails of water.

The Greeks have it that the first cornel (*cornus mascula*), or Cornelian cherry, sprang from the grave of Polydorus, who was slain by Polymnestor, and that it dripped blood when Aeneas tried to tear its limbs from the trunk.

CORNFLOWER

Since the German imperial family's adoption of the *centaurea kyanus*, it has gained in popularity on both sides of the sea. Queen Louise, of Prussia, flying from Berlin before the advance of the first Napoleon, hid in a field of grain with her children, and beguiled the tedium by braiding cornflowers into wreaths for their little heads. The blue flower was remembered by one of those children, the gruff old Emperor William, who, when he retaliated on the French by conquering the third Napoleon, made the centaurea his emblem, and it was adopted by his people, in whose fields it grows abundantly. Like the poppy, which also grows in the grain, the cornflower is thought to have its origin in the east. Among its names are blue bottle, blue cap, blue bonnet, blue bow, bluet, flake flower, bachelor's button, and hurt sickle. In its name it commemorates the centaur Chiron who, poisoned by an arrow dipped in the blood of the hundred-headed hydra, covered the wound with its flowers and so recovered. The hydra legend persists vaguely in a belief that if cornflower is burned snakes will fly the premises. The qualifying adjective, kyanus, commemorates a Greek youth who worshiped Flora with ardor and was forever gathering flowers for her altars. When he died, in a field, with unfinished garlands strewn about him, the goddess gave his name to the blossoms, and they were known as the kyanus.

COTTON

According to the story of a colored "auntie," this is the beginning of cotton: Many years ago there lived at a swamp's edge a tiny fairy who occupied her time in spinning, and made the most beautiful and delicate fabrics imaginable. Her wheel whirled so fast that it was nothing but a blur, such as a fly's wings make when he is tangled in a flower, and her spindle was the sting of a bumblebee- her uncle- who had left it to her, for any good use, in amends for a life so grouchy that none of the other creatures would have anything to do with him. Still, one inhabitant of the swamp was worse than the bee, and the fairy was as mightily disturbed when she discovered that he had taken up his abode on the very next bush. He was an enormous spider, big as a bird and hideously gorgeous with red, blue, and yellow. He took some pride of himself as a spinner, but when he saw the shining tissue that the fairy was weaving, he realized that his own art was cheap and poor in comparison, and he was jealous, and determined to destroy her. She caught up her wheel and spindle and ran, with the spider in pursuit. She asked the mouse for shelter, but he was afraid and shut the door; she begged the toad to protect her, but he only ran out his tongue. Finally a firefly came along, with his lantern lit. He saw the fairy; he saw the spider; and, calling on the fairy to follow, he fled with her across the field, lighting the way, for it was now night. They soon reached a bush that bore a handsome pink blossom. "Jump into the flower!" commanded the firefly. Still clutching her wheel, the fairy put her last strength into a spring and alighted in the heart of the blossom. The spider was close upon her, but as he put his ugly claw on the lower petal to draw himself up after her, she gave him such a stab in the leg with her spindle that he lost his hold and fell to the ground. In another second the flower closed over the fairy, gathering its petals so tightly that the spider could not get in. He wove his web about it, believing that he would catch her when she ventured out in the morning; but when morning came, she did not appear. The spider kept watch; but finally the petals dropped to the earth, and when he saw no fairy he knew it was all up, so he bit his own body, and died. But the fairy was not dead. She remained snuggled in the little ball that the plant put out behind the blossom, and in a few days the ball opened, and all the beautiful fabric she had been spinning while in hiding poured out in a tassel of snowy white. And men wove the threads to make garments for themselves, and they bless the fairy of the cotton plant and are glad when she escapes the weevil as well as the spider.

CROCUS

The crocus, first gem of the earth in spring, we prize for its beauty only; but the little bloom was once valued for other reasons. The stigmas of the saffron crocus, the fall variety, were a cordial, and the juice of the flower was esteemed by the women of Rome as a hair-dye, for which latter reason it was disapproved by the fathers of the Church. Henry VIII. forbade the use of crocus as a dye for linen by the Irish, who had formerly employed it for this purpose, believing that cloth so colored did not require to be washed as often as white, and that the stain had some sanitary virtue. Until recently, saffron gave a lively hue to cakes, and in cookery during the six weeks of Lenten fast it kept up the spirits of the public, although the faith that it would do so may signify no more than that the ancients used it to decorate their banquet-rooms and tables and wreathe about their wine-cups, for the effect of banquets and wine is to lift the spirits. In Cashmere, saffron was long a monopoly of the rajah, but an English traveler, who penetrated the country as a pilgrim in the day of Edward III., stole a bulb at the risk of his life, concealed it in his hollow staff, and so reached his home in Walden, where he planted it, and such a harvest of flowers came from that single root that the place has been Saffron Walden ever since. The plant and its dye were greatly esteemed in India, and it is said that when in their wars the rajahs saw themselves doomed to defeat they put on their saffron robes of state, gathered their unhappy wives about them, and submitted to be burned to death. The spring crocus was so named by the botanist Theophrastus, who applied the Greek word kroke, or thread, to its stigma, but tradition, old in his day, had it that the flower sprang from the warmth of Jove's body on a bank where he had lain with Juno on Mount Ida. Yet another legend has it that saffron is that child Krokos who, being accidentally killed by a quoit flung from the hand of Mercury, was dipped into celestial dew and changed into a flower, while our spring crocus came from some drops of the elixir of life that Medea was preparing for the aged Aeson.

CROWFOOT

This cheery yellow flower from Illyria has its counterpart in the buttercup, or, if you like the old English names better, the king's cup, gold cup, gold knobs, leopard's foot, and cuckoo bud. These ranunculi- the botanical name from rana, a frog, shows that they like to grow where frogs are plenty- are acrid, and cattle avoid them, as a rule; but the crowfoot is alleged by Pliny to have this merit: that it stirs the eater into such a gale of laughter that he scarce contains himself; in fact, unless he drinks pineapple kernels and pepper in date wine, he may guffaw his way into the next world in a most unseemly manner. With

MYTHS AND LEGENDS OF FLOWERS

one species of the plant the ancients smeared their arrows, to poison them, yet the root of another kind, the double crowfoot, or St. Anthony, would cure the plague if rubbed on the spot most affected, and was good for lunacy if applied to the neck in the wane of the moon, when it was in the sign of the bull or the scorpion.

CROWN IMPERIAL

The golden cups of the crown imperial, or fritillary, are held to resemble a crown when viewed in mass, and the commanding aspect of the plant lends color to its claim of empire over the lesser creatures of the garden. This Persian lily was a queen whose beauty, instead of contenting her husband, the king, made him jealous, and in a moment of anger and suspicion he drove her from his palace. She, conscious of her innocence, wept so constantly at this injustice, as she wandered about the fields, that her very substance shrunk to the measure of a plant, and at last, in mercy, the Divine One rooted her feet where she had paused and changed her to the crown imperial, still bearing in its blossoms somewhat of the dignity and command she had worn in her human guise.

CUCUMBER

As a phallic emblem, the cucumber symbolized fecundity, and of the sixty thousand offspring of Sagara's wife, in the Buddhist legend, the first was a cucumber, whose descendant climbed to heaven on his own vine. Jews and Egyptians reveled in cucumbers, but at the contemplation of them, the English owned to a fright, that lasted for centuries, not daring to taste lest they should "kill by their natural coldness.", "Cool as a cucumber" is a common saying, and as the fruit is mostly water its malignity has been exaggerated.

MYTHS AND LEGENDS OF FLOWERS

CYPRESS

Cyparissos, a boy much liked by Apollo, was in turn attached, not to a god, but to a stalwart playmate- a stag that grazed on sacred Ceos. Having killed the animal in an accident, he begged the gods to let him mourn forever, and, that he might do so comfortably, Apollo changed him to a cypress, dark, drooping, distilling tearful dews. Venus wreathed twigs of the cypress for her brow when she mourned Adonis; the tragic muse, Melpomene, was crowned with it; and its wood coffined the Egyptian mummies. Still, it was also used for roofing temples, which are for the worship of the principle of life, no less than for consolation in death, for it was fragrant and strong and lasting.

A cypress near the tomb of Persian Cyrus had the unhappy faculty of leaking blood every Friday- the Mahometan Sabbath- hence it was an object of veneration; but elsewhere it was freely cut and is thought to be the gopher wood of which Noah's ark was made. As its cone shape suggested flame to the Oriental, it was planted before temples of the fire worshipers in Persia, and Zoroaster himself lived in its shadow. Even in Cyprus- so named for the tree- it was worshiped as the symbol of a god. Ceres plugged the crater of Aetna with it and thus imprisoned Vulcan at his forges beneath the mountain. The oldest tree in Europe is held to be a cypress at Somma, Lombardy, one hundred and twenty-one feet high and well grown in Caesar's day. Napoleon, who spared so little, allowed it to remain when he built his road across the Simplon.

DAHLIA

Josephine, empress of the French, was born on the West Indian island of Martinique, but though this is within easy reach of Mexico, the birthplace of the dahlia, she never knew the

MYTHS AND LEGENDS OF FLOWERS

flower till she had gone to France. The Swedish botanist, Dahl, had done so much for its cultivation and improvement that his name was bestowed on the plant, and it bloomed in such splendor at Malmaison, where Josephine planted it with her own hands, that she declared it her favorite flower. She invited princes and ministers to visit Malmaison that they might see it, but she would not allow a bloom, a seed, or a root to go out of her possession. A Polish prince who possibly would not have lifted his hand to pick one of the blossoms had they been free for all comers bribed a gardener to steal a hundred of them, paying him a louis apiece. After this Josephine petulantly refused to cultivate them any longer.

DAISY

The wee, crimson tippit flower of Burns, and known to the English as the daisy, is with us a pot and bedding plant, save where it has made an escape from gardens, which is not to a large extent as yet. Our own daisy is a more glorious creature-the white weed, detested by farmers, but beautiful in their fields in June. It is near to the chrysanthemum in form and height and leaf, and is so plentiful and so lovely that it should have a better consideration in the discussion respecting the choice of a national flower. The French and German name of marguerite is permissibly applied to the daisy because that means pearl, and signifies the delicate whiteness of its petals. It also wears that name in honor of one of the six Saints Margaret: the daughter of a heathen priest who drove her from his home in Antioch when she would not renounce the Christian faith. The devotee became St. Margaret of the Dragon, and her flower appropriately bears her name because in her prayers and meditations she always kept her face toward heaven. Various Marguerites of history have made the daisy their flower also. She of Anjou had her courtiers embroider it on their cloaks and robes. Queen Margaret, mother of Henry YII., wore three white daisies. Margaret, sister of Francis I., wore it. And it is also claimed as the flower of the

MYTHS AND LEGENDS OF FLOWERS

"maid Marguerite, meek and mild," of Antioch, whose prayers for women about to become mothers saved many lives and enshrined her in their loves. Bellis, the botanical term for the old world daisy, comes from the Belides, dryads of the mythologic age, one of whom, while dancing on the green, was seen by Yertumnus, god of spring. That observer, smitten with a sudden passion, ran forward to clasp the white and graceful creature in his arms, when, to his grief and wonder, she turned an eye of fear and aversion on him, and, through divine aid in the transformation, sank to the earth in the form of the little daisy. The daisy has several names in Europe that commend themselves for quaintness or poetry. The Welsh call it trembling star; the Scottish gowan means the same as bellis; the French have christened it the little Easter flower, and the German name of Easter bowl also allies it to the Norse divinity, Ostara, goddess of spring- whence our word Easter.

Other German names are little goose flower, Mary's flower, a-thousand-charms, meadow pearl, and measure of love. The last name comes from the practice of maids who have given their hearts, without knowing whether they are to get them back again, and who resort to the flower to read the fortune of their affection, repeating Marguerite's formula, "He loves me- loves me not," as they pull off petal after petal. The last petal and the last phrase determine the situation- unless the young man in the case determines otherwise.

DANDELION

An Algonquin tale of the love of the south wind for the dandelion, which is made in likeness of the sun: Shawondasee, the south wind, heavy, drowsy, lazy, likes to lie in the shade of live oaks and magnolias, inhaling the odor of blossoms and filling his lungs so full of it that when he breathes again you detect the perfume. One day Shawondasee, gazing over his fields with a sleepy eye, saw at a distance a slender girl with yellow hair. He admired her, and but for his heaviness he would even have called her to his side. Next morning he looked again, and she was still there, more beautiful than ever. Every day he looked, and his awe sparkled when he saw the maid in the warm green prairie. But one morning lie rubbed bis eyes and looked hard a second time, for he did not trust them at first: A woman was standing where the maid bad been at sundown, but what a change! The youth was gone, the brightness fled. Instead of a crown of golden glory, here was a faded creature wearing a poll of gray. "Ah," sighed Shawondasee, "'my brother, the North Wind, has been here in the night. He has put his cruel hand upon her head, and whitened it with frost." Shawondasee put out such a mighty sigh that it reached the spot where the girl had stood, and behold! her white hair fell from her head, tossed off upon that breath, and she was gone. Others like her came, and the earth is glad with them; but in the spring Shawondasee sighs unceasingly for the maiden with the yellow hair as he first saw her.

Dandelion is a corruption of dent de lion, or lion's tooth, and the plant is so called because the leaf does not in the least resemble a lion's tooth or any one else 's. As a lion was once a symbol of the sun, and as the flower suggests that luminary, the association of the plant with the lion is more excusable on such a ground than on that of a resemblance between its leaf and teeth.

DHAK

The palassa, or parana, or dhak tree of India (hutea frondosa), sprang from the lightning, and its triple leaf is held to typify the thunderbolt, therein resembling the rod of the fire-carrier, Mercury. It is employed by the people of the east in such ceremonies as the blessing of cattle and sheep, to make them rich in milk and wool. In some accounts the dhak yields the nectar of the Hindu gods, the soma (see soma), which perpetuates life, and in the Vedas it grew from a feather dropped by a falcon that had stolen soma from the demons who guarded it. One of the angry fiends shot an arrow after the bird, causing the plume to fall, take root, and yield the fluid for which the gods were athirst. It yields red sap and red bloom, symbols of the divine fire, and as the falcon was sacred, the tree born of its feather became sacred also.

EBONY

The heavy black wood of which so many canes and batons have been made was the subject of an uncanny superstition in the time of Sir John Mandeville, that ready believer, or awful prevaricator. It was that the wood changed to flesh at certain times, and yielded an oil which, if it were put away and kept for one year, would change into "good flesh and bone," though of what animal the historian forgot to tell us. The blackness of ebony has made it a frequent figure in our language, as when we speak of ebon night and the ebon-hued negro. It was fitting that the throne of Pluto, in the nether world, should be carved from this timber, and the Pythian Apollo is also said to have been shaped from it, as were the statues of many of the Egyptian gods.

EDELWEISS

Edelweiss (noble white), a velvet flower, greenish-white, and of unobtrusive aspect, is by reason of its modesty overlooked, save by thrifty urchins who gather it to sell, and travelers, who regard it as the type flower of the Alps. In one legend the edelweiss is related to heaven, so near to which it grows, for an angel, wearying of her celestial home, longs to taste once more the bitterness of earth. She receives permission to take her shape of flesh again, but, unprepared to mingle with a humanity that even to her sympathetic eyes is enacting a tragedy of poverty, crime, oppression, misfortune, and discontent, she chooses a home among the highest and wildest of the Swiss

MYTHS AND LEGENDS OF FLOWERS

mountains, where she may look off upon the world, yet be not of it. The angel soul of the visitant illumines her face and transfigures her form to marvelous beauty. Having been seen by a daring climber, the icy fastness where she hides her loveliness is invaded by men eager to behold, and, from the joy of beholding, doomed to love her, hopelessly. She is kind but cold to all, and, unable to endure the sight of so beautiful a presence and be separated from it, her lovers join in a prayer to God that as they may not possess her they may at least be relieved from the torment of her loveliness. The prayer is answered; the angel is taken back to heaven, leaving her human heart in the edelweiss, as a memento of her earthly residence.

EGG-PLANT

As the Arab women use henna juice to redden their palms and soles, so the egg-plant is used to blacken the teeth of women in Japan, but for a different purpose, for whereas the henna stains are regarded as beautiful, the blackened teeth are a confessed disfigurement. Tradition says that the custom arose from the wish of a handsome young wife to cure her husband of a causeless jealousy. The color is obtained by dropping peel of egg-plant into water that contains a red-hot iron. After applying it to the teeth, they are brushed till they shine like metal. The practice was continued until the empress appeared in public with white teeth, when society in Tokyo dutifully followed the example. Among the commoners, however, the use of toothdye is continued to a considerable extent. The variety of egg-plant known as the apple of Sodom, or Dead Sea fruit, is often pierced by an insect, whose sting has the effect of shriveling it and converting its inside to bitter dust. The name of Dead Sea apple, however, is applied to a gall nut, like that borne on our oaks, which also results from the stings of insects. The true egg-plant which bears that name because of its shape, and not for its flavor, was anciently believed to be a poison, especially to wits, wherefore it had the names of raging apple and mad apple.

MYTHS AND LEGENDS OF FLOWERS

ELDER

Lurking in swampy isles and borders, and hiding unknown things in its shadows, the elder came to be regarded as having a supernatural consequence: it was possessed of a spirit, and none might destroy it without peril to himself. Its name associates it with Hulda, or Hilda, mother of elves, and the good woman in northern myth. In Denmark Hulda lived in the root of an elder, hence the tree was appropriately her symbol, and was employed in the ceremonies of her worship on the Venusberg. If the forbidden wood is used in buildings, the occupant will presently complain that mysterious hands are pulling his legs. The dwarf variety is believed by some to grow only where human blood has been shed, and in Welsh its name signifies plant-of-the-blood-of-men. Yet the elder has its virtues, and on the night of January 6 you may cut a branch from it, first having asked permission, and spat thrice if no answer comes from the wood. with the branch you will mark a magic circle in a lonely field, stand at the center, surrounded with such kinds of bloom and berry as you have saved from St. John's night, and, so prepared, you will demand of the devil, then abroad, some of his precious fern-seed that gives to you the strength of thirty men. Though the evil one is foot-free on that night, he is still under the spell of the good Hulda, and when a wand of her wood is directed against him he must obey, and the fern-seed will be brought by a shadowy somebody, folded in a chalice cloth.

Incidentally elder wood cures toothache, keeps the house from attack, fends off snakes, mosquitoes, and warts, quiets nerves, interrupts fits, removes poison from metal vessels, keeps worms out of furniture, and guarantees that he who cultivates it shall die in his own house. If this cross be planted on the grave- as in the Tyrol, where peasants lift their hats to the elder- the beatitude of the buried is understood when it bursts into bloom and leaf; if it fails to flower, the relatives may draw their own

MYTHS AND LEGENDS OF FLOWERS

conclusions.

ELM

America claims the elm, though its original is said to have come from Italy, where it was often used as a support for vines. As it yielded no fruit, the ancients had but a small opinion of it, and, like other such trees, they put it under protection of the infernal gods and made it a funeral emblem, as we afterward made the willow. To our Indians, it was a demulcent, even a food, and the Iroquois called the red or slippery elm "oohooska," meaning "it slips." In classic legend the elm was a creation of Orpheus, or a gift of the gods to him, for when he had returned from the vain attempt to release his wife from Hades and betaken himself to his harp for consolation, the listening earth took new life, and crowding over it came a grove of elms, marching to his song, and forming a green temple in whose shade he often pondered, and uttered melody while he remained on earth. Thus it should be the tree of Orpheus, but by some strange perversion it became the tree of Morpheus, god of sleep, and dreams hovered and roosted in its branches, ready, it would seem, to pounce on the unwary who stole a nap beneath it and fill him with conceits and terrors. In saintly heraldry the "attribute"' of Zenobio is an elm putting forth fresh leaves, for this holy man restored so many from the dead and lived so prayerful a life that the people crowded about his body at the funeral, exactly as they crowd today about the hearse of a beloved rabbi in New York, to touch his coffin and obtain healing. In the crush the corpse of Zenobio was thrown against a withered elm and instantly on this contact the tree put forth a crown of leaves, showing that he had brought the tree to life as he had raised men and women from the tomb.

It has been claimed that the lotus, which, being eaten, causes the traveler to forget his native land and be content forever in the country of the stranger, is no lotus at all, but the species of elm known as European nettle, also called hackberry and sugarberry. Sundry of the famous trees of this country are elms. Such was the Penn treaty tree, which stood in a suburb of Philadelphia until 1810, marking the spot where the only fair agreement was ever made between white men and Indians. That under which Washington took command of the American army in Cambridge is still standing, despite the appeals of a street railroad company for more track room. Our New England green with its border of monumental elms, has a likeness and precedent in old England, where an elm on a village common was a gathering place for the people when they were to debate public matters, or hold court for the trial of minor cases. In at least one instance it served as a stake for the burning of a poor wretch "for the profession of the gospel." There are not infrequent instances in folk tales of the dependence of human lives on those of plants and trees, and one such instance has been noted in the superstition relative to the great elm of Castle Howth, near Dublin.

For years this tree received care, its limbs being propped or tied when threatened with decay, in the belief that whenever a branch was broken the head of the house would die, and that when the tree itself should have lived out its life the family would become extinct.

ERYNGO

The hapless maid Sappho loved a boatman, a stalwart, handsome fellow, and to compel his love she wore sprigs of eryngo, or sea holly, for it was a faith of that age that whosoever would conceal this upon him and set his mind on the object of his affection would clinch that object to him as with bands of steel. But the boatman was of low tastes, and when she read odes to him he responded with indifference. Sappho could not abide these rebuffs, and ended the pain of them by rejecting the eryngo, singing her death-song on a cliff, and casting herself into

MYTHS AND LEGENDS OF FLOWERS

the deep. Eryngo was formerly used as a tonic and confection. Lord Bacon is authority for it that when taken with ambergris, yolks of eggs, and malmsey, eryngo roots are nourishing and also strengthen weak backs. According to Plutarch, if a goat took a sea holly into her mouth, it would not only bring her to a standstill, but affect the whole flock, so that they would remain like a group of statues, gazing into vacancy, till the herdsman, discovering the cause of the trouble, violently possessed himself of the herb and so broke the spell.

FERN

Few ferns have commercial value, though a New Zealand variety is used as a food, and the fragrant shield fern, yielding an odor that is compared to both primroses and raspberries, is boiled by the Siberian Yakoots as a substitute for tea. The commoner brake, or bracken, or eagle fern- *pteris aquilina*- so called from a fancied likeness between its frond and an eagle's wing, and which grows to seven feet in British Columbia and fourteen feet in South America, is believed to be the "fearn" of old England that gave to the villages such names as Landisfearn, Femham, Fernhurst, Farndale, Farnham (fern home), Farnsfield, Farnsworth, Feamall, Feamow, Farningham, and the like. Rarer than this variety is that known in old times as lunary and martagon, but in our day as moonwork, rattlesnake fern, and (in extreme cases) hotrychium lunaria. This would have been a most unsafe thing to have growing about one's doorstep, because on putting it into a keyhole, it will open a door; it will unlock fetters; it will loosen the shoes from a horse's feet if he but cross a pasture where it grows. Indeed, one of its ancient names is unshoe-the-horse. But rarest of all is the fern of Tartary called the barometz, or Scythian lamb, the root whereof, with its hairy rootlets, is likened to a sheep or dog.

Lucky-hands is the name given by a limited number of people to that fern which is called *aspidium filix mas*. Its unexpanded fronds resemble hands, and fronds as well as roots were used to keep off spells of warlocks and witches. Glass made from the ash of it had magic properties. Some say that the ring of Genghis Khan contained it, for whenever he wore it he could understand the ways of plants and the speech of birds. But the really precious part is the seed, for the plant flowers only once, and then in the dark. If you are abroad on St. John's night and look closely, you may see the dark red blossoms open, but only then, and at dawn they have fallen and been wholly absorbed into the earth. In the belief that it is good to see them, Russian peasants spend that night tramping through dells where the pretty plants are found. If the flowers do not appear, you may still, possibly, see the fern seed, shining like molten gold in the dark, and the seed is most precious of things, for if you scatter it, at the same time making a wish that the treasures of the earth be revealed, you shall see these treasures in a dim, blue light, as if the earth were glass. The sap of the flowering fern, when drunk, confers eternal youth. This seed can be gathered only on Christmas, just before the clock strikes midnight; and keep your wits about you, for the Devil has the care of it. At the appointed time take your stand at a lonely cross road, where a corpse has recently been carried, and where uncanny things are flocking, half visible to you. These creatures will sometimes cuff your ears, or knock off your hat, or will try to make you speak or laugh by making mysterious noises in the shrubbery, or by whispering fantastic ideas into your head. You must resist all temptation to make a sound with your lips, for if you do, either you will be changed to stone or torn to pieces. Just go forward silently till you find the fern with its seed glowing and sparkling, lay a chalice cloth under, lest the devil extend his hand to catch it, and collect such of the seed as falls before sun-up. When you begin the search you will see hideous snakes running over the frozen earth, yet they are only guides that lead the way to what you seek, and in following them should you become entangled in that fern which causes one to lose his way and sense of distance, change your shoes, putting that of the left foot on the right, and

MYTHS AND LEGENDS OF FLOWERS

vice versa, and you will regain the road.

The invocation of the spirit of the plant against magic seems to be indicated in a practice among the Syrians of printing the form of the lady fern on the hand of a woman about to be married. A leaf of this fern, known to them as bride's gloves, is laid on the hand, bound into place, then the ruddy dye of the henna tree is washed over the skin. The back of the hand, covered by the leaf, is protected, and the form of it remains as long as the stain. It is obviously the thin, black, shining stalk that gives to the adiantum its name of maiden hair, for the Greek adiantos signifies dry, and refers to the hair of Venus, which was not bedraggled when she arose from the sea, wherefore this fern was anciently Venus 's hair, and also. Virgin's hair, and, for unguessable reasons, was dedicated to Pluto and Proserpine, the gods of hell. Was the Greek myth carried to England, or how came it that in that country the fern was still a plant of mischief? True, the male fern averts sorcery and the evil eye, but you must not carry a fern, or snakes will chase you till you throw it away. All ferns are haunts of the fairies, who in Cornwall are the spirits of such as died in paganism, before the coming of Christ, and are punished for lacking the true faith by the shortening of stature and the strange life of the woods.

FIG

The fig, first known, probably, in the east, is relative of almost as many useful forms of vegetation as the rose. In its family are the famous but now little dreaded upas, the nettle, the Indian hemp, the hop, the breadfruit, the mulberry, the rubber, and other plants of milky sap. Fig wood was used by Egyptians for mummy cases, better wood being scarce in their almost treeless country, and roaming tribes have pitched their camps in its shade. The fruit still forms an important part of the diet of these wanderers, especially that of the ever-blooming species, known as the sycamore-fig or mulberry fig- to primitive tribes, as sacred as the oak to the Druids. Beneath it the nature worshipers performed rites, some of which were better unperformed, for which reason, no doubt, as well as for Judas's choice of it to hang himself upon- he seems to have destroyed himself on all the trees in the wood, from the rose-bush to the palm- imps have been hiding in it ever since: "Obscene monsters," St. Jerome called them. Yet another saint, Augustine, to wit, found it no such matter, for when he had cast himself, despairing, under a fig tree, unable at the moment to believe some statements in the Scriptures, the fig spoke to him in a child's voice, bidding him read anew: which he did, and his doubts were solved. It is dangerous for some people to sleep under a fig, for they will be waked by a spectral nun, who offers a knife and asks how it will be taken. If the victim offers to take it by the blade, she will pierce his heart with it, but if he grasps it by the handle, she is compelled to give him good fortune. Christ deepened the fig in disrepute when he cursed it for its barrenness, with the result that it lost its leaves and died. Even its wood was worthless, for when they cast it into the fire it merely smoldered and would not burn. The fig furnished our first parents with what one old Bible called "breeches," and some scholars claimed it as the original tree of knowledge, instead of the apple. When Mary sought shelter for the infant Jesus from the soldiers of Herod, it was a fig that opened its trunk to hide them till the pursuers had gone by. And in eastern mythology we also find the tree associated with the divine, for Gautama dreamed of his approaching empire under that form of fig known as the banyan or peepul, "the sacred tree of many feet," and when he had achieved deity he sat beneath it as enthroned. Vishnu, too, was born in the cathedral shade of the peepul. These trees grow to vast size and vast age, the Holy Bo, of Ceylon, grown from a scion of Buddha's tree, being "the oldest and most venerated idol in the world," according to Kipling. The banyan near Surat, India, is held to be three thousand years old, and is never touched with steel, lest the god who lives in it be offended. One near Patna spread over nine hundred and twenty feet and

MYTHS AND LEGENDS OF FLOWERS

was supported by sixty stems growing downward to the earth from its horizontal branches. Another immense ficus in the ruins of Padjajarian, Java, "The Vegetable Giant," is visited by many pilgrims, who believe that the souls of the dead occupy its branches.

In classic myth the fig is Lyceus, a Titan, changed to a tree by Rhea, while another story ascribes its invention to Bacchus. It was growing on the site of Rome when the cradle of Romulus and Remus stranded under its branches, and was worshiped there, down to the time of the empire, the women of the city wearing collars of figs as symbols of fecundity in the Bacchic feasts and dances, and the men carrying statues of Priapus carved from its wood, in the holiday processions. In Rome, when Calchas challenged his fellow prophet, Mopsus, to a test of soothsaying, and the latter, answering his question, told him, "Yonder fig tree has 9999 fruit"- which proved to be the case- Calchas, unable to guess anything of equal importance so nearly, hated himself to death.

FIR

The fir, which has been a sacred tree ever since it was hewn for the ceiling of the Temple at Jerusalem, was Atys- he whom Zeus changed to a tree, that he might thus appease the anger of Cybele, for Atys, a priest of Cybele, had lapsed from virtue: hence his punishment. So strong was the regard for the tree in France that when St. Martin arrived and began to raze the temple erected to heathen gods, his proposition to destroy the firs roused such anger that he was forced to desist. Some remains of its heathen association linger in the Hartz, where girls dance about it in their religious festivals, singing songs that are not Christian, and decorating it with lights, flowers, eggs, and gewgaws. In circling about it thus, they prevent the escape of an imp concealed among its branches, who must give to them whatever is in his keeping or resign hope of going free. This is held to be the origin of the Christmas tree, and the imp has grown to the benevolent St. Nicholas, Santa Claus, or Old Nick, who is believed by Grimm and other students of folk-lore to be no other than Odin himself. Christianized somewhat out of likeness. When you light up the tree on Christmas eve, making sure it is a fir and not a pine or spruce or hemlock, for we use all sorts of evergreens in our celebration, you may learn your fate, if you have courage to look at your shadow on the wall. If the shadow appears without a head, it signifies that you are to die within the coming year. If you will cut off a branch and lay it across the foot of your bed, it will keep away nightmare. A stick of fir, not quite burned through, fends off lightning, and a bunch hung at the barn door keeps out evil spirits that want to steal the grain.

In Christmas celebrations in the neighborhood of the hill in the Hartz mountains known as the Hubinchenstein, cones gathered from the firs growing thereon are silvered and used for ornament, and if you ask why, you learn that long ago, when a miner fell sick, leaving his wife and children in straits for food and fuel, the wife climbed the Hubinchenstein, intending to pick up cones, which she might possibly sell for another day's living. As she entered the wood, a little old man with a jolly face and long white beard emerged from the shadows and pointed to a fir tree that he said would yield the best seeds. The woman thanked him, and when she reached the tree there was such a downfall of cones that she was frightened. The basket was extraordinarily heavy, too; indeed, she could barely reach her home with it, and the reason for this was soon evident, for when she emptied the cones upon the table, every one was of silver.

In the northern countries respect for the fir, as king of the forest and home of the wood genius, is so genuine that some choppers refuse to cut it, and when a monster fir is thrown down by storm in Russia the wood is not sold, but is given to the church.

MYTHS AND LEGENDS OF FLOWERS

FLAX

Hilda, the earth goddess, having taught to mortals the art of weaving flax, revisits us twice in the year, emerging from her cave near Unterlassen, in the Tyrol, and going about to see if the people are still profiting from her instruction. She comes in answer to the summer's call, when the flax is putting out its blue, and her first concern is to know if enough has been planted. In winter she looks to see if the women have flax enough for spinning on their distaffs, or if there are hints of a proper industry in the fresh linen of the household. If she fails to find these tokens it means that the family is thriftless, lazy, or unfit, and she inflicts punishment by blighting the next year's crop.

Because Hilda is the goddess of plenty, flax, in the regard of some of the northern people, has become the type of life. When a German baby does not thrive they place him naked on the grass and scatter flaxseed over him, in the belief that such of the seed as, falling on the earth, takes root and flourishes, will join his fortunes to the plentiful life that is everywhere about him; so he must begin to grow when the little plants appear.

FLOWERS OF PARNASSUS

Legend clothes Parnassus with poetry as nature clothes it with beauty. Many flowers of our gardens were born there, and they come to us bearing not only color and perfume, but history and allegory. This storied hill loomed above Delphi, where Apollo spoke through his oracle. It towered into a region of snow, but its sides were green with olive, myrtle, and laurel; and on a ridge of the mountain the Thyades held their revels in honor of the vine. Here grew the narcissus, translated body of that swain who wept himself to death for love of his own image. When Adonis died he became the adonium (in one version of the story), and the tears that Venus wept for him changed into anemones. The *adonis autumnalis* also known as May flower, pheasant's eye, and rose-a-ruby, is stained red with his blood. Here grew the beech, wherewith victors in the games were crowned, till Daphne had become a myrtle, when the leaves of that tree were substituted, since Daphne was loved of Apollo, god of arts and grace and light. Here sprang roses, first white, but changed to red for shame and pity when Venus, running toward the dying Adonis, was pricked by their thorns. The snowdrop bloomed here, but to the Greek it was the magic moly, wherewith Ulysses protected himself and his companions from the spells of Circe, when they had been wrecked on her island. Those who had drunk from the cup she offered became swine, but Hermes had provided the hero with a moly root that Niade it safe for him to drink.

Here grew the elichrysum, an "everlasting" named for the nymph Elichrysa, because she had woven it into a wreath for Diana; here grew mandragora and enchanter's nightshade, of evil note; the dark hellebore, the fatal hemlock, and the agrimony wherewith Mithridates countered the poison administered by his courtiers; here was the eyebright, or euphrasy, named for the grace, Euphrosyne, and restorative of sight to hurt eyes; here the yellow gentian and vervain used by Medea in her enchantments; here grew the filbert which is the metamorphosed Princess Phyllis; the fleabane that drove vermin from couches; the gilliflower, called clove for its spiciness, and blooming for men in paradise; the mullein or hag taper, a funeral torch and gathered by witches for their incantations; and the hawkweed, dedicated to the bird that names it and eats it to clear its sight. Juno's tears (*coix lacryma*) bloomed among the trees sacred to the gods who sat on Olympus, not far distant. Daphne's chase by Apollo is recalled by the laurel, for she was transfigured into that tree. The orchis commemorates the assault of the satyr Orchis on a priestess of Bacchus, his death at the hands of the outraged worshipers, and the conversion of his body to this flower. Parsley gathered in Parnassus's shadow wreathed the conquerors in the

MYTHS AND LEGENDS OF FLOWERS

Nemean and Isthmian games, for it was chosen by the strenuous Hercules as his first garland; yet it decorated graves and biers, and was so commonly accepted as a funeral plant that a body of Greek troops was once thrown into rout by meeting some mules laden with parsley- a certain forecast of ill fortune. With the loosestrife, or lysimachia, growing here, king Lysimachus found that he could quiet unruly oxen, if he placed it about their necks. Here might be plucked the primrose, the florified Paralisos, the poppy created by Ceres that she might forget grief in the sleep it induced, and the violet wherewith Diana changed the nymph she would save from the embraces of her brother Apollo. To his Delphian temple, they carried the rampion, or *campanula ranuculus*, on golden plates, to be eaten as food or used as a funeral decoration.

Here Syrinx, chased by Pan, was rescued from him by a sudden conversion either into a reed, or the syringa that still blooms for Greece; and tansy, bearing its old name of athanasia, recalls Jove's command to give eternal life to Ganymede, his cup-bearer, by causing him to drink of it. Thyme, which also covered Mount Hymettus, renewed fainting spirits, and symbolized vitality. The country hereabout is also favorable to the growth of quinces, which were consecrated to Venus and called golden apples. It was possibly with this fruit, not with apples of real gold, that Hippomenes won his race against Atlanta, for she could not forbear to stop and pick them up when he threw them to the ground. It was fondness for them that induced Hercules to fight the dragon of the Hesperides gardens.

FORGET-ME-NOT

Not many of the flowers retain their legends in their names, but the forget-me-not indicates its own history: A young man walking beside the Danube with his sweetheart notes her admiration for some flowers- blue as her eyes- that grew on an islet in the stream. He tosses off his shoes and hat and coat, kisses her hand laughingly, and leaps into the river to pluck them for her, regardless of the current, the fangs of rock that lift through the foam, the cold of the evening, and the protest of the girl. He crosses safely, plucks the morsels of color, and is almost at the bank again when he is wrung by a cruel cramp, and can no longer hold his way against the whirl and surge of the rapid. The roar of the fall, not far below, is in his ears; he realizes that his hour is come. Looking into the white face of his beloved, he flings his bouquet at her feet with his last strength, cries, "Forget me not!" and disappears. She never does forget him, but wears the flowers in her hair till her own death.

The flower was adopted by the fourth Henry of England in his exile, with the motto, or petition, "Remember me." An order of knighthood in the fourteenth century wore the flower as a device. In Italy they tell you that it is a flower of love, and is the changed form of a pretty maid who was drowned. In France, where it likewise symbolizes affection, it is sometimes known as "the eyes of our lady." An old tradition cites that when Adam- one version says, God- named all the plants in Eden, as he supposed, he overlooked this plant because it was so small. Afterward, as he passed through the groves and gardens, he called these names, to find if they were accepted, and every plant bowed and whispered its assent. His walk was almost over when a small voice at his feet asked, "By what name am I called, Adam?" and, looking down, he saw the flower peeping shyly at him from the shadow. Struck with its beauty and his own forgetfulness, he answered, "As I forgot you before, let me name you in a way to show I shall remember you again: You shall be forget-me-not."

A Persian relates how in the world's morning an angel sat weeping at the gates of light, for he had loved a daughter of the earth, and so forfeited his place in heaven. He had first seen the girl at a river edge, decorating her hair with forget-me-nots, and as punishment for losing his heart to her he was barred from

MYTHS AND LEGENDS OF FLOWERS

paradise till the woman had planted forget-me-nots in every corner of the world. It was a tedious task, but for great love she undertook it, and so for years, in all climes and weathers, they wandered over the globe together, planting this little flower. When the task was ended the couple appeared once more at the gates, and behold, they were not closed against them. The woman was admitted without death. "For," said the keepers of the way, "your love is greater than your wish for life; and as he on whom you have bestowed yourself is an angel, so love of the heavenly has raised you above corruption. Enter, therefore, into the joys of heaven, the greatest of which is unselfish love."

GENTIAN

This lovely flower has its American analogues in the fringed gentian, the inspiration of Bryant's poem, and the closed gentian, with its strange, unopened, bud-like prominences of intense and glorious blue. Physicians of old held the plant to be "sovrayne" for poisons, pestilences, indigestions, dog bites, stubborn livers, weariness, lameness and other maladies. It bears the name of Gentius, king of Illyria, who discovered it to be useful in medicine. In Hungary the plant was *Sanctus Ladislas Regis Herba*, in honor of Ladislas, the king, whose reign was vexed by a plague. In despair, Ladislas went into the fields bearing his bow and arrow, and prayed that when he shot at random the Lord would direct the shaft to some plant that might be of use in checking the ravages of the disease. He shot, and the arrow was found sticking into a root of gentian, which he immediately culled, and with which wondrous cures were wrought.

GERANIUM

The geranium has many forms, ranging in showiness from the much cultivated garden varieties to the humble crane's bill of the shadowed roadside, and in the old world common among hedges. It is a splendid thing in the east, is our geranium, almost worthy to be called a tree. There heaven created it to honor the virtues of the Prophet, for when Mahomet washed his shirt one day, he hung it to dry on a lavender mallow at the water's edge. It did not take long for the moisture to evaporate, but in that time a wondrous change had taken place, for the plant was no longer a mallow: it was head high, adorned with flowers of brilliant red and exhaling a spicy and piquant odor. It had changed into a geranium, the first of all its tribe.

Of the wild variety common in England and America and known as herb Robert, statements conflict as to the meaning of the name. Some hold that it was intended to commemorate certain concealed virtues of the highwayman Robin Hood, but in the belief of others it bears the name of a gentler Englishman, Saint Robert, founder of the Cistercian order, who was born on the 29th of April, when this herb commonly unfolds in the mild air of the old country. At all events, it was this saint who used it as a cure for Ruprecht's plague. An easier solution of the name is offered by a Scottish botanist, Dr. Macmillan, who traces it to the Latin rubor, or red.

GINSENG

Ginseng is in demand by the Chinese, and the plant is gathered for export by American rustics, from Vermont to the hills of Georgia. The Chinese carry the dry root as an amulet, and their name for it is genshen, meaning man's wort. The roots, which affect rocky places, are compelled to turn and twist in getting into the ground, that they may avoid stones and enter crevices. In appearance it is somewhat like the mandrake, and as the mandrake is held to be shaped like a man, it follows, according to the doctrine of signatures, that appears to be still effective in the east, that it is intended for men's use; hence it is esteemed not merely as a prophylactic and demulcent, but as a charm against evils. It is good for ills and weaknesses that have

MYTHS AND LEGENDS OF FLOWERS

been inherited; it refreshes memory, calms passion, and begets pleasant dreams. Though the Tatars would shoot an arrow at random, saying that where it fell ginseng would be found, it is so no longer, for the Chinese have as industriously rooted the plant out of their dominions as we are destroying it today, we being a reckless race that seldom thinks to sow where it reaps. Our shipments of it aggregate probably fifty thousand dollars a year, but the individual earnings of the gatherers seldom amount to as much as they could make in an equal time in the fields. A hunter may tramp over wooded hills and undergo much hardship in collecting a dollar's worth.

GRASSES, GRAINS AND REEDS

The most common form of vegetation in all parts of the world, a form that is familiar in poetry and art, pervades tradition to but a slight extent. It appears as a simile in our own and other religious teachings and histories, and wherever the Bible is read the sayings will be recalled, "All flesh is grass," "If God so clothe the grass of the field, how much more will he clothe you!" Grass-blades were once eaten to achieve second-sight and prophecy, and sods were thought to be barriers against witches. Sods were also given with title deeds as proof of a valid transfer. Conquerors exacted grass and water from the enemy in token of submission. In some of the wars in India, when a tribe was overcome, the fighters would go upon their bellies and eat grass from the ground, as an assurance that they had become as cattle under the hands of their enemies. Indeed, when the Cid surrendered to King Alfonso, he and his fifteen knights knelt and ate grass. The Masai hold grass in the hand or tie a wisp of it to the dress when they would denote welcome, they throw it over one whom they wish to bless, and they cast it into rivers as a peace-offering to the water spirits, tokening therein an appreciation not unlike that of the Romans, who gave a crown of it to the captain who should deliver a town under siege, the trophy being known as the *corona obsidionalis*, or siege crown, and also the *corona gramiriea*, or grain crown. It was woven of grass that grew in the beleaguered camp.

The Hindus, who speak of kusa grass as the ornament of sacrifice, and the purifier, use it in fires of incense on the altars of the Hindu trinity, Brahma, Vishnu, and Siva. As Brahma once sat on a tuft of it, and thereby made it holy, so the wise and wonderful, who in the east, as elsewhere, live to meditate, strew their floors with kusa, and carry blades of it for good fortune, as harder-headed people carry four-leaved clover. Albeit grass is the commonest of weeds, and witch grass is one of the worst pests with which the farmer has to contend, there is only one poisonous variety, namely the *lollolium temulentum*, which is the tare of Scripture, that the enemy sows in the night. In a Welsh superstition there is danger in tussock grass, because it is occupied by fairies, who must be treated with consideration or they may revenge themselves.

Early botanists, who formulated the doctrine of signatures, observed in the shaking of grass a token that it must be usefully employed in human diseases, so the kind known as quakers, or shaking grass, became a cure for chills and fever. In an English tradition of last century, the grass did not merely tremble on the happening of a tragedy; it refused to deck the grave of a man unjustly put to death. In the churchyard at Montgomery is a bare spot of the size and shape of a coffin. It is told that a young farmer incurred the enmity of two prosperous neighbors, who brought a false accusation and had him arrested for highway robbery. He was convicted and sent to his death- for in those times robbery was a hanging matter. Before the execution he said, "If I am innocent of the crime for which I suffer, the grass, for one generation at least, will not cover my grave." So soon as the bell began to toll for the hanging, the sky darkened, and as Davies put his foot on the scaffold there was a glare of lightning and an appalling roar of thunder that struck terror to his accusers, and the multitude that had assembled to see the killing fled, crying that the end of things had come. In 1852, thirty years after the hanging, a village clergyman in Montgomery wrote that the grass had not yet covered the grave, and that, although attempts had been made to induce a growth, it always died, leaving the soil cold and bare, as if burned off by lightning. The rush, or reed, came into existence when the burly, jealous Cyclopes, Polyphemus, found Galatea in the arms of the shepherd Acis, whom she loved. Polyphemus crushed his rival with a stone, and Galatea, unwilling to leave him in his gory state, yet unable to restore his life, caused the blood of the shepherd to change to water and flow forever.

When it had completely lost its color a form like that of the dead youth appeared waist deep in the stream, and while the weeping nymph looked on the arms began to lengthen, the shoulders to sprout green blades, and presently the brook was edged with a growth of rushes. The reed or rush, long associated with kingship, seems to have represented the royal scepter. We learn that Moses's cradle anchored among rushes that beaconed above his head, as pointing the way to high station among his people. We see the reed placed in the helpless hands of Christ as he is mocked before his death. It is reported that William the Conqueror fell on the floor at his birth. It was then the fashion, and for long after, to strew halls and churches with rushes, to relieve their bareness and collect dirt, it being easy to change them for cleaner. The little William, rolling among these rushes, grasped a number of them in his tiny hands, whereupon all the bystanders who had been invited to witness the function, broke into a cheer, for this was promise of kingship. When Isis set sail to recover the body of Osiris she wove her boat of papyrus, and the crocodiles respected it, allowing it to proceed along the Nile in peace. It was of this great water-grass also that the basket boat of the little Moses was made, when he was committed to the river, and boats of the same grass have been made in our day, though its more important use is the making of paper, sheets of which made from papyrus two thousand years ago are still in existence.

Bamboo represents shelter and friendship, in Indian symbolism. Though its flowers irritate delicate noses, producing something like hay-fever, its huge stems are used for houses, corrals, fences, furniture, and furnishings, and we are told how Chinese not rich enough to own a garden make a raft of bamboo which they cover with earth, and so raise vegetables on lakes and rivers. Our Indians of the southwest relate the preservation of man and the brutes through the deluge to the canebrake: When the earth was about to be overwhelmed, the red Noah called his family and the representative animals to enter the hollow of a monster cane-stalk with him, and, closing the break, they mounted higher and higher into its wood as the waters spread and deepened. Now and then the big rush threatened to break in the sway of the storm, but by repeatedly strengthening it with scarfs of cloud they kept it fast. At last the flood had reached its height, and, crawling up on the side of the cane, the preserver of the race reached its tip, and, pulling off the feather he wore in his hair, he swept it against the sky, in memory of which act the canes have worn feathers ever since. In the cosmogony of Japan it was a bulrush, budded at its tip and piercing the misty heaven from the misty earth, that carried the seed of life into the infinite. The bud opened and from it came four pairs of heavenly beings, the last couple, Izanagi and Izanami, god of the air and goddess of the clouds, undertaking the creation of the earth. They first cast rice grains abroad, to dispel the darkness that prevailed; then the air god let down his spear and stirred the sea, which began to eddy, turning faster and faster till by its speed it had brought up land from the bottom and thrown it out at the feet of the gods.

When this earth had dried a little, the rice had root-hold, and so the means of supporting animal life was provided, while the spear remained where Izanagi had thrust it and became the center of the earth, around which all things turn. Then the gods begat the sun goddess, who in turn begat all the flowers that lend

MYTHS AND LEGENDS OF FLOWERS

beauty to this whirling sphere. This rice-straw figures curiously in one of the Japanese legends, for it is because the straw held firm that Japan has a summer: Amaterasu, goddess of day, had fled, discontented, to a cave, to escape the persecutions of her jealous brother of the dark- he known as Susano, the moon god. So long as she hid her lights there could be no warmth, no vegetation, not even any water, for in the chill did not the springs freeze fast? A conspiracy was planned among the earth dwellers to lure her from retirement. Eight hundred girls were assembled before the cave and told to laugh their heartiest. Amaterasu, startled from her melancholy, stepped into the air for a moment, and so soon as she was at a little distance from the grotto and the world was filled with light again, they held a mirror to her face and bade her look at her new rival. Never before having seen her own countenance, the goddess stood admiring it long enough for the plotters to close the cavern's mouth with a stout rope of rice straw. Finding the way into the earth barred, realizing, too, how prettily she had been tricked, the sun goddess laughingly confessed the cleverness of the earth people, and mounted again to her place in the sky. Then, as if to amend for the suffering she had caused by withdrawing light and warmth from her worshipers, she sent her grandson, Prince Plenty, the Rice Prince, to live among them, granting into his keeping the magic mirror, from which all Japanese mirrors have been designed for centuries, and which indicate the sun in their round and shining shape. This Rice Prince lost hold on the heavenly life by coming to our planet; he was the son of gods, made man, and he devoted his life to the teaching and guidance of the human race. Although generations of kings come and go in other lands, the Prince's line has continued unbroken, the oldest royal family in the world; for the Rice Prince is ancestor of all the mikados who have ruled Japan. Japanese farmers who have not been reached by the missionaries still pray to the god of rice for plenteous harvest, and hold the grain as a symbol of generation as well as of abundance- a symbol that has extended to other lands, for even in our own country bridal couples are showered with rice when they set off on their wedding journey.

In India the Brahmins throw the rice over the shoulders of the couple after they have mixed it with saffron, and when the children arrive the little fellows are taken into an apartment where the father empties a quantity of red rice over their scalps, to keep off the evil eye. Long ago the priests of Japan lived on roots and plants, but while meditating on the ineffable, one of the brotherhood found his thoughts drawn to earth by the behavior of a mouse that was scurrying to and fro, carrying something to its nest. The priest set a trap, caught the little creature, and, having tied a thread to its leg, followed it as it scuttled across the hills and into a watery country he had never seen before, where wild rice grew plentifully. This the priest found so good that he sent for his people to cultivate it, and when it had become the food of the nation the mouse entered into the respect of the public to that degree that you shall find him in bronze, paint, ivory, and porcelain, for he, too, is sacred. The Arabs do not admit this: they claim the first rice grains to have been drops of sweat from the brow of Mahomet.

The other nations have their lore of grain, which in the north was under protection of Hulda, or Bertha, benevolent earth mother. In her anxiety that her fields should have a plentiful crop of seed, she protected them against damaging visitors by stationing were-wolves at the boundaries. Loki, the mischievous fire god, would sometimes steal past the wolves and sow his wild oats; and when heat shimmers over his farm the Jutlander says, "Loki is sowing his wild oats." Two weeds still carry his name, in the north: the polytrichium commune, which are Loki's oats, and the yellow rattle, or rhinanthus, which is Loki's purse. For some reason rye-fields at that time were affected by devils, of whom the peasantry were so afraid that when they reaped the harvest they left the last sheaf for these imps to quarrel over while they hurried the rest of the crop into the barn. But demons never quarreled over the bed straw, *galeum verum luteum*,

MYTHS AND LEGENDS OF FLOWERS

because it was too holy for their touch: it filled the manger where the child Jesus lay; hence it became a custom to strew such of it as had been used in the Christmas festivities over the fields, to bless them and increase the harvest; also to spread it in the stalls as a litter for cattle, to keep them from disease, and lastly, to heap it on the floor as a bed for the whole family on Christmas night.

When the Spanish adventurer Cortez came to this western world, he was more concerned for gold than he was for grain, yet he became the unwitting agent in the begetting of more wealth for us than he could ever have taken away, had he lived till now: for it was from a few kernels of grain, brought by one of his party through sheer oversight, and shaken upon the earth of Mexico, that the crops of this country are alleged to grow. So largely is our wealth a matter of wheat, rye, oats, and barley, that if we were a more imaginative people, we should be justified in a revival of the ancient festivals, held at harvest time, in honor of the goddess of grain, who in her various names and aspects is Ceres, Rhea, Hera, Demeter, Cybele, Tellus, and Isis. Proserpine, passing six months on earth and six in Hades, types the plant that sleeps in winter and flourishes in summer, and this tale of the nymph who is spirited away to lightless depths to emerge again for a season has its complete or partial likeness among primitive peoples, east and west; in fact, a survival of the ancient rites of Greece is found in India, where the bride is crowned with corn as a symbol of fertility. Grain was Egypt's wealth, and in many tongues we read the parable of the man who bade his son search diligently, for there was buried treasure in his field. The son plowed and dug for years, and discovered no buried coin, but his plowing resulted in splendid crops, and from these he earned much money, so that he was content; and when he had become so, and had earned the right to rest, he understood that the treasure was the earth's fatness, and that in increasing its yield of yellow grain he had lived more happily and usefully than if he had uncovered gold. It has been claimed for millet that if eaten on New Years' day it will make the eater rich, and this despite the poverty of many whose diet is millet, mostly. The unaccountable wanderings and shiftings of these fancies, as we deem them, but of symbols and figures as they often are, discover connections in beliefs that appear widely unrelated at first glance. For instance, this belief in New Year luck relates millet to an earlier faith among the Germans that it was the food of the great storm dragon, and also to the fancy that grain took its color from gold. For when the thunder beast, from his hiding in the clouds, dropped red lightning, it signified that gold had fallen on the earth where the bolt had struck, whereas if he spat blue fire it meant that he had sown millet for his own eating. Hence gold and millet, being made by the same power and process, were in a measure transmutable. In Persia, the myth takes a different form, yet is recognizable as a relative, for there the dragon is still an inhabitant of the sky, and is a more pleasing object than the lightning: he is the rainbow. And instead of throwing gold to the earth, he drops it gently, so that you shall find treasure where the end of his body rests upon the ground.

No amative significance attaches to grain in America, but there is a custom in New England of pairing young men and women at the corn huskings, when neighbors aid one another to strip the ears of maize, and this carries with it the privilege of a swain to kiss the girl beside him if he finds an ear with red kernels. In old England the last ear of grain in harvest is cut by the prettiest girl, who permits no such consolation to her admirers. There is one grain known to every city child: the sesame; for was it not by that magic name that Ali Baba opened the cave of the forty thieves? The sesame, or sesamum, is described as an oily pulse that is sown before the rising of the seven stars, and was created by the god of death, whence the orientals use it in services of repentance, expiation, or purification. Sesame is mixed with rice and honey in the cakes offered to the dead, and "the offering of the six sesames" being duly made, at six different times, the giver believes that the

MYTHS AND LEGENDS OF FLOWERS

departed has received his admission to heaven. When an Hindu funeral is over and the body is burned, the friends leave half a pound or so of sesame on the bank of the river where the burning has occurred, and on which the ashes are drifting, that the dead may feed on it and gather strength for the long journey into the hereafter.

HAWTHORN

While Christ was resting in a wood during the pursuit prior to his crucifixion, the magpies covered him with hawthorn, which the swallows, "fowls of God," removed as soon as his enemies had passed. From this circumstance the plant gained holiness, and in the chapter on Christian legends may be read how Joseph of Arimathea planted the white thorn of Glastonbury, which, to prove its saintly association, flowers on Christmas eve, no matter what the weather. A kindred instance is recorded in the life of Charlemagne, when he knelt before the crown of thorns, which is alleged to have been fashioned from the hawthorn.

The wood, dry for centuries, burst into bloom and the air was filled with a wondrous fragrance. After thousands of Calvinists had been put to death during the St. Bartholomew's massacre, the wearied slayers, surfeited with slaughter, were fain to allow the survivors to escape. But the priests spurned the flagging spirits of the people by declaring that heaven applauded the stamping out of heresy, and had proved it by kindling into new life the hawthorn bush in the cemetery of the Holy Innocents, "as if it had drunk the blood of heretics and gained new strength from it." So the populace marched to the graveyard, where, true enough, the hawthorn, or "holy thorn," had put forth a wondrous mass of bloom; and, seeing it, the men who had done what they truly believed to be the will of heaven, fell on their knees and worshiped the innocent flowers of the "albespyne." At Bosworth field the crown of Richard III. was hid in a hawthorn, and, being recovered after the death of that misshapen monarch, was placed on the head of Richmond, who thereon took as his device a crown in a hawthorn.

HAZEL

Moncure D. Conway associates the name of hazel with the Syrian hazeh, meaning hazy, since mysteries associated with the ancient religions were of that effect on beholders and participants. He also believes that our word hazing is derived from the same root, that being a process of induction into the mysteries of study, the excesses of which were best corrected with the hazel rod of the schoolmaster. The hazel, too, was a tree of Thor, and protected buildings and graves against lightning. It took on sanctity because the holy family was sheltered by a hazel in the flight to Egypt. It is used as a means of securing crops, warding off lightning, curing fever, and driving devils out of cattle. It takes only three hazel pins to preserve a house from fire, if they are driven into its beams; also, a hazel cut at twelve o'clock on Walpurgis night and carried in the pocket will prevent the one who carries it from tumbling into holes, though never so drunk. If you cut it on Good Friday or St. John's eve, you can lash your enemy with it in your own apartments, and without seeing him. Merely name him and lay stoutly about you, and your foe will dance and bellow, no matter if he is a thousand miles away.

The hazel is the caduceus of Mercury, which roused in all who were touched by it love of kin, country, and the gods; and, as everybody knows in our time, it is the divining rod, cut in a Y from a dividing branch, one handle held in the right hand, the other in the left, its point toward the ground, and so held it is to indicate hidden springs, or gold and silver. It is told that Linnaeus, having no belief in these tales, hid a purse of a hundred ducats under a ranunculus, and bade a fellow find it with a hazel wand, if he could. An unasked company, hearing of money in the ground, tore up the pasture and destroyed the

MYTHS AND LEGENDS OF FLOWERS

ranunculus and other plants, so that the owner of the ducats could no longer tell where he had hidden his wealth; but the man with the hazel, disregarding all guesses and advice, presently marked the spot where, sure enough, the coin was hidden, and from which it was safely removed. Another such experiment, said the botanist, and he would believe in the witchery of hazel himself. But it was observed that he risked no more of his ducats in experiments. When Adam was expelled from paradise God pitied him to the degree that he allowed him to create new animals by striking water with a hazel rod; and he, having so produced a sheep. Eve, forsooth, must try her apprentice hand and bring a wolf into the world, which forthwith sprang at the sheep. Adam regained the rod, and with it summoned into existence a dog that conquered the wolf. The first Christian church at Glastonbury, England, was a wattled house of hazels; it was a wand of hazel with which St. Patrick drove the Irish snakes into the sea ; and the pilgrim's staff was made of this wood and often buried with him when he died of disease or exhaustion on his way to Jerusalem. Magicians used it also in summoning fiends; Circe employed it in turning her lovers into swine; in one version of the legend, Aaron 's rod was made of it; and such was the sanctity it obtained from that circumstance that oats fed to horses in Sweden are touched with hazel boughs, in God's name, that no harm may come to them from the eating. In that country, too, the hazel nut is one of the magical agents in making its carrier invisible. Divining rods must there be cut at night on the first of the new moon, or on Good Friday, or Epiphany, or Shrove Tuesday, the cutter facing east and lopping a branch from the east side of the tree.

HEATH

The heath, or heather, that decorates the Scottish hills, commemorates in its name the efforts of the Christians to convert the Picts. When the latter were visited by armed missionaries who ordered them to cease the worship of false

MYTHS AND LEGENDS OF FLOWERS

gods, the Picts unreasonably gave battle, and the plants that were bedewed with the blood of the heathen became the heathen, or heath, for short. When all except two of the tribe had been killed, these survivors- father and son- were taken before Kenneth, the conqueror, who promised them life if they would tell him how to make heath beer. They remained silent. Thinking to force the older man to compliance, the king put the son to death before the father's eyes. In anger and disgust, the old man refused to grant any favor to so brutal a victor, and the secret of the drink was never known, although, for shame's sake, Kenneth suffered his prisoner to live. In the Jura the secret still survives, for the peasants of that region continue to make a beer in which two parts of heath tops are combined with one of malt. But the heath of the Jura is not stained with a people's blood.

HELIOTROPE

The Greek word heliotrope means to turn toward the sun. We apply the name to a modest flower of purple color and delightful odor, that came from Peru, and, being adopted into France, was called there herb of love. What the original heliotrope was, we do not know with certainty, but it is supposed to be a plant known in Germany as God's herb, and to have many healing qualities. In the Greek myth the sun god Apollo is loved by Clytia, for whom he cares so little that he goes a-wooing the princess Leukothea. Clytia reveals the liaison to the king, who, furious at the misconduct of his daughter, buries her alive. Apollo returns to the heavens without so much as a look for the unhappy Clytia, who, bitterly conscious of the mischief she has done, falls to the ground and lies there for nine days, watching the passing of Apollo in his chariot, and praying for a look of pity. Seeing her wasted with privation and sorrow, the gods have mercy and change her into the heliotrope. She still lies at length upon the earth and looks toward heaven with half averted eye, as waiting complete forgiveness and acceptance. So our purple heliotrope is wrongly named, in that it does not turn toward the

MYTHS AND LEGENDS OF FLOWERS

sun. Various plants have been instanced as foundation for Ovid's story: sunflower, wartwort, spurge, salsify, anagallis, elecampane, aster, marigold, and blue marigold.

HELLEBORE

This plant (see early Christian legend of the Christmas rose) is commonly called black hellebore, because of the color of its root. It was a cathartic medicine so long ago as medicinal use was made of plants, and it also purged human habitations of such evil spirits as had gained entrance, provided the perfuming of the house was accompanied by proper rites and hymns. Cattle were blessed with hellebore that had been dug within a circle drawn on the earth with a sword, the digger first asking leave of Apollo and Asklepias. Arrows were rubbed with hellebore, that the flesh of animals to be killed with them should be tender. The plant cured insanity; and one of the earliest instances of a care for the soul-sick is found in the shipping of patients of a gloomy temper to Anticyra, where the herb grew plentifully.

HEMLOCK

Hemlock- *conium maculatum,* not the tree we call hemlock- was prescribed instead of the gallows and the ax as a means of death for certain political offenders in the past, and was a common drug of suicide, since it was supposed to give a painless death. The plant was considered by the ancients as so deadly that snakes would wriggle away even from a leaf of it as fast as their ribs would carry them, lest they be chilled into a paralysis. It was mixed with the hell broths and ointments brewed and blended by witches for mischief, and in Russia and Germany it is still regarded as the devil's own property. It was by means of hemlock that the philosopher was put to death, after having annoyed Athens beyond endurance by exploiting his love for argument.

MYTHS AND LEGENDS OF FLOWERS

HEMP

"To stretch hemp" is a cant phrase for hanging, hence the plant that furnishes the means for death might be thought to be of evil omen; but since more rope is used for goodly purposes than for shutting off the wind of rogues, the weed has a kindly aspect, especially for maids who wish to see their future husbands before they are led to the altar, that they may make their plans wisely and put in train their fascinations. The damsels must run around a church at night, scattering hemp seed as they go, and repeating, "I sow hemp seed. Hemp seed I sow. He that loves me best, come after me and mow." And, looking over her shoulder, the sower experiences a pleasing terror, for she will behold the wraith of a man, chasing her with a scythe which he swings through the phantom crop that springs in her footsteps. Sicilians use hempen threads as a lure for lovers, for there would seem in this to be a suggestion of the tying of hearts together. An ill use that is made of hemp is that of extracting the hashish. The eater of this intoxicant bewilders his brain with grotesque and unearthly visions. Under its influence the Arabs believe they can hear the words and even read the thoughts of others at a distance.

HOREHOUND

Horehound candy was popular in our fathers' day, because it was "good for the system." Horehound, horseradish, coriander, lettuce, and nettle are the five bitter herbs ordered to be eaten by the Jews at their Passover feast, and the name of the first also bespeaks antiquity of service, for it is the seed of Horus, which the Egyptian priests dedicated to that god; but how the name of hound attached to it nobody knows. In Egypt horehound was likewise bull's blood and eye-of-a-star. It was one of those many plants that defended the eater against poison.

MYTHS AND LEGENDS OF FLOWERS

HOUSE-LEEK

The house-leek, which is not a leek, and grows in old gardens and on old walls as readily as in houses, may have taken its name from a command of Charlemagne that it should be planted plentifully on the roofs of houses in his kingdom that it might protect them against "thunder."

This curious little plant, with its rosettes of leathery leaves, was anciently known under the names of Jupiter's beard- not in the least like anybody's beard- Jupiter's eye, ayegreen, and thunder flower. It cured fevers inflicted by witches; babes dosed with the juice of it were assured of long life; and if a person rubbed it over his fingers he could then handle hot iron- once.

HYACINTH

The hyacinth symbolizes misfortune and sadness, though to the gardener none is more welcome than this early visitor, with its luscious perfume and softly radiant color. The name was borne by a handsome boy, who was beloved by both Zephyrus and Apollo. The lad preferred the god of day to the inconstant master of the winds, but in expressing his preference he did not realize what danger he incurred. Apollo having challenged the young fellow to a game of quoits, Zephyrus lingered in the wood, resolved to take his revenge. When Apollo hurled his discus at the mark, the wind god deflected it full against the brow of Hyacinthus, and killed him. But the sun god declared that while the beauty of the boy had departed, it should be recorded in the finer beauty of a flower, and he summoned the hyacinth out of the earth, sighing upon it "Ai, Ai!" which words of grief some will affect to see, in Greek character, on hyacinth blooms. Yet because the sound is like that of AEi (eternal), the plant has come to signify remembrance; hence it used to be sculptured on tombs. The wild hyacinth, or bluebell, otherwise known as wood hyacinth, St. George's flower, and bending Endymion, represents benevolence in florography, and all hyacinths expressed affection of old, no less than ill ending, for Venus bathed in their dew to increase her beauty, and they formed the couches of Jove and Hera, and of Adam and Eve.

HYPERICUM

Like fern seed, the hypericum, or St. Johnswort, has a way of revealing itself on the eve of St. John in a golden glow, surpassing the brightness of its flowers in the sun. It was the early missionaries to the north who, finding this plant devoted to witches that fought against the sun (darkness and ill weather in symbolism), gave to it a new and wholesome consecration, which was no doubt suggested by its ruddy sap. This, the good fathers said, indicated the blood of the martyred John the Baptist, and, thus blessed by name, it began to bless in purpose in that it keeps off the witches who, of all nights in the year, are abroad on Walpurgis night, the eve of St. John. When a sprig of St. Johns wort is placed above the door, along with a cross, no witch or demon can enter. The Tyrolese mountaineer puts the wort into his shoes, believing that so long as it is there he can climb or walk without fatigue.

INDIAN PLUME

An Indian girl living near Lake Saranae loved a youth whose straightness of form and swiftness in war and the chase had caused him to be named The Arrow; but before the time set for the wedding a fearful pestilence appeared and ravaged all the Adirondack villages. The Arrow was among the first to die. The people implored the Great Spirit to be merciful, whereupon he showed himself on the crest of the Storm Darer. It was their sins, he said, that had brought punishment on them; they had grown too fond of war and bloodshed; they had held too lightly their pacts with other tribes; they had been careless in good deeds;

MYTHS AND LEGENDS OF FLOWERS

they had grown haughty and selfish. Nothing but the blood of one much beloved would appease his wrath. The people of Leelinaw's village gathered to consider this revelation. After a time Leelinaw arose and entered the circle. "I am a blighted flower," she said, "it is my blood that shall flow for you. Place me beside The Arrow." So speaking, she caught a stone knife from the belt of the priest, and slew herself.

The Great Spirit saw from his mountain top, and his heart was softened. He swept away the pestilence; but he did more, for he eternalized the memory of the sacrifice by causing the flower we call the Indian plume, or Oswego tea, to spring from the spot where Leelinaw's blood had been shed.

IRIS

No plant more sweetly recalls the gardens of our grandmothers than the iris, or fleur-de-lis. Though showing by its hollow stem that it prefers to be near water, it grows in all manner of soil, and was generally to be found near the porch of the farm-house, where its blossoms, blue, purple, white, or yellow, were eagerly looked for as the spring advanced. It vies with amethyst in the depth of its color, and with the lily in its delicate, almost watery texture. In flower poetry it typed wisdom, faith, and courage; but in the rude medical practice of earlier days it cured "spleens," coughs, bruises, fits, dropsy, snake-bites, and anger, and one had only to lay its petals on a black-and-blue spot for a couple of days to restore the bruised flesh to its natural condition. Scrofula and other blood diseases were cured by creating an open wound and inserting a bead of iris root. The root was also to be used for infants to cut their teeth upon, and the practice of placing beads of iris, or orris, as it is oftener called in the drug-shops, about the necks of the little ones extended itself to adults, who wear them for ornament. Leghorn and Paris export twenty millions of these beads in a year. Orris is also used to throw upon fires and give out a pleasant odor; to remove the smell of liquor, garlic, and tobacco from reformable breaths; and to simulate violet in sachets.

The Iris is really meant when we speak of the lilies of France and Florence. Near the Italian city, it is raised for the sake of its fragrant root, while in France it was conventionalized on the royal arms and standards. King Clovis, of France, had for his coat-of-arms three black toads. In peace they served him well enough, but every time he went to war the toads on his shield were soundly battered, and some fear was felt lest the swords of the enemy pass through them and pierce the body of his majesty. But one day a holy hermit, gazing from his cell in contemplation, was startled by the appearance of an angel bearing a shield as blue-bright as was the sky, with three flowers of iris enameled on it and shining like the sun. The old man took the shield, with news of its heavenly origin, to Clotilde, the queen, who gave it to the king. Clovis expunged the toads from his armorial bearings, and in his next fight bore the angel's shield, observing, when it was over, that all stains of battle had disappeared, and that the lilies shone. From that day his armies triumphed in every field, and France, inheriting not only his prowess and his fame, but the shield itself, adopted the lilies for the royal standard. The iris then symbolized Christianity, which faith Clovis at once adopted, in accordance with his vow to do so if he should win a victory against the Germans.

Doubters say that he never wore the toads as a blazon, but took the iris on his accession to the throne. The blossoms, being badly represented by the rude artists of that day, were mistaken for toads. At all events, they became more like lilies as time went on, and kept their place till the Revolution brought in the symbolism of the cock, the eagle, the Roman fasces, and the bee. The seventh Louis adopted the iris in his crusades of 1137, for it appeared miraculously pictured on his white standards; hence it became known as the flower of Louis, though its earlier name may have been flower de luce, or flower of light. At first the royal standards were thickly sown with this emblem, but Charles V. reduced them to three, to typify the trinity.

JAMBU, OR SOMA

A huge tree bearing a great fruit, known to the Hindus as the jambu but to botanists as *eugenia jambo*s, is the "fruit of kings" that gave its name to the continent Jambduvipa, and was one of the four trees- ghanta, kadamba, ambala, and jambu- that marked the cardinal points where the four giant elephants held up the world. Four great rivers run from this tree, in the cosmogenic myth, for its fruit was then as large as elephants, and breaking as they fell, when ripe, they released the flood now called the Jambu River. This stream, fed expressly from its fruits, is therefore sacred, and a stream of health, as near to the precious soma of the gods as mortals may hope to know. Brahma having breathed upon the tree and imbued it with eternal life, it exhales the perfume of his breath. The dead climb into its branches for new strength as they begin the journey to the sky where the immortals are. It is as the soma, however, that the tree is king of plant life in the world, for soma yields the divine ambrosia, the drink of eternity. When the gods arrived on Mount Himavant in their boat of gold, the costus, or kushtha, threw forth such a light that it revealed this neighbor tree, which, in its earlier aspects, yielded night and day before the sun and stars were created. It formed a visible body for Brahma himself, bore every kind of fruit known to the world, and the gods sit in its shade drinking soma and constantly renewing their youth.

The Hindu soma is thought by some scientists to be *asclepias acida*, a name that seems to relate it to our milkweeds. In the Punjab, where it is known as the moon plant, it represents or emblemizes the moon god, who seems, in turn, to have a care for it, and the sap, fermented and described as "a very nasty drink," is an elixir of life. The juice is variously called sharp and acid, and astringent and bitter; hurtful in large doses, because it is a narcotic, and, without inducing sleep, benumbs the body and dangerously lowers vitality. To the Oriental mind, always eager for equivalents and parables, the milkiness of its sap symbolizes the motherhood of nature, while the division of its blossom into five petals has a mystic meaning for the Indian; hence, the yogi, or wise man, drinks soma at his initiation into the mysteries of priesthood, and sees that which the common man may not, who is unworthy to taste it.

JASMINE

We who know the jasmine only as a greenhouse plant with a few white blossoms do not realize the possibilities of the species, for in tropical lands it becomes a tree-cloud of flowers, white and pink, and deliciously fragrant. And in spite of the abundance of flowers in the hot countries the people prize them as we do not always prize our sunsets and our northern lights. True, we are developing a better appreciation of the common and neglected beauties of the wood and wayside, but we make no such use of flowers, even in our social functions, as the Mexicans and Central Americans make of rose, flamboyant and jasmine. They are sold in the towns for little money, hence the people can afford them for decorations as we can afford the goldenrod and daisy, and they use them lavishly in their churches and homes on feast days.

Many flowers died of sorrow on crucifixion night, but the jasmine merely folded its leaves and endured its pain, and in the morning, when it reopened, it was no longer pink, as it had been before: it had turned pale, and was never to show color again. In the east it is highly esteemed, and the Indian women braid it into their hair when they receive it from their lovers, inasmuch as it promises long affection. It is worn in bridal-wreaths for that reason, though its oriental name of dark-and-thoughtful suggests no connubial delights, nor is its legend gladsome, for that represents the despair and suicide of a

MYTHS AND LEGENDS OF FLOWERS

princess who discovers that the sun god has transferred his love from her to a rival. From her tomb sprang the night jasmine, known as the sad tree, whose flowers still shrink in reproach and horror from the sun, shedding their petals at the dawn. To the Arabs, again, it is a flower of love, imaging the charm of a sweetheart, though they call it the yas min, which means, despair is folly, and suggests an Omar Khayyam mood of heedlessness rather than the tenderness of love.

JUNIPER

Venerable antiquity pertains to the German tradition of the juniper; that a boy entering a chest to pick up an apple is caught and killed by his step-mother, who boils his flesh for soup, and buries his bones under a juniper. She is disconcerted when the tree takes fire and a bird leaps from its branches, flying over the land and spreading the story of the murder. The bird carries gifts to the boy's sister, and breaks the head of the wicked woman by causing a mill-stone to drop upon it; after which exploit the bird reenters the flames of the juniper and takes on human shape; he is the boy once more. Under the following circumstances, the juniper serves as a thief-catcher: Bend a young juniper toward the earth and hold it down where you have placed it with two weights: a big stone and the brain-pan of a murderer.

You are then to say, "Juniper, I bend and squeeze you till the thief" (here you name the suspect) "returns what he has taken, to its place." So soon as the rascal feels an unaccountable impulse coursing through his legs and mind to restore the abstracted property, your injunction is in process of fulfillment, and you are then in all speed and kindness to release the tree from its cramped position. To the Greeks the juniper was a tree of the furies, though it had not then been distilled to gin. Its berries were burned at funerals to keep off demons, while its green roots smoked as incense on offerings to the god of hell. It is one of the trees that opened their arms to afford hiding to Mary and Jesus in the flight to Egypt. It sheltered Elijah, too, from King Ahab; and the idea that it is a refuge for the weak or hunted continues in the supposition that hares find safety in its shadow when hounds pursue, and that its odor will kill any scent that dogs can follow. In later years it was burned in, or its sap was smeared over, dwellings and stables, to keep off evil spirits, and in Italy it is a protection against witches, because when they find one at a door they are compelled to count all its leaves before they can enter- a task so hopeless that they usually give it up.

LARCH

Have a larch about the house, for when burned it disturbs snakes. Sundry Romans built their bridges of this timber, because they regarded it as almost fire-proof. A ship of larch that had been floated after sinking in twelve fathoms of water was declared to be absolutely indestructible by fire, so hard had the sea made it. To the French, this tree, the *pinus larix*, yields a manna that would appear to be little different from the gum that keeps so many American jaws wagging, for it is chewed by mountaineers in order to "fasten their teeth." This gum was also used by witches, along with the blood of basilisks, the skin of vipers, the feathers of the phoenix, the scales of salamanders, and other commodities that were commoner once than they are today, in the dreadful stews which were boiled at midnight as a preliminary to cursing the neighborhood.

LARKSPUR

This flower had on its petals the letters A I A, signifying Ajax, terror of the Trojans. Disappointed in a division of the spoils after one of his battles, this hot-tempered soldier rushed into the open and wreaked his anger on a flock of sheep, stabbing several with his sword before he recovered from his madness. Ashamed of the spectacle he had made of himself, he

MYTHS AND LEGENDS OF FLOWERS

turned his sword into his own vitals and perished. His blood, pouring over the sod, flowered into the air again as the delphinium Ajacis, but some who are able to read only so far as the first two letters of his name on the petals, construe them as the wailing cry of Ai, Ai! still to be heard in the east when Fate oppresses. The name delphinium is applied because the buds were held to resemble a dolphin; but it has suggested many things to many eyes, for it is also known as lark's heel, lark's toe, lark's claw, lark's spur, and knight's spur.

LAUREL

However it came by its symbolism, the laurel, or sweet bay, was prized by the Greeks as an averter of ill, and hung over their doors to keep off lightning. From a token of safety, it became a badge of victory. Generals sent dispatches to the emperor encased in laurel leaves. The leaves were woven into garlands and crowns for victors in the games, as were myrtle, olive, pine, and parsley. If laurel were put under a rhymester's pillow, they made a poet of him, and if he read his verses in a university he was crowned with the leaves and berries, so we have the word baccalaureate, which means, laurel berry; and as the student was supposed to keep so closely to his books that he had no thought for matrimony, the derivative word bachelor came to be applied to an unmarried man. Laurel also gave power to soothsayers to look into the future. The Delphian oracle chewed its leaves before seating herself over the volcanic fumes on the tripod, and those who asked her service appeared with laurel crowns and nibbling the leaves that grew about Apollo's temple, It shocks us a little to discover of the emperor Tiberius that his faith in the protecting power of laurel was such that whenever a storm blew up he clapped on a laurel crown and crawled under the bed, remaining in this unkingly attitude till the trouble was over. While standing under a bay tree one was safe against wizards; and the berries kept off various diseases, at least, Nero believed so, for during a pestilence he retired to

MYTHS AND LEGENDS OF FLOWERS

Laurentium that he might save his precious health by breathing air that the laurels had purified.

We should be in an oratorical plight indeed if we were deprived of our laurel. It is long since we have used it for personal decoration, though at intervals the triumph of a musician is confessed in the laurel wreath that is passed across the footlights. Where did the fashion begin? Uncountable years ago, when Apollo chided Cupid for wanton conduct, and the boy revenged himself by shooting the god with his golden arrow, dooming him to love the first woman he should meet. Not content with that, he sped a second shaft, with a leaden tip, into the breast of the offended deity, so branding him that he was bound to create a feeling of repugnance in whomsoever that woman might be. Ere long Apollo met the wood nymph Daphne, and laid siege to her heart, but Daphne was repelled, and the more eager he became, the more frightened and indignant she. At last she found that her only safety lay in flight, but Apollo was close at her heels, and when it became plain that her pursuer must overtake her, she prayed to the gods to take away the form that had enchanted him and deliver her from his persecutions. Hardly had that wish been uttered ere her feet struck into the earth; her arms, that she had flung aloft in appeal, began to thicken, and they, too, became immovable; her face disappeared in knots and wrinkles; her fair skin turned brown; her hair, that a moment before had been streaming on the wind, now rustled as leaves; and Apollo, coming up with outstretched arms, clasped nothing but a laurel tree. Though the god was cast down in sorrow, his love was unquenched. He still preferred his Daphne to all the trees of the field, and he ordained that locks of her shining hair- the leaves that should be borne in winter as well as summer- should crown all who excelled in courage, service, or the creation of beauty.

MYTHS AND LEGENDS OF FLOWERS

LEEK

The Egyptians and the Druids viewed the bulbs of the allium species- lily, onion, garlic, and leek- as representing the universe. Each successive layer about the center corresponded to the successive heavens and hells of ancient cosmogonies. The leek was much used in secret ceremonies in the temples of the Nile. "To eat the leek," which is synonymous with eating crow pie and humble pie, is a phrase that extends into the antiquity which saw the rising of the pyramids, for an inscription uncovered in one of those monuments shows that the leek was a common food of the poor; hence its association with humility. In the Egyptian legend, Dictys, who corresponds to the Greek Endymion, was drowned while gathering the leek from a river, to the grief of Isis, the moon goddess, who loved him. Greece respected the leek because Latona, having lost her appetite, found it again when she had eaten freely of leeks. The leaf of the leek, too, is "the ribbon of Saints Maurice and Lazarus," and it is the cord by which St. Peter's mother sought to be lifted out of hell, in an odd legend of the Sicilians. It appears that this woman was stingy and grudging to a degree, and in all her life had never given anything away except the leaf of a leek, which she threw to a beggar to quiet his pleading. When she died and was consigned to eternal torment, she begged her son to intercede with the Lord in her behalf. Peter begged the favor, but was coldly received. Said the Lord, "The woman never did a particle of good; still, I will send an angel to her with this leek leaf, and if it is strong enough to lift her out of hell, let her be free." The angel flew to the pit and offered the end of the leaf to Peter's mother, but no sooner had she risen a few feet than all the rest of the damned laid hold on her so that they might be lifted, too. She kicked wildly at the host, and struggled so viciously that the leaf broke and she fell into gloomier depths than ever.

The Poles assume that the leek was the reed borne as a

mock scepter by Christ when He was crowned with thorns, and they place its flower-stalk in the hands of His statue on certain holy days. White and green, the hues of the leek, are the Cymric colors, and on the 1st of March the Welsh wear them in celebration of St. David. It has been alleged that St. David, being a holy and frugal man, subsisted considerably on leeks, inasmuch as they grew wild in his neighborhood. On leaving his cell to engage the Saxons in battle, he ordered his soldiers to put leeks into their caps, that in the turmoil, when men were striking at close quarters, the Welsh might not only spread terror into the ranks of the foe by charging the air with this most appalling smell, but could also know one another. The device was not unusual, and several heraldic cognizances had their beginnings in the custom, notably that of the Plantagenets in the planta genista. As the Welsh carried the field on this occasion, they continued to wear leeks in memory of their victory.

LILY

Because of its purity, it is especially fitting that the lily should represent the Virgin and decorate her altars, for her tomb was found to be filled with lilies and roses after her ascension. This miracle was accomplished in order to allay the doubts of St. Thomas, who could not be persuaded that the Virgin had really risen from the dead; but, standing beside her flower-filled tomb, he saw her hovering in the air; and when she had flung her girdle to him he was forced to believe. In the symbolism of the Church, the lily is also the "attribute" of St. Francis, St. Joseph, St. Barnard, St. Louis de Gonzague, St. Anthony, St. Clara, St. Dominick, St. Katharine of Siena, and the angel Gabriel. The lily fell from grace in Gethsemane when Christ walked there on the night before his death, for every other flower in that garden bent its head in sympathy and sorrow as he passed. The lily, shining in the darkness, said in the conceit of her own beauty, "I am so much fairer than my sisters that I will stand erect on my stalk and gaze at him as he goes by, in order that he may have the comfort of my loveliness and fragrance." As he saw the flower, he paused before it, for a moment, possibly to admire, but as his eye fell upon it, in the moonlight, the lily, contrasting her self satisfaction with his humility, and seeing that all other flowers had bent before him, was overcome with shame, and the red flush that spread over her face tinges it still. We call it the red lily for that reason, and it never erects its head as it did before that night.

The decorative qualities of the lily have always been appreciated. In our own days Mr. John S. Sargent has introduced it abundantly in his celebrated painting "Carnation Lily, Lily Rose." Like Diana and Juno, Lilith, the first wife of Adam, carried the lily as an emblem. The Greeks and Romans regarded it, as we do, as a symbol of purity, and they crowned the bride and groom with wreaths of lily and wheat, indicating a cleanly and fertile life. Among older nations, it typed virginity and innocence, like most of the white flowers; hence the lilies on our altars at Easter- relics of a sun worship begun in Egypt- will sometimes have their anthers removed, that the lilies may remain virgin. The symbolic use of the lily persists, and it was long regarded as of good fortune, Judith wearing it on the night when she went to Holofernes, to keep off the evil she intended to inflict on him. In Spain it was held that the lily could restore human form to any who had fallen under enchantment and been changed to beasts.

In a garden in that land, in 1048, an image of the Virgin was seen to issue from this flower, and as a sequence to this apparition the king, who lay ill of a dangerous disease, suddenly left his bed as sound as ever he was. In recognition of the divine help, he organized the Knights of St. Mary of the Lily, three centuries before a similar order was instituted by the ninth Louis of France. Under the rain the lilies of the Caucasus used to change, sometimes to red, sometimes to yellow. Maidens tell their fortunes in these revealments, for, having chosen a bud, they look at it after the shower, and if it has opened yellow they suspect their lovers of unfaithfulness, but if it is red they know them to be true. In an eleventh-century legend of that land, an officer returning to his home in the hills, after the pains and trials of war, brings with him Plini, son of a fellow soldier, whom he adopts. The lad, introduced to the general's home, meets his daughter, Tamara, a blushing damsel who has known so little of the world that she is as innocent as the birds that sing among the vines and trees at the door. Plini, finding her ignorant of books, teaches her to read and speak the Greek, even as the poets spoke it. He finds her unskilled in music, but under his instruction she learns to sing and play on the harp. They study together, they walk the fields hand in hand; time is not for them, for the world rolls on in an eternity of happiness. But Tamara has been promised to an official of consequence in the Georgian state, and, learning of this, Plini and Tamara realize that they love each other; that apart they can hardly endure to live. Still, the girl is dutiful, and will not listen to her lover when he pleads with her to fly with him to Greece. She promises only to pray for a way out of the difficulty, and, hoping to obtain it, she visits a monk who lives alone in the mountains. Her retinue remains outside while she questions the old man in his hermitage, and it is thrown into terror by a storm in which the place is pelted with lightnings and shaken by thunder. When this has passed Tamara is no longer seen. The attendants rush into the presence of the monk and demand that she return to them. "God has heard our prayer," he answers. "Tamara is no longer troubled. Behold her!"

The people follow the monk's gesture with their eyes and observe a splendid lily in his garden where none grew before, and its fragrance comes to their nostrils like incense. But the people are doubters, and they will not believe the miracle. They drag the recluse from his cell, search the building and the shrubbery, and with cries of anger fall upon and kill him. Not content with this, they set fire to all that will burn, destroying the house, its statues of the saints, its ancient trees, its library, so that

MYTHS AND LEGENDS OF FLOWERS

when they go to break the news of the girl's disappearance the lily stands alone in a field of ashes. In the excess of his grief Tamara's father dies, but Plini hastens to the scene of the floral transfiguration and, standing before the flower, cries, "Is it indeed you, Tamara?" And there is a whisper, as of wind moving through its leaves: "It is I." The youth bends above the lily, and his tears fall on the earth beside it. Yet, blinded as he is by grief, he cannot but observe that the leaves turn yellow as with jealousy. The next drops fall into the flower itself, and it flushes red with joy. That night he falls into such a passion of weeping that the Lord changes him into a rain-cloud, that he may the oftener refresh the lily that was his love. And in after years, when dryness bakes the earth, the girls go out from their villages and strew lilies over the fields, singing Tamara's song as they march. Seeing these flowers, the cloud arises and pours warm tears over the land.

A boy regarded as an "innocent" or imbecile, was accepted by a kind abbot as an inmate of his monastery near Seville. The brethren did their best to instruct him, but as he seemed to remember nothing from hour to hour he was put at work in the fields and about menial tasks in the building. He did with patience what was expected of him, but was shy because of his infirmity, and at every chance would steal into the church, where he might sit alone, murmuring to himself, "I believe in God; I hope for God; I love God." And there, after a day in the garden, they found the guileless fool, his hands folded, a serene smile on his face: dead. The words he had so often repeated were carved on the cross at his head when they buried him. Shortly a lily sprang from the grave, and, curious to know its origin, the abbot ordered the body to be exhumed, whereupon it was found that the heart of the innocent had become the root of the flower. In a folk-tale of Normandy a knight who had resisted the charms of the sex till he had acquired a reputation for coldness that exempted him from its assault, was accustomed to spend much time in graveyards, where he would be seen in a listening attitude, as if he expected some message from the dead which would show him the way to happiness. And the way came as he did not expect it, for, so wandering among the tombs, he met on a fair morning a woman of beauty such as he had never before imagined. She was sitting on one of the marbles, dressed in precious stuffs, with glowing jewels at her waist, and hair as yellow as the pollen of the lily she held in her hand. Her presence breathed a sweetness that filled him with admiration and awe, and, kneeling, he kissed her hand, at which salute the lady woke, as from a dream, and, smiling on him, said, "Sir knight, will you take me to your castle? You have sought me long, and I have come at last, for I have been waiting the hour when I might disclose myself. That happiness you have denied to yourself so long, it is mine to give. But before I go with you I must exact one promise, and it is that none shall speak of death when I am near. Think of me as representing the life of the world, the bloom of youth, the tenderness of love, and think of this as yours forever."

The knight, enraptured, lifted the maid to his horse; the animal cantered away without seeming to feel her added weight, and as they rode through the fields the wild flowers bent their heads, the trees murmured musically, and fragrance filled the air, as from unseen beds of lilies. So they were married, and were very happy. If now and then some touch of his old sad manner was seen in the knight, his wife had only to place a lily against his brow and all melancholy disappeared. Christmas eve arrived, and a great banquet was ordered. Flowers of magic size adorned his table, the dames sparkled with smiles and jewels, and the lords wore so brave a mien it was inspiriting to look at them. And while they feasted a minstrel sang, now of love, now of war, of knightly adventure, of noble deeds and high resolves; then, tuning his harp to a more reverent strain, he sang of heaven and the earning of it through death. At the word the lily wife turned pale and began to fade like a flower touched with frost. Her husband caught her in his arms with a cry of anguish, for

MYTHS AND LEGENDS OF FLOWERS

now she began visibly to shrink, and in a few moments grief and bewilderment possessed him, for, behold, he was clasping a lily in his arms, and its petals were dropping to the floor. A great sighing was heard in the air, and the room was filled with a sweet odor. The knight turned away with a despairing gesture and went out into the darkness, never again to be seen by those about his board. And out of doors a change had come. It had grown cold and bleak, and the angels were scattering over the earth the lily petals of the snow.

LILY OF THE VALLEY

No sweeter flower blooms than the lily of the valley. It expresses the virtues of purity and humility. There is somewhat calming in its whiteness, and something holy in its perfume. It seeks quiet, half-shaded places, as if avoiding the ruder contacts of the world. Little May bells is one of its German names, and in England the old names of May flowers and May lilies are still applied, but these are trite, and "ladders to heaven" commends itself as a better. To the French, a tender meaning tells itself in "the tears of Holy Mary." Ostara, Norse goddess of the spring, was a patron of the flower that marked her coming. We find a fitting use of it in the Saga of Frithjof, where Ingeborg, lamenting her hero, describes his grave as covered with these tender blooms. Lilies of the valley are appropriate gifts to be offered by young swains when they visit their ladies; and, indeed, the homage and implication of purity and sweetness is poetry in itself. Is it any wonder that the perfume distilled from these holy flowers should have been held so precious in other times that only gold and silver vessels were fit to receive it?

In the allegory which has been localized as a legend in Sussex, England, St. Leonard met the frightful dragon, Sin. For three days he struggled against it, sometimes almost fainting, often desperate and fearing, yet never giving over the fight. On the fourth morning he had the satisfaction of seeing the creature trail its slimy length into the wood, weak with pain, never to encounter with him again. Yet it had left its marks. Wherever its claws or tusks had struck him and his blood had dewed the earth, heaven marked the spot and sanctified it, for there sprang the lily of the valley. Pilgrims might trace his encounters in white all about the wood; and those who listened could hear the lily bells of snow chiming a round to victory.

LILAC

The lilac, which comes from Persia and retains the name it bears in that land, lilag meaning flower, was carried to Europe in the sixteenth century and brought to this country by the Puritans. It grows wild in southern Asia and southwestern Europe, but with us, who have known it as prince's feather and duck's bills, and also as laylock and blow-pipe tree, because pipe-stems were made from its smaller branches, it is a loved occupant of the garden; and what more beautiful than a lane of lilacs in May with heavy heads nodding over the walk and dripping dew and perfume? Though picked for May festivals it was introduced charily indoors, for to many it was a flower of ill luck- a result of the association of its purple color with the hues of mourning. An old proverb declares that she who wears lilacs will never wear a wedding ring, and to send a spray of lilac to a fiance was a delicate way of asking that the engagement be broken. An English nobleman having ruined a trusting girl and caused her death of a broken heart, a mound of lilac blooms was placed upon her grave by friends, who averred that in the morning the flowers had become white, though when put upon the grave they were rosy mauve. This, the first white lilac, is pointed out today in the churchyard of a hamlet on the Wye, in Hartfordshire.

MYTHS AND LEGENDS OF FLOWERS

LINDEN

To the old Germans, the lime, or linden, was a holy tree, yet a haunt of dwarfs and fairies; and under it the dragons lay so often, for the shade, or for some protecting property, that they became known as lindenworms. The custom of magistrates of sitting beneath it to give sentence also lent importance to the lime and caused it to be known as the tree of judgment. In the mythology of the north, when Sigurd, after killing the dragon Fafnir, bathes in its blood, a linden leaf falls on his shoulder and makes it vulnerable to Hagen's spear, since it prevents the blood from touching the skin at that point; hence the linden was a tree of ill-fortune. Like other trees, it is occasionally bound up in the fortunes of a family or tribe, an instance being that of the "wonderful tree" of Susterheistede, which was to be green so long as the Ditmarschens kept their freedom, but was doomed to wither when they lost it, as the event proved; but the people say that the day is coming when a magpie will build in its branches and rear five young, and the ancient liberties will then be restored to the land.

A tradition of the tree had fresh telling in America when Prince Henry came to us on his friendly errand, with Admiral Baron von Seckendorff as chief of his suite, for the history of the Seckendorffs begins in the year 1017 in this wise: When Henry II. was on the throne, the favorite pastime of the court was hunting. In one of his expeditions, the emperor roused a bull, which attacked him fiercely. Henry had only a sword for his defense, and had nearly given up hope, when the underbrush was shaken, and a young man bounded into the clearing with a lance, which he cast into the body of the bull. As the animal sank with a groan, the young man respectfully uncovered, while the king mopped his brow, and gazed from the bull to the spearman, as if doubting their existence. On coming to himself, he embraced his preserver, crying, "So brave a man is destined to father a race of heroes;" and led him to a linden, where his retinue had now assembled. There he related the incident, his story being greeted with applause. "What is your name?" asked the king. "Walter," replied the stranger.

Henry reached into the tree and, breaking off a branch with eight leaves, bent it into a wreath and placed it on the young man's brow. "I have no chain of gold to give to you here," he explained, "so take this spray of linden as a sign of better favors from your emperor." Then, commanding him to kneel, the monarch dealt the accolade, saying, "Rise, sir knight; and because you have risked your blood for mine, be your device a red linden branch on a white field. The lands and castle of Seckendorff are yours."

The linden is one of the elements in the well-known tale of Philemon and Baucis, the contented old couple who served Jove and Mercury in their humble cot, when those gods descended in disguise, and who, in recompense, were spared from destruction in the deluge that overwhelmed their neighbors in Phrygia. Their home was transformed into a temple, and there they served as priest and priestess to the end of their days, which were long in the land. That neither husband nor wife might survive after the other was gone had been their prayer; so at the appointed time, when they came into the morning light, they knew that they should never see the sun again through human eyes, for on the head of each was a crown of leaves, not new placed, but growing. There was time for a last embrace. "Good-by, my love," said Philemon, and "Good-by, my dear," said Baucis. Then, hand in hand, they faced to the east and spoke no more. Slowly their human guise was lost. Their forms, bent and withered, passed into the shapes of trees with corrugated trunks, but not trees that expressed age. On the contrary, they ascended high and higher, unfolding large and larger crowns of leaves to the sky, and so they stood for ages and may stand yet: Philemon an oak, Baucis a linden. Something of human spirit lingered in both and the Scythian soothsayers turned to the linden when they were to prophesy and twined its leaves about their fingers when they sought inspiration, as if it spoke to them.

LOTUS

The symbolic use of the lotus is various and remarkable. It is the representation of the sun and moon; the attribute of silence; the symbol of female beauty; the breath of gods; the source of nectar that gives eternal life; the cradle of Moses; the seat of Buddha; a memorial of the ark; the resting place of great spirits. Lakshmi, the Hindu goddess of love, is couched upon it, the fragrance of her body filling the heavens; Kamadiva, the Hindu Cupid, floats down the Ganges on this flower; the Japanese Mercury, Fudo, glides through the air on lotus sandals; the new-born Buddha, in setting foot on earth causes a lotus to spring from it, and in his first seven steps northward a lotus marks each footfall. With the Egyptians it is the flower of Osiris, the sun god; and Horus, or Harpocrates, son of Osiris and god of silence, sits like Buddha, on a lotus, with finger on his lip, enjoining peace. This peace of eternity is expressed in the contemplative figures of Buddha, which the Japanese carvers have put into such exquisite form, and which represent the god as seated on an opened flower, ready to listen to the prayer of the faithful, that begins, "O God, the jewel of the lotus." In the Greek legend this "bride of the Nile" is the body of a lovely nymph, who, deserted by Alcides, flung herself into the river and was drowned; but among the mystic orientals it is an emblem of the world, for Brahma, springing into life from the navel of Vishnu, alighted on a lotus, and from that rostrum commanded all worlds into being.

This flower, simple, decorative, and attractive in its form, appears in the architecture of Egypt, in the capitals of its temple columns, in paintings and wall ornaments of the east, in the carpets of Turkey and Persia. No doubt it was first regarded merely for its beauty, and painters and sculptors used it as we might use the daisy or the maple leaf, without a thought of symbolism; but its petals, flaring to the light, suggested sun rays, and so it entered into the aspects and appliances of sun worship. Professor Goodyear, in his "Grammar of the Lotus," gives to it a high place in the arts of thirty centuries before Christ. He evolves the Ionic capital from its twisted sepals; the Greek fret or meander he also traces to that; and the fret or key pattern doubled is the swastika, earliest of symbols and ornaments, to be found in pottery and on the temple fronts of the old world and the new, where it represents light and dark, death and life, male and female, good and evil. The triangle of its calyx has doubtless served, like the shamrock, as text for those who expounded the Trinity, and the old figure of the cornucopia, showering plenty on the world, may easily have come from these seed vessels.

The seed were closed in balls of clay and thrown into the water, that they might root and create new plantations; hence the saying, "Cast thy bread on the waters and thou shalt find it after many days." For, despite the sanctity of the lotus, the Egyptians, Chinese, and others eat the bread made from its kernels; but in their case it seems to exercise none of the spell ascribed to it by the poets, who tell of lotus-eaters that care for no other food and so remain where it grows, forgetting their own countries and all pertaining to them. The lotus was a sacred flower in Egypt four thousand years ago, and was used to decorate guests at banquets, the stem being wound about the head and the bud hanging on the forehead. The Japanese still make ceremonial use of the lotus, which they buy on holidays for temple decoration, and they use its leaves or pads to wrap up food that is offered to the dead. In Siam, where the lotus is the national flower, this heaven is suggested in the great ponds of lotus in the king's park near Bangkok.

MYTHS AND LEGENDS OF FLOWERS

MAGUEY

Maguey, or agave, is often known as the century plant, because it blooms so seldom that most people believe it flowers only once in a hundred years. As a matter of fact, it blooms once in eight years in its own country, but in a cooler climate can be persuaded not to bloom at all. In Mexico it throws its leathery leaves to a height of fifteen feet, and its stalk, a veritable candelabrum, bearing about four thousand white blooms, is twenty-five feet high. When it has flowered it seems to have fulfilled its mission and dies down, leaving the ground to be occupied by sturdier offspring, often from the old roots. Miles of country are covered by the maguey, for it has a commercial value in that it is food for cattle, its cores are baked for food, it furnishes thatch for cabins, fuel for kitchens, and fiber for thread and paper. The spike at its leaf-tip is used as a needle, its flower-stalk is a house-pole, and it stores water for the thirsty. These sweet juices, the *agua miel*, or honey water, that would otherwise go to the making of flowers, are drawn from a hollow cut in its heart, fermented, and made into pulque, or native beer. A plant will yield six quarts a day for four weeks, and is then exhausted. Pulque induces laziness and sleep, but the more fiery mescal, also made from a variety of this plant, involves the applicant in riot.

The maguey is associated with the Virgin of Totoltepee, where the Aztecs had reared a temple to their gods, but which the Spaniards invaded to place the Virgin among the ruder statuary-a thing allowed, for peace's sake. When the people, unable to endure the arrogance, the persecutions, and the looting any further, arose and drove them forth, the Spanish troopers hid the image beneath a maguey, near the top of Totoltepec. Twenty years afterward a Christianized Aztec, wandering near the hill, was dazzled by a light, and, looking up, beheld the Virgin, who, smiling at him kindly, said, "Dear son, my image is hid near where you stand. Find it and enshrine it."

Cequauhtzin found it under the maguey, and took it home for safe-keeping. In the morning it was gone, but an "'inward voice" told him it had gone back to the hill, and sure enough he found it once more, under the maguey. Again he took it to his house and put it into his stoutest chest, making his bed on the lid; yet in the morning the figure was gone again, and he found it a third time under the maguey. To the Fathers he went and told all that had happened, and they saw that the Virgin's wish was that a shrine should be built over the plant in whose shade she had rested for so many years; accordingly, the splendid church of Our Lady of the Remedies was erected on the hill-top, the Aztec temple being destroyed to make room for it. This church is now a resort of thousands seeking health and pardon. The slab in the altar records that "this is the very spot where the Holiest of Virgins was found under a maguey by the chief, Don Juan Aguila" (the Indian's Christian name), "in the year 1540, where she told him, on appearing before him, that he should seek her."

A curious mark of patriotism was shown by the Mexican congress in 1830, when it ordered that no legal document should be written on any other material than the paper of the national plant, the maguey. One writer offers a theory that Mexico means no more than the land of the maguey, the word mex-tli signifying a maguey, personified.

MAIZE

It was a common belief among the American Indians that corn was of divine origin; that it was the food of the gods that created the earth, and when they flew back to heaven, pained by the ingratitude of men, seeds of maize fell from their hands, and, rooting on the earth, sprang up to be the food of millions. Our farmers kill the crow, but some of the Indian tribes protect it, for this bird was the seed-bearer who brought the corn from heaven. But two legends of the Iroquois tell another story. One is, that a chief, having climbed a mountain where he might be alone with the Great Spirit, begged the deity to give more food to his people, for they wearied of meat and berries, and longed for the food of the gods. The Great Spirit bade him go to the plains with his wife and children in the moon of rains, and wait for three suns. This the man did, and while waiting he and his family slept. Others came to seek them, and behold, the old man and his wives and children had changed to corn. The prayer had been answered. The other tale is of a man who for love of a beautiful girl would sleep in the wood near her wigwam, fearing lest some accident might happen, or a daring hostile creep into the camp and steal her. On a summer night he was awakened by soft footfalls leaving her lodge, and, springing up, he saw her walking in her sleep. He followed, but the faster he pursued, the faster she ran, till at last, in a field, he overtook her and clasped her in a strong embrace. It was Apollo and Daphne again, for, to his astonishment, he grasped, not a girl, but a plant such as he had never seen before, a tall and graceful stalk, with leaves as long as grass. The fright of waking far from home, and in the grasp of a man, had caused the girl to pray that she might be so changed, and her hair became the silk and her lifted hands the ears that are now eaten. It was a common belief among our eastern Indians that human beings could change their shapes in time of need, unless they were under the spell of an evil spirit.

Corn dances, celebrating the bounty of nature, are practiced among many tribes, and among the Hopis of the southwest there is perpetuated a drama which symbolizes the growth of corn and the beneficent and malefic powers that affect it, figured in the appearance and conduct of strange creatures, represented in part by the Indians themselves and in part by rude figures operated from behind a screen. The front of the stage represents a field of growing corn, with actual blades in mounds of earth, and this field is swept by the demons of storm and drought, while shamans perform saving incantations, and heroes end the play by overwhelming the demons.

In one of the earliest of the Indian corn legends, the First Mother was born of a beautiful plant. Seeing her children suffer during a famine, she begged her husband, the First Father, to kill her and scatter her body over the fields, so that the distress of hunger would be ended. The First Father appealed to the Great Spirit, who bade him do as his wife desired. So he scattered the fragments far and near, and after a time green blades came up, ripened, and were corn. So it is that the wise say, "A man is a grain of corn. Bury him and he rots. Yet his spirit lives and leaps from the earth again, to make him as he was." The Chippewas tell how the demigod Wunaumon, son of Hiawatha, lived alone, a mighty hunter, from whom the beasts flew or slunk away when they saw his shadow on the earth. He roamed freely through the forests of the Mississippi, and in one of his long tramps reached the prairies, which were like an endless lake of land save that far away he saw a strip of wood. "I will know what is there" he said, and with great strides gained the other side of the country. As he stood under the trees a stranger came to meet him- a stranger with a shiny coat which was hard, like husks, and a flowing, ruddy feather in his scalp-lock. He was short and stubby, not likely, one would say, to offer battle to the big Wunaumon; indeed, he seemed to have no such intent, for after a short talk he produced a pipe and exchanged a whiff or two with the hunter. But the spirit of fight was in Wunaumon, who, looking down at the stranger, remarked, "I am very strong. Are you?"

"I have the strength of a man," said the little fellow candidly. "I am Wunaumon. What is your name?" "I will not tell unless you beat me in wrestling. Throw me, and you shall find out. And it will be worth while to try, for you shall win more than the knowing of my name." "Come, then, Red Feather!" cried the hunter, stripping off his ornaments. "I am not Red Feather. Try me, and perhaps you shall know. If you conquer, it will be for the good of all your people."

They struggled, feinted, broke away for breath, and went at it again, without the slightest advantage of one over the other, for hours. Wunaumon looked at his little adversary with astonishment. At last, as the sun began to sink, he braced himself for a mighty effort. He planted his feet far apart and threw his arms about the other wrestler with a hug like a bear's. Something seemed to burst, and the man collapsed. "Ha, Red Feather, I have beaten you!" cried Wunaumon. "Now tell me your name."

"I am Mondahmin. I give my body to your people. Where I have fallen cover me with fine earth; then come back to me often. You shall see me again, and I will bring gifts out of this land for you." Wunaumon laid the body in the earth, covered it with dust, and in a month he came back to see two green feathers waving on the grave. The wind passed, and a voice like singing came from the plumes, saying, "This is corn, the gift of Mondahmin. Watch it, take the seed to your people, and tell them to make a feast to Mondahmin in the Moon of Fruits." This did the hunter god, and the seed sprang up in strong, tall stems, bearing store of delicious grains that people planted, so that in times of famine it might save the lives of many. For this was that Mondahmin, who, after the Great Spirit had destroyed all men but one, by dropping the world into the great lake, came from the unknown and won the new-created sister of the survivor. He was the fifth of the spirit suitors for White Earth, and her brother had told her to keep silence till the fifth had come. The first was Usama. When White Earth refused him, his blanket fell from his shoulders and he became tobacco. The second was Wapako, and when she turned from him, this round and pudgy man rolled down the hill, a pumpkin. Next came Eshkossim, the melon; and Kokees, the bean; and they too fell as if dead when White Earth refused them. But at the call of the fifth voice, which was like a musical rustling in the trees. White Earth looked the new-comer in the face and took him for her husband. After the wedding feast great rains fell, and from where the other suitors had disappeared sprang up the leaves of tobacco, pumpkin, melon, and bean, but tallest and most prized were the stems of corn, the plant of Mondahmin.

MALLOW

Our common little mallow, whose seed-pods- the "cheeses" of children- are eaten seriously in the east, appealed to Mahomet so greatly, through his joy in a rope woven of its fiber, that he glorified a plant of it into the pelargonium- an achievement worthy of Burbank. Taken in the morning, the mallow protects one from disease for that day. Marsh mallow, however, was held to be "Twice as good" a medicine, and nobody is much hurt by eating the confections sold as "marshmallows," even in these days of adulterations. As ointment, the mallow cured those affected by witchcraft, and it had the more wonderful effect of protecting from hot metal.

MANDRAKE

Because of its supposed power as an aphrodisiac, the fruit of the mandrake was apples of love to the Greeks, but devil's apples to the Arabs. More than twenty solemn books have been written on the medicinal, spiritual, and diabolical nature of this plant, with its forked, flesh-colored roots that were carved into figures of men and carried as charms. It was a most dangerous plant to dig, hence it had to be pulled from the ground by a dog, that died of fright on hearing it scream- the shriek "like mandrakes torn from the earth"- for the sound was death or madness to any that heard. The dog's owner tied the tail of his faithful animal to the stem, first making the sign of the cross thrice over the plant, retreated to a safe distance, whistled to the dog, closing his own ears tightly, and up came the angry vegetable. In time men acquired a better control over the plant, or themselves, for it sufficed to pry it out with a sword, if the

MYTHS AND LEGENDS OF FLOWERS

digger would keep to windward of it and direct his face to the west. If he failed to dislodge it, the earth opened and he disappeared forever in the grasp of a fiend. Having taken the root, the owner is to keep it in a white cloth, in a box, bathe it every Friday, and save the water in which it is washed, as it has medicinal properties. This "earth manikin" brings luck to the house, and, carried under the coat, protects one against reverses in courts of law. Possibly for this reason it was a more than suspicious circumstance to have a mandrake about one's premises. It branded the owner as a wizard, and in 1630 three women were put to death in Hamburg on no other charge than that of having mandrake roots in their homes. The devil had a special watch upon these objects, and unless one succeeded in selling one for less than he gave for it, it would stay about him till his death. Throw it into the fire, into the river, smash it, fling it from a cliff, lose it in the woods, so soon as you reached home there would be the mandrake, creeping over the floor, smirking, human-fashion, from a shelf, or ensconced in your bed.

After dread of the mandrake had worn away to some extent, it was still observed with respect, was handed down from father to son, and in one case was kept in a coffin and enfolded in a picture representing a thief on the gallows, with a mandrake growing at his feet. Sometimes the root bore a startling likeness to a human head, one such specimen being shown in the College of Surgeons, in London: a double bulb, each showing every feature of a human countenance, including a beard. German miners said that the root went far into the ground, and that it was the kobolds who cried when they saw it disappearing upward. The merits of mandrake became practical, as years went by, and referred less to fortunes than to health, since it tended to cure barrenness, nightmare, cramp, and toothache, and protected the owner against robbers and bad weather. A common association of the plant with a buried corpse is thought to arise from the burial of Medusa's head under the Agora at Athens; whence its name of mandragora, and it may be because of the stupefying

MYTHS AND LEGENDS OF FLOWERS

and fatal effect of Medusa's gaze, while she lived, that this output from her tomb should be regarded as an opiate and poison.

Shakespeare speaks of "poppy, mandragora, and all the drowsy spirits of the east." In Iceland, where it is thieves' root, because it grows from the mouth of a rascal who has been hanged, it will draw to itself the money from unguarded pockets if the owner puts beneath the mandrake a coin which he has just stolen from a poor widow at a high festival of the church, between the chanting of the Epistle and the Gospel.

MANGO

Travelers in the tropics endure mingled emotions in their experience with the mango, the exceeding juiciness whereof suggests that it be eaten in overalls, and which, when all is said, tastes to most of us like a door-mat soaked in turpentine. But the mango is prized by the blacks and the browns who live in the shade of it, and in a Canarese legend it is the tree of life itself. In that story a king had a magpie that flew up to heaven, and returned bringing mango seed, which it gave to the king, saying, "Plant this, and when it has grown, eat of its fruit; for it will give everlasting life to all who taste it." The king put it into the ground forthwith, and in due season the tree had grown large, fair, with glossy leaves and glowing, ruddy fruit. It chanced, however, that the first mango he chose had been poisoned, for a snake in the grasp of an eagle flying overhead had dropped some venom on it. In some doubt as to its wholesomeness, the king ordered an old man in his court to eat the mango, and, the poison working in his vitals, he fell in torment and died. The king, astonished and angered, took the unfortunate magpie by the neck and beat its life out, and for a long time after nobody dared touch the tree. It was called, in fact, "the poison mango," and might have been cut down and burned had it not been for an old woman who had been flouted and whipped by her son and his

MYTHS AND LEGENDS OF FLOWERS

wife, and had resolved to commit suicide by eating a mango, that her death might be charged upon the undutiful pair. She ate the fruit and instantly was as a maid in her teens. Others, hearing of the wonder, ate also of the fruit, became young, and rejoiced. But the king did not eat. He thought on his wickedness in killing the affectionate bird that had brought to him the tree of eternal youth, and in remorse he slew himself. In a Hindu parable a mango tree is denoted, filled with fruit. A black man chops at it with his ax; a blue man tears off a branch; a red man pulls off fruit; a yellow man perches on a bough, eating ripe mangoes; and a white man pauses on his way to pick up a fruit that has fallen to the ground. This is an allegory of life, and the use we make of it. The black one, with his ax, seeking only destruction, is the conqueror, or criminal; the blue man is the careless egotist who spoils, but in smaller measure; the red man will not injure the tree, but he is still greedy enough to require the best; the yellow man is temperate and wise, taking only what he needs and leaving enough for others; but the white man shows humility and accepts what the rest neglect, living content with the smallest share, pausing in his walk and service only long enough to take a single fruit, for the hungry will afterward pass that way. Yet the fruit he eats is sweetest.

MAPLE

Various legends concerning Manabozho- or Hiawatha, or Hoyawentha, or Glooskap- relate to trees and plants. For example, it is said that he flogged the birch, so often used in the flogging of others, and left the rings about its bark; that he gave thorns to the roses, out of his love for them, that the animals might not eat them; that he stole the first tobacco from a giant, and that the smoke of it, as he blows it abroad in the fall, makes the haze of Indian summer. The blood from sundry cuts in his flesh flowed to stain the red willow, which has never since lost its color; blisters from his burned back have become lichens on the rocks. As a crowning gift to his people, he created maple sugar, though this latter tradition is disputed by some eastern tribes, who assert that the sugar was discovered by a squaw who, having to cook moose-meat in early spring, and being at a distance from water, tapped a maple-tree and drew enough of the sap to fill her kettle. Having run away from her domestic duties to gossip with the neighbors, she was horrified, on her return, to discover that the liquid had boiled to nothing, and that the meat was immersed in a sticky mass of unpleasant aspect but inviting odor.

To offer such a joint to her husband, whose step was even then heard in the wood, was to endure a beating, so she fled. What was her astonishment, on creeping to the camp, a little later, to discover her lord luxuriously seated at the fire, licking his fingers, which were coated with the brown substance, and quite neglecting the burned and hardened meat. She made bold to approach and was about to apologize for her neglect when the brave arose and, throwing his hands about her neck, addressed her in terms of thankfulness and endearment; for she had discovered what was worth much moose-meat, and should continue to be his bride forever. In that episode was discovered a solace and a source of revenue that has advantaged good New Englanders and Canadians to this day, and may have had its influence upon the latter in their choice of the maple leaf as the provincial insignia. When frosts touch the earth, and the year fades to its sunset, it is the maple, more than all other trees, that glorifies the landscape and turns the hills to heaps of ruby and topaz.

Anciently, the maple was an emblem of reserve, because of the quietness of its flowers. Its root cures lameness of the liver, says Pliny. Cicero had a table of maple-wood that cost ten thousand sesterces, and another was sold to an opulent Roman for its weight in gold. Maple, too, was a common material for cups, in the scarcity of gold and glass, and the fair Rosamund drank her fatal draught from such an one. The Hungarians tell how a king's blonde daughter falls in love with a shepherd, who has charmed her with a maple flute- still blown in Cornwall on May day to bring in the spring with music. This daughter went into the fields with her two sisters to gather the first strawberries of the season, their wretched old parent thinking so much more of his victuals than of his kingdom or his kindred that he promised his crown to the first who should return to him with a basket of the fruit. The blonde's basket being first filled, her prospects maddened the brunettes with jealousy; hence, they killed her, buried her under a maple, and divided her berries between them, returning with a probable story that a deer had eaten her. Vain were the lamentations of the king; vain, too, the pipings of the shepherd on the hill, for, blow as he might, the maple-wood made no answer, nor would his lady appear. On the third day the sheep-herder, passing the maple where the princess had been buried, noticed a fair new shoot that had sprung from the tree. He cut off the branch and fashioned a new and better (flute), which began to sing when he put it at his lips, not in wordless notes, but in downright speech:

"Play, dearest! Once I was a king's daughter; then a maple shoot; now I am a flute." Astonished at this disclosure, he rushed to the palace, demanding audience of the king, who was amazed, as well he might be, when, on putting the wood to his own mouth, he heard it say, "Play, my father! Once I was a king's daughter; then a maple shoot; now I am a flute." Wishing to test his senses, he called the wicked daughters and commanded that they blow into the instrument, but as each did so it cried, "Play, murderer! Once I was a king's daughter; then a maple shoot; now I am a flute." Realizing what a crime had been committed, the king drove them from his home, while the shepherd went back to his sheep and solaced his loneliness with the voice of his beloved.

MYTHS AND LEGENDS OF FLOWERS

MARIGOLD

Like other yellow flowers, the marigold was an expression of light- "the bride of the sun," "the golden flower"- yet, strangely enough, it has been chosen to express jealousy and fawning. In one legend it is a girl who, consumed with envy of a successful rival in the affections of a young man, lost her wits and died. But while in one floral dictionary it stands for envy, it more clearly means constancy, because of its bright face, its devotion to the sun, its cheer. Odd are the names the members of this family have borne; death flower, cowbloom, gouls, goulans, goolds, king cups, butterwort, bull flower, pool flower, care, horse blob, water dragon, drunkard, publican-and-sinner, yolg of eggy Mary bud, gold flower, shining herb, and lefthand-iron, the latter name coming from Provence, where it was suggested by the likeness of the open blossoms to a shield. The Greek name, kalathos, or cup, from which its botanic name of caltha is derived, may indicate that the Greeks had their own story of its origin, and in Germany a tale survives that strongly recalls the Greek: A maid, Caltha, fell in love with the sun god- so deep in love that she lived only to see him. She would remain in the fields all night, that she might meet the first glance of his flashing eye. So consuming was her love that she wasted till she had become entirely a thing of spirit, rising from the earth and losing herself in the rays that shone about the being of her adoration. And where she had long stood the first marigold appeared, its form and color recalling the sun, and on its petals a drop that might have been dew or a tear of happiness at the maid's translation.

Quite other is the marigold of Mexico, for its petals are red- the blood of Aztecs put to death by Spaniards in their eagerness for land and gold. It was alleged that the Virgin wore the plant on her bosom; hence the name of Marygold; but a likelier origin is marais (marsh) or meer (pond, or lake,) since

MYTHS AND LEGENDS OF FLOWERS

the marsh marigold, so called, elects damp places to enliven with its color.

MARJORAM

Marjoram is one of those rare plants that yield no poisonous quality. It not only gives spice and savor to viands, but was believed to have antiseptic value, and was therefore used in chambers of the sick and for strewing over church floors at funerals. The German name of the plant, "happy-minded," and its older name of joy-of-the-mountain, indicate a festal rather than funereal significance. In Greece and Rome it was one of the hymeneal flowers, because Venus created it, and it is the touch of her fingers that lingers as a perfume. In Cyprus they ascribe its origin to Amarakos, a page in the household of the king, who, passing through the palace with a jar of perfume in his arms, slipped on the marble floor, and dropped the vase, which was shattered into a thousand pieces. The king arose to chide him, which so terrified Amarakos that the life instantly went out of him, and he lay white and still in the bath of floral essence. From his burial-place arose the plant we call marjoram, corrupting it from his name- when we do not ruthlessly dub it *origanum vulgare*.

From Cyprus the marjoram found its way to the mainland, and as dittany it blooms as far away as England and Germany. In those countries it was formerly prized as a charm against witchcraft, for no person who had sold herself to the devil could abide it.

MELON

For some reason this fruit stirred the ire of Elias, possibly because he had eaten thereof and they disagreed with him, and on Mount Carmel, when you climb to the top, you shall see a field of stones which were melons once, but which he cursed so bitterly that they became more indigestible than ever and hardened into their present shape. A king of Tuscany was once father to triplets, whom he never took the trouble to look at, because his sisters, jealous of his queen, told him they were not human, but were a cat, a snake, and a stick. The king believed them, cast his wife into prison as a witch, and ordered the progeny to be thrown into the sea. The gardener, to whom the last task was allotted, took the poor little people to his home, reared them as if they were children of his own, and taught them to raise flowers and fruits. One of the first fruits that came from their garden was a watermelon, so big and tempting that it was deemed fit for the king, so to his table it went. When he cut it, behold, its seeds were precious stones. "Oh, wonder!' roared the monarch. "Can a melon produce stones?" "As easily as a woman may give birth to a cat, a stick, and a snake," declared a maid of honor. "What do you mean?" blustered the ruler.

Then they labored with his primordial intellect till at last he understood; whereupon he released his wife, took his children home, and, instead of drowning his sisters, ended the scandal by making a public show of them at the stake- and incidentally exposing his preceding imbecility.

MIGNONETTE

To work in the garden of a summer morning, when the breeze, blowing over the mignonette, brings the delicate rapture of its odor and the hum of bees who are plundering its sweets, is to know a moment of old paradise. To be sure, the charm of the flower is in its perfume; it has no splendor for the eye; but its constancy and generosity of bloom endear it to every one whose patch of ground is big enough for heaven to brood upon. The mignonette, or sweet resada- meaning, to soothe- is one of the blessings we owe to the Orient, where it expresses health. Nor is it difficult to imagine, if, indeed, it is imagination that affects us in this case, that lesser aches and ills are charmed away by

MYTHS AND LEGENDS OF FLOWERS

inhalation of its fragrance. There are subtleties of cure, of stimulation and narcosis, in odors that our nose-blind race has forgotten. Because of its modesty, mignonette can be blent with almost any combination of blossoms, and because of the readiness of its growth, it is a favorite wherever it is known.

MIMOSA

Most curious among forms of vegetation is the sensitive plant, that folds its leaves together and hangs as if wilted when it has been pinched or struck. It seems as if it were moved by an instinct to "play possum," as animals will do to prevent their falling prey to carnivorge that will not touch a dead body. The sensitive plant has sturdier relatives, however, to whom a pinch is no great matter. One of these is the Egyptian mimosa, which supplies the gum known as frankincense. In a Greek legend, the sensitive plant was the maid Cephisa, who inspired Pan with so violent a passion that she fled from him in terror. He, pursuing, caught her in his arms just as her appeal to the other gods for protection was answered in her transformation to the mimosa. In an old belief, the delicacy of the plant was so extreme that if a maid passed by after a sin, it would fold its leaves as if it had been touched.

MINT

Pluto was not a deity to inspire love, even in the heart of his wife, when, after long waiting, he was able to steal one. Men figured him as a dark and angry god, who flourished a staff as he drove unruly spirits to their last abodes of gloom. Pluto spent most of his time in the underworld, yet he did visit the light occasionally, and on one of his emergings he saw and loved the nymph Mintho. Now, his wife, Proserpine, watched him more closely than he knew; not that she was fond of him, but, being a woman, she could not endure to divide the affections of her lord. Hence at the first opportunity she revenged the slight he had put upon her by turning her rival into an herb, in which guise she lost some outward beauty, yet still attracted men by her freshness and fragrance.

Of the several varieties of mint, the catmint, or catnip, commends itself especially to the feline race. In an old belief this herb will not only make cats frolicsome, amorous, and full of battle, but its root, if chewed, "makes the most gentle person fierce and quarrelsome." The mint called pennyroyal, which has value in the rural *materia medica* because it purifies the blood, disperses fleas, and, smeared on the face with vaseline and tar, keeps off gnats and flies, was used by witches in a malignant medicine which caused those who swallowed it to see double.

MISTLETOE

Our custom of decorating the home with mistletoe goes back for centuries, to the ceremonials of the Druids, and is a reminder of their winter custom of keeping green things indoors as a refuge for the spirits of the wood, exiled by the severities of cold and snow. Because of its pagan associations, mistletoe was long forbidden in the church. Five centuries ago, however, assemblies were held in public squares to greet the sacred plant, and its continued use as a protector against spells is reported in Worcestershire, where the farmer offers it to the first cow that calves after the new year, thereby securing his stock against illness and trouble for a twelvemonth. In Germany, if you will take the trouble to carry a sprig of mistletoe into an old house, the ghosts who live there will appear to you, and by means of it you may force them to answer your questions.

The symbolism of mistletoe in Druid rites was spirit, hence its relation to spirits, for, like the orchids, it grew not on the earth, but in the air, on the sacred oak; at least, it was most prized when found clinging to that tree. "When the Druids required it at the end of the year, it was cut by a white-robed priest with a golden sickle, and was not allowed to touch the ground, a white cloth being held for it as it fell. Two white bulls were then slain beneath the oak where it had grown, and the twigs of the parasite were distributed among the people, who placed them over doors, or twined and carved them into rings and bracelets, to keep off evil; for it is a remedy against fits, witches, apoplexy, poison, tremors, consumption, and the like. The wide extension of the plant is due to the birds that eat its sticky berries and carry its seeds from tree to tree. Its fruit ripens after snow begins to fly, for which perversity it may be said to entitle itself to renown for strength.

Virgil says that Aeneas could go down into Tartarus only on condition that he bore a mistletoe in his hand. Probably it kept off devils. The old Saxon name of mistl-tan means "different twig"; that is, it differs from the twig of a tree to which it may affix itself. But it was not always the lean parasite that it is today; it was a tree till its wood was used for the cross of Christ, when it shrank to its present proportions. The old-time monks named it "wood of the cross," and swallowed chips of it, or water in which it had been steeped, or wore fragments about their necks as cures for all diseases. Mistletoe was common in America before the landing of old-world peoples, and is not, therefore, an introduction from Europe. It was better known abroad, however, and to the Norsemen, as to the Druids, was fateful.

Freya so loved her son Baldur that she asked all things of earth and air to cherish him. But one plant she overlooked: the mistletoe, hardly seen in a notch of a tree, even when its berries whitened. This plant grew on an aged oak, near Valhalla, and in the shadow of the oak Baldur dared the gods to harm him, offering himself to their rough sport, standing unmoved and unhurt when they shot their spears and arrows against him. Loki, jealous of the favor and beauty of Baldur, disguised himself as a woman and asked Freya why her son never suffered pain. Freya told him it was because the creatures and things of the earth and air and water had promised to be kind to him; therefore nothing would bruise him or cause his blood to flow. "And there is nothing that can touch him?" Loki asked. "Nothing," answered Freya, "except the mistletoe. But that is so small and feeble it could hurt nothing." Loki went back to the wood in his own shape, plucked the stoutest twig of mistletoe he could find, trimmed off its leaves and berries, and sharpened its end to a point. Soon after, the gods again assembled about Baldur, testing his invulnerability against bows and slings. Hodur, the blind one, stood apart, and Loki went to him. "Why don't you share the sport?" he asked. "I can not see, and, besides, I have nothing to throw," answered Hodur. "You can at least play at the game," insisted Loki. "Throw this, in fashion of a spear." He put the weapon fashioned from the mistletoe into Hodur's hand, and turned his face toward the spot where Baldur stood. Hodur threw, and the point pierced the breast of the young god, stretching him lifeless on the earth. By the combined power of all the gods, Baldur was restored to life. They made the mistletoe promise never again to lend itself to harm, and, to make sure that it kept its vow, they dedicated it to Freya and gave her special authority over it. It promised never to do harm to any so long as it did not touch the earth, and that is why, thousands of years after, people who have never heard of Baldur and Hodur and Loki, hang the mistletoe in their houses in the season of gladness, and kiss one another as they pass beneath it, for it brings happiness, safety, and good fortune so long as it is not beneath our feet.

MORNING-GLORY

Looking up to the new day with its mild eyes, and plentifully starring its vine with color, the morning-glory needs only perfume to be of exceeding value. It is one of the most persistent of plants, and, once sown, is sure to continue itself without other attention than the planter may give to uprooting the thousand offspring that gather about it when life renews at the

MYTHS AND LEGENDS OF FLOWERS

end of winter. It should be the emblem of courage and energy, despite the transiency of the flower. That wild form known to the English as large bindweed, but to the French as belle of the day, appears less beautiful when we learn that, mashed or boiled, it was applied to vulgar swellings that disfigure the human countenance. Poetry should have dissevered morning glory from the mumps. Gerarde, however, will not sanction it for even this purpose, for, says he, "It is not fit for medicine, and unprofitable weeds and hurtful to each thing that groweth next them, and were only administered by runnagat physickmongers, quacksalvers, old women leeches, abusers of physick and deceivers of people." Still, the English country folk were not afraid of it: they even pickled the young shoots of sea bindweed as a substitute for samphire.

MOSS

The modesty of moss has not led to its neglect by the myth-makers, for we know that the *supercilium veneris*, the hair moss used by Lapps for bedding, is claimed for both Freya and for Thor's wife, Sif. We are told, also, that the hyrum, now spread over walls of Jerusalem, is the hyssop of Solomon; and as hyssop had a medicinal worth, it may have been the particular moss that covered the cross of King Oswald, in Northumbria, and worked miracles after his death. For example, a citizen crossing the ice toward this venerated object fell and broke his arm, whereupon a friend tore some of the vegetation from the cross, clapped it upon the injured member, and the bones knit instantly. Another moss of a marvelous sort is that which grows on a human skull in a church-yard, for this is a cure for "chin cough" and fits.

Lycopodium selago, or club nose, probably the golden herb or cloth of gold of the Druids, was likewise remarkable, not as a medicine, but as a protection against unearthly creatures and black magic; only, it must be gathered by a person whose feet were clean as well as bare, and who had offered sacrifices of bread and wine. Thus qualified, he picked the moss with his right hand pushed through his left sleeve, and placed it in a new cloth. The Druid nuns on the island of Sain, in the Loire, made the gathering yet more difficult and interesting when they required the moss for the altars of Ceridwen, the Isis of their faith, or their warriors asked it to poison arrows. The maid who gathered it was stripped of clothing, that she might better personify the moon. She must avoid iron, for if that touched the moss, calamity was near. The selago being found, a circle was drawn about it, and she uprooted the moss with the tip of her little finger, her hand being covered, meantime, with a white cloth never used before. Until our theaters were "electrified," lycopodium was an agent in imparting the delightful terrors of a storm- that, and cannon-balls rolling down zigzag troughs to simulate thunder, and peas shaken in a box to imitate the sound of rain; for dried club moss ignites almost like powder. The moss wives of German lore are good fairies who live in hollow trees, couch on moss, and when startled hide themselves in this green growth. Their time is largely occupied in weaving moss into the most delicate fabrics, soft as silk, luminous as velvet, and colored in the green, gold, brown, and red of the woods. When a person has done a kindness to them, or they have taken him under their protection, they prove their interest by embroidering for him one of these moss cloaks. They give other benefactions, too, for a poor child who had climbed the Fichtelbirge to gather strawberries for her sick mother, was met by a tiny moss wife who asked for some of the berries. The child cheerfully allowed the little creature to take her fill from the basket. On reaching home she found that all the remaining berries had turned to gold.

MOTHERWORT

Drink motherwort and live to be a source of continuous astonishment and grief to waiting heirs. Its English name denotes its medicinal value for women, and in Japan it is also a herb of

MYTHS AND LEGENDS OF FLOWERS

life. A certain stream in that country courses down a hill that is covered with this plant, and people drinking of the waters are wonderfully preserved and endowed with long life. Saki, or Japanese brandy, is supposed to contain a wee bit of motherwort, its flowers being dipped into the liquor; and a beer is also brewed from them. The Japanese motherwort festival, on the ninth day of the ninth month, is signalized by the drinking of these fluids, and mixing flowers of the wort with rice. Cups of saki are dressed with the flowers that neighbors pass from hand to hand with wishes for a long life.

MULBERRY

The Greeks dedicated the mulberry to Minerva, because of some attribute of wisdom that its growers have not always shown, for when James I. introduced the tree into England in 1605, to raise silkworms and create a new industry, he brought in the black mulberry, which the worm will not eat, instead of the white. An equally disastrous attempt to introduce it into the United States involved many farmers and nurserymen in loss. One of the trees early grown in this country was planted at Clay Court House in 1840 by a Scotch peddler who was taken ill in that place, and in the intervals of his gripes he prayed for some sedative, or even poison, for he was so deep in misery that he desired his death. As if in answer to his prayer, a small plant intruded itself on his notice; a plant of minty and therapeutic odor- pennyroyal, probably- which he eagerly bit upon. His torment was appeased, and in gratitude he marked the place by planting a mulberry seed he had brought from Scotland. Milton 's tree at Cambridge still bears fruit, but the mulberry planted by Shakespeare in his Stratford garden was cut down by the man who bought the property, because people bothered him so by asking to look at it. The mulberry is worshiped outright in Burmah, where the European superstition is not shared; namely, that the devil blacks his boots with the berries. In the east it is an innocent custom to make a thick preserve from it on the 15th of the first month, because a fairy, in payment for that dainty, engaged with one Chang Ching to make his mulberries yield an hundredfold more than they had ever done before, and he had a wondrous crop of silk in consequence.

Pyramus and Thisbe are the classic forerunners of Romeo and Juliet. These two young Babylonian lovers were parted by their cruel parents, yet contrived to meet secretly, and between-whiles they breathed affection through a chink in the dividing wall. Their favorite tryst was in the shade of a white mulberry at the tomb of Ninus, outside of the city gates. One day Thisbe, having first arrived, was frightened by a lion that made its appearance, fresh from the plunder of a sheepfold. She sought refuge in a cave, but in her haste she let fall her veil. It was torn by the claws of the beast and drabbled in the blood of a lamb it had slain, and when Pyranus discovered it, he set up a loud lament, convinced that he had lost the maid. "Since you are gone," he cried, "my blood shall mingle with yours." After moistening the veil with his tears, he plunged his sword into his heart. After waiting till she felt sure the lion had gone, Thisbe ventured from her hiding place and came to the tree once more. A human form was lying under the mulberry. It was her Pyramus, and as she caught his head to her bosom the last glance of his glazing eye was fixed on her. Exclaiming, "As love and death have united us, let us be buried in one tomb," she struck the steel into her own soft breast, with such force that the blood spouted over the berries hanging overhead. As her eyes turned toward the heaven, blue and calm beyond the branches that shadowed her, she gasped, "You tree, bear witness to the wrongs our parents have done to us. Let your berries be stained with our blood in token of their misdoing." The lovers were buried together and since that day the mulberry has been red.

MYTHS AND LEGENDS OF FLOWERS

MUSTARD

As a condiment, mustard has been known to men for centuries. It is noted in parable, for the smallness of its seed and the comparative consequence of the plant make it a type of small beginnings and large endings. There is a parable by Buddha which tells how a mother, bereft of her child, carried the little body from house to house, imploring the people to heal it. To a wise man she put her constant inquiry, "My lord and master, what medicine will heal my boy?" Looking on the still face, he answered, "He requires a handful of mustard-seed from a house where no child, husband, parent, or servant has died." She hurried on, but wherever she asked, "Has there been no death in this house?" the answer would be, "Assuredly, for the living are few and the dead a multitude." Day followed day; still her search promised no ending. She understood its uselessness at last, and knew the wisdom of the physician, for she realized the selfishness of her grief.

Others had suffered and sorrowed as much as she. So she parted from the dead child in a wood, and, going back to the wise man, confessed that she had not found the mustard-seed, but had found his meaning. "You thought that you alone had lost a son," said he, "but death rules all."

In India the mustard symbolizes generation, and it is told that a farmer, having plowed over the site of a temple in which the nymph Bakawali had dwelt immovable for twelve years, her body having been transformed to marble, sowed mustard over the freshened earth. This, ripening, was eaten by his wife, who till then had been childless. The pair soon became the parents of a little one, lovely as a nymph, whom they named Bakawali, and who was believed to be no less than the original Bakawali, still in progress through the states of being.

MYTHS AND LEGENDS OF FLOWERS

MYRRH

Gum of balsamodendron is one of the precious substances used in religious observances, and its employment for this purpose began at least two thousand years ago. It blended with the oil wherewith the priests were anointed, anciently, and ran down the beards of Aaron and his sons when they were exalted to leadership. With it the Jews gave fragrance and sanctity to the tabernacle, the ark, the altars, the cups, and other holy vessels. During the year required for the purification of women, myrrh was employed for the first six months and other perfumes after. It is a tradition that Nicodemus bought a hundredweight of myrrh and aloes in which to embalm the body of Christ, following a custom of the Egyptians. Incense smoked before the sun god at Heliopolis thrice a day, myrrh being chosen for the noon offering, another resin at daybreak, and a blend of aromatics at evening; and the Persian kings regarded themselves as sufficiently holy to wear myrrh and labyzus in their crowns. Indeed, the ceremonial use of the gum by royalty occurred so lately as the reign of George III., who made in the royal chapel a "usual offering" of gold, frankincense, and myrrh, in memory, ostensibly, of the gifts that the wise men laid at the feet of the infant Christ.

Yet, if ancient legend be true, myrrh is a sufficiently irreligious matter, being no less than the tears of that wretched Myrrha who, conceiving an unnatural attachment for her own father, the king of Cyprus, was pursued by him out of his kingdom. Recovering her reason in exile, and wandering for months in hostile deserts, she came at last to the Sabaean fields, in Arabia, and there, her strength gone, she implored the gods both to pardon and to punish. The gods changed her into myrrh, in which guise she remains, weeping tears perfumed of repentance.

MYTHS AND LEGENDS OF FLOWERS

MYRTLE

Myrtle, which figures so largely in poetry and myth, is thought by some to be the bilberry or whortleberry, or bay. Indeed, the bay is a variety of myrtle, and has among its congeners the giant eucalyptus, the guava, pimento, clove, and pomegranate. There is reason to assume, however, that the myrtle of the ancients was the myrtle that abounds in southern Europe and has extended into other lands. In its human origin it was Myrtilus, the rogue son of Mercury, who took a bribe from Pelops to pull a pin from his master's chariot-wheel. This enabled Pelops to win a race and thereby claim his master's daughter.

The master showed scant gratitude, for he seized the astonished young rascal and incontinently flung him into the sea, scorning the traitor he had made. But the sea would none of him, either, and tossed him ashore, where, in mercy, his human form was taken from him, and he became a tree. In another legend the myrtle, which loves salt air, is a creation of Venus, who was known in some states of Greece as Myrtilla, or Myrtea, and whose head was decked with it when Paris judged her most beautiful of the gods. In that legend a girl Myrene, who had been carried from home by a robber band, was rescued by Venus, who made her priestess in her temple. During one of the festivals, Myrene chanced to see a member of the pirate crew, and in her rage for vengeance pointed him out to her lover, promising to yield to his entreaties if he would put the robber to the sword. The lover succeeded, but Venus, angered by her priestess's desertion, cast the young man into a fatal illness and changed Myrene into the myrtle. When Venus found that her wayward son, Cupid, had fallen in love with Psyche, it was with a myrtle rod that she beat the weeping nymph, and again, when pursued by satyrs, it was a myrtle that received her into its friendly shadow. In a legend possibly yet older, the myrtle was created by

Minerva, and the subject of the metamorphosis was Myrsine, a sprightly maid who had beaten the goddess in a foot-race. Rogero, the Moorish knight, landing from his hippogriff on an unknown coast, tied his steed to a myrtle tree, while he slaked his thirst at a fountain that bubbled forth in a neglected garden. He had laid aside his helmet, shield, and weapons to rest, when a voice issued from the tree, saying, "Do I not suffer enough, that I must endure this rudeness?" The knight, hurrying to untie his winged monster, answered, "Whatever you are, tree or mortal, I ask forgiveness for my unwitting fault, and am ready to do what I can to repair it." Tears, like thin gum, trickled down the bark, and the tree spoke again: "I am Astolpho, paladin of France and by renown one of the bravest. Returning from the east, we reached the castle of dreaded Akina, who took me, a willing subject, to her island seat. There we passed happy days till, tiring of me, as of all who yield to her, she changed me to this form; a myrtle. Of my friends, some are here as cedars, olives, palms; some she changed to springs and some to rocks and some to beasts. Beware, for this may be your fate."

Rogero attached too little importance to the warning. He, too, met Alcina, and, bewildered by her beauty, suffered himself to be led to her palace, with its walls of gold and pillars of diamond. In the end he also was changed into a myrtle; but, recovering his human form through white magic as powerful as her black, he avenged himself on the enchantress and released Astolpho and his friends. To the Greeks, myrtle was an emblem of immortality, because it kept green throughout the year; and because the work of great men is immortal, in humanity's conceit, the populace bound myrtles on their favorites' brows when they had produced successful plays and epics. In the markets a large space was always reserved for the sale of these shrubs and they figured in feasts and ceremonies. One of the wreaths of myrtle carried in the procession of Europa at Corinth measured ten feet in diameter. Being a tree of love, the myrtle was viewed askance by the pious of the ancient world. When the

MYTHS AND LEGENDS OF FLOWERS

festival of the Bona Dea came around, it was allowable for the Romans to use every plant, flower, and leaf in the decorations, save only the myrtle, which was barred on the ground that it encouraged sensuality. Yet the Greeks wore the leaves not only in their celebrations, but in their religious mysteries.

The custom of crowning people with myrtle, especially brides, was passed on by the Romans to the Jews, and by them to the Germans, who are fond of it as a wedding ornament, and to the Bohemians who employ it contrariwise for funerals- a lovely custom, this bowering of the dead in green, signifying immortality. To the Jews, who used myrtle in their feast of tabernacles, and to their relatives, the Arabs, the myrtle was reminder of the bounty of deity when Adam was expelled from paradise, for the first father was allowed to take with him wheat, chief of foods; date, chief of fruits; and myrtle, chief of scented flowers.

NARCISSUS

Narcissus is that Narkissos of the ancients, a seemly youth who won the love of Echo, but did not love her in return. In despair, she faded to a voice, and you shall hear her calling, sadly, in waste places. But the youth had his punishment; having caught sight of his own reflection in a spring, he was lured back to lie on its brink for hours, admiring the face he saw there. He would not eat nor sleep for love of the image, and worshiped so ardently that he died of sheer weakness; or he may have fallen forward into the spring and been drowned. When the nymphs came to remove the body to the funeral pyre, they found no corpse, but in its stead the white flower we call poet's narcissus. It came at once into the favor of the gods and men and was planted everywhere. Pluto used it to entice Proserpine to hell, or else to so dull and drowse her senses and those of her attendants that her danger was not seen. In the Greek belief, it wreathed the harsh locks of the Eumenides. It also starred the brows of the

MYTHS AND LEGENDS OF FLOWERS

Fates, and when the dead went into the presence of the gods of the underworld, they carried crowns of narcissus that those who mourned had placed in their white hands when the last good-byes were said. We learn from Sophocles that narcissus was the crown of the goddesses on Olympus, blooming constantly, moist and fragrant with the dew of heaven. If the Greeks wove the narcissus about the brows of dreaded Dis and the Furies, if they placed it in the coffins of their dead, it was because it gave off an evil emanation, producing dullness, madness, and death. Indeed, narhe, the Greek word from which the flower really takes its name, signifies narcotic.

NETTLE

Tender-handed, grasp the nettle, and it stings you for your pains. Grasp it like a man of mettle, and it soft as silk remains. This ancient saw many good people believe and take on other men's authority, for the nettle is an irritating plant, its stems being covered with fine, sharp hairs that have a poisonous effect on the skin they pierce. It is, or was, occasionally stewed into a tea by country women and administered to the helpless and unfortunate as a cure for anything that might be the matter with them. It is one of the five bitter herbs which the Jews were commanded to eat at the Passover. The Roman nettle, that thrives in England, was planted there by Caesar's soldiers, who, not having breeches thick enough to enable them to withstand the climate, suffered much in the cold, raw fogs; so, when their legs were numb they plucked nettles and gave those members such a scouring that they burned and smarted gloriously for the rest of the day.

OAK

In the speech and letters of all men, the oak is the symbol of strength. It was Jove's tree; the Thunderer's of the North, no less; Merlin worked his enchantments in its shade;

beneath it the Druids held their mystic rites. The Hebrews held it in liking, for under it Abraham received the angels; Saul, his sons, and Deborah were buried beneath it; Jacob hid in one of them the Shechem idols; it was an oak from which Absalom was hung by the hair; the anger of Ezekiel was roused by the images of wrong gods that "stood in every thick oak"; and in its shadow towered the angel who spoke to Gideon. Doubtless it was the service which this excellent tree has given to mankind that keeps it in use in oratory and poem, as it is useful in the arts. It has furnished us with house, ship, arm, tool, funnel, and food. Back in the golden age the oaks dripped honey, and men lived in peace and comfort with no shelter but their boughs.

In the silver age they left these coverts and stripped away the branches for their huts, thus isolating themselves and departing from their primitive communism. In the brazen age they shaped from the wood handles for their weapons. In the iron age, the age of crime and violence and greed, the oaks were wrenched from the hills for battle-ships, aiding to curse where once they blessed. Erisichthon, the lawless and irreverent, ordered his servants to fell an oak that stood in a grove of Ceres. They, fearing the anger of the gods for such a sacrilege, debated till Erisichthon, whose anger was not to be slighted, either, grasped the ax from the hands of the unwilling woodmen and assailed the trunk himself. A spectator who reached forward to take away the implement caught the blow of the ax on his neck, so that his head rolled at the tree's foot and bathed the roots in blood. Now furious, Erisichthon attacked the oak with such energy that it fell, amid the cries of the beholders. But he enjoyed no triumph from this act. From the fallen body of the tree came a voice saying, "I who live in this tree am a nymph of Ceres, and in my death hour I warn you of punishment."

Retribution came speedily. The goddess whose nymph had been so cruelly slain condemned the cutter to unending hunger. He squandered all his fortune on food; he ate continually; yet nothing nourished him, and he died at last, gnawing at his own flesh. Another instance of the speaking tree is found in the oaks of Dodona, which retained their power to talk, even after cutting, for the prow of the Argo, being fashioned from one of them, directed the crew and warned Jason to purge himself of the murder of Absyrtus. Of old it was noticed that oaks were oftener struck by lightning than were most other trees, hence it was supposed that Jupiter launched his arrows at them in warning, when he would express his displeasure at the perversity of the human race, the oaks being worthier and stronger to receive these bolts than other objects. The oak known as the holm, or ilex, a funeral tree in which the ravens croaked forebodings, "drew lightning" to that degree that ancient farmers planted it as a lightning rod, or spite vent for the gods, which may account for its somber reputation. When Christ's fate was known in the forest the trees held council and resolved not to lend their wood for the execution. Every tree that the ax-men tried to cut, splintered and broke, or dulled the tool with knots, till the ilex was reached. That alone remained whole, and of that the instrument of death was shaped; but though it thus became accursed, Jesus forgave it as content to die with Him, and in the shade of an ilex he reappeared to the saints. The Greek drus, a tree, gave the name to dryads, and later to Druids; and belief in dryads merged into a faith in fairies, the northward progress of this belief being traceable into far countries. These fairies affected oaks, making their homes in hollow trunks and going in and out by the holes where branches had fallen; hence it is healing to touch the "fairy doors" with a diseased part, if church-bells have not driven the elves away. The barbarians thought so much of a certain oak in Hesse that St, Boniface swore to cut it down. A tree so esteemed could be nothing less than an idol. As he laid his ax to the trunk, the heathen stood afar off, looking to see him maimed or blinded, cursing him under their breath, yet too frightened for interference.

When half-severed the great creature trembled, and it

MYTHS AND LEGENDS OF FLOWERS

seemed as if a blade had flashed from the sky, for of a sudden it split into four equal pieces, and came to the earth spread apart, like petals of a great flower. Now, there may have been some who saw in this no greater favor for the new gods than the old, but the saint claimed it as a show of approval for his effort, and several were converted on the spot; so in a few days the timbers of Thorns oak were hewn into an oratory, where they celebrated the new faith. Other oaks were resanctified from the worship of Thor to that of Christ by carving crosses on their stems, and legend confuses us when we find that whereas the fairies avoided the signs of the Christian faith in some parts of the world, in others they fled to these protected trees, even as men did. In one pathetic happening, we find the tale of Apollo and Daphne transferred to Germany: A young farmer marries an elf, believing her human, but when he embraces her she changes suddenly into an unresponsive oak. If we pass eastward from Germany the oak is still a tree of legend, and among the blonde Lithuanians we discover traces of their ancient forest worship. They were a quiet people, even when savagery encompassed them, and were much buried in woods, which they worshiped as abodes of deities-secretly worship to this day in isolated communities. Offerings from the people were placed at the feet of the biggest oaks, and the chief priest, or krive, known also as judge of judges, headed a hierarchy of no less than seventeen orders of priests and elders of forest worship.

Lithuania was not christened till the fifteenth century. Despite these heathen practices and associations, despite the ancient belief that from it came the race of men, the oak presently became acceptable to disciples in the new faith, and was early regarded as the tree of Mary. In a Greek legend its roots went down to hell; but in early Christian lore its boughs are heard praying to heaven. The druids, as the Gaels called the oak, was sought by the very ones who had rebuked the popular affection for it. In Ireland St. Bridget at Kildare abode in "the cell of an oak" and founded there the first religious community of women in that island; at Kenmare, St. Columba had her favorite oak, and a tanner who had impudently peeled the bark from it to season leather for shoes was smitten with leprosy for his insolence; another saint, Colman, was the guardian of an oak, a fragment of which kept in the mouth, safeguarded the faithful against hanging, if they had been forgetful in their morals. Augustine chose an oak for his oratory, also, when he addressed King Ethelbert to convert him. The chair of St. Peter, in the Vatican, is an oak board in a frame of acacia. It was to be expected that superstitious people would ascribe virtues to a tree that meant so much for their faith, their practices and their history, hence even in our country we find survivals of that belief in the curability of diseases by pushing the patient no longer through the "fairy doors," but through the forks of an oak, or a gap made artificially, with axes, and thereafter to be repaired with loam. The tree is benignant even to the Wandering Jew, for he can have no rest unless he finds two oak trees growing in the form of a cross. There he can fling himself to the ground and take the sleep that has been denied to him for months. St. Anthony's fire, toothache, and other disorders were cured by the wood, bark, or even by the moral influence of the oak, and people fastened locks of their hair to it when they sought its help, and fed its galls to spavined horses.

In Finland they tell of an oak so tough that it grew only bigger and stouter when attacked by woodmen with their saws and axes- a legend that embodies popular respect for the tree: a respect that in Saxony took shape in a law forbidding its injury. Similar protection was given to the Stock am Eisen, in Vienna, an ancient tree into which every apprentice, starting on his year of wandering, after the good Teuton fashion, thrust a nail for luck. It is the survivor of a holy grove in which, originally, the cathedral stood. Many are these oaks of history and observance: the Parliament oak; the oak of Robin Hood; John Lackland's oak in Sherwood Forest; William Rufus's in New Forest; the Volkenrode oak of Gotha; the oak at Saintes, France, estimated

MYTHS AND LEGENDS OF FLOWERS

to be two thousand years old; Westman's oak of Dartmoor; the oak of Dorset, sixty-eight feet around, with a chamber sixteen feet wide in its trunk, that was fitted as an ale-house; the Wadsworth oak on Genesee river; the oak at Flushing, New York, that served George Fox as a Quaker meeting-house; the oak at Natick, Massachusetts, a "peace tree" of the Indians and a shelter for Eliot when he translated the Bible into Algonquin. The oak that inspired Morris to his adjuration, "Woodman, spare that tree," grew, not as might be supposed, on his premises, but in St. Paul's churchyard, a few steps from roaring Broadway.

In a tradition of the Mission Indians, Wyot, son of Night and Earth, guardian of all things, told of his death ten months in advance- "when the great star rises and the grass is high." He bade his people gather shoots of bushes and make a basket for his ashes, for he had taught the arts to them; and when they burned his body and entered on a season of mourning his spirit did not suffer in the fire; it ascended to the skies and became the moon, or, in another version, a bright star, believed to be Vega. The frog, then a creature fair to look on, with flesh white and red, and big eyes, had yet thin and ugly legs, and the sight of men with legs more shapely made her jealous and wishful to injure them; hence, when Wyot was drinking at a spring she fouled the water and spat in it three times, accusing him of her defects of shape. Wyot drank the water and became ill, dying as he had said, in May, with a promise that from his ashes should spring a precious gift to all his children. And while his soul went skyward his mortal part became the oak. Seeing it fair and strong, the people who had cherished it said to the crow, "Go to the great star and find Wyot, that we may know all the uses of the tree he has given to us." The crow flew high, but came back; then the eagle was dispatched, and he, too, returned without a message; all the birds in turn undertook the errand, but none was strong enough to reach the star. Finally the hummingbird was told to seek the absent one, and he flew from the earth with the speed and straightness of an arrow.

MYTHS AND LEGENDS OF FLOWERS

After some days he reappeared and gave the words of Wyot: "The tree I have given to you with my body is for the sustenance of all people and animals and birds. Men will make flour of its nuts and this flour can be made into cakes." So the feast of acorns became a yearly ordinance, and the acorn is still a food of the Mississippi Indians. It is recorded that Jeanne d'Arc went to her death the sooner because she had been accused of frequenting the Fairy Oak of Bourlemont, hanging it with garlands, dancing and skipping about it during mass, and reviving the worship of its spirit, who in return, had given to her the charmed sword and banner with which she led her countrymen to victory. But of late centuries it is oftener the saints who have appeared in the trees, and so late as the nineteenth we hear of a girl, frightened by thunder, taking refuge under an oak on the Roman Campagna- the most dangerous place one can choose in a storm, for tall trees draw the lightning- and begging the Virgin to save her from the elements. The Virgin, neglecting the rest of Italy to protect one who had presence of mind to pray to her, appeared and remained beside the young woman, allaying her fright and keeping every drop of rain from the leaves, although it poured a deluge roundabout.

There used to stand in Bologna a famous cork tree, a variety of oak, in which a pious shepherd placed a statue of the Virgin. That was well enough, save that the young man had thoughtlessly borrowed the image from a church, without asking leave of the clergy, because he conceived that they were neglecting it. And to this tree he would repair every day and play his flute before the Virgin. Having been caught in the act, and the robbery being brought home to him, he was sentenced to death, and the statue was taken back to the church; but that night it indignantly stalked out of the building, away from the keeping of the neglectful fathers, and, opening the prison door, released the innocent thief, so they were found together in the tree next day. They were taken down, locked up, but the miracle was repeated, until the people were convinced that it was the Virgin's will, so the tree became a shrine. Perhaps from that incident began the practice of hanging small images of the Virgin in oak trees in country districts. Father Bernardo, a holy hermit who lived far from cities, was often besought to solve moral problems and guide his people in worldly transactions. Though his time was mostly spent in prayer, he derived comfort from his "two daughters": terms playfully applied to little Mary, the daughter of a vine-dresser, who brought delicacies to soften the hardness of his fare and cheer him with her prattle, and a big oak that defended his hut from snow and rain.

This oak was his daily companion. He watered its roots if it thirsted, talked to it, caressed it, and fancied its thanks in the murmur of its leaves. Once, when the country had been devastated by freshets that swept away his cabin, he found refuge in the tree, and thither went the speaking "daughter," carrying food and cover, for after three days of imprisonment among the branches he was like to die. Several lumbermen wanted to cut the tree into beams, but Bernardo would never consent, and during his life the oak suffered no injury. As his last days drew near he implored heaven to mark "his two daughters" in some way to signify the use and beauty of their lives, but at first it did not appear as if this were to be done, for Mary became the wife of an artisan, and the big oak was at last sacrificed for its wood, which Mary's father converted into wine casks. As the young woman sat nursing her infant before one of these casks a handsome stranger drew near, just as the older boy of Mary ran to her with a little cross he had fashioned from a couple of sticks. As if struck by the incident, the young man asked leave to make a picture of the group. Hardly waiting permission, indeed, he seized the cover of the cask and on its smooth surface outlined the picture known to the world as the "Madonna delle Sedia." For the young man was Raphael. And thus the prayer of Father Bernardo was answered, for the two "daughters" became elements in one of the highest expressions of beauty.

MYTHS AND LEGENDS OF FLOWERS

OLEANDER

In an humble home in Spain a girl lay ill of fever. Her mother had done what her small means allowed for her comfort, yet the patient made no gain toward recovery. Reduced almost to illness herself by the sense of unavailing service, the mother fell on her knees at the bedside and offered a fervent prayer to St. Joseph for the sufferer's recovery. A reviving shock of joy went through her when she raised her head and found the room shining in a rosy light that seemed to emanate from a figure which bent above the child- a man of lofty aspect. The stranger placed on the child's breast a branch of flowering oleander, pink and unfading, as if freshly plucked in paradise. Then the light faded, and when the mother rubbed her eyes to see the man more clearly and thank him for his coming, the chamber was empty, save of the patient and herself. But she saw that the girl was in a calm sleep, the first since her illness, and bowed her head anew with tears of gratitude. The recovery was swift, and from that day the oleander became the flower of St. Joseph.

In spite of this legend, the plant has an unpleasing reputation. We of the north, who prize it for its beauty and spend much for greenhouse specimens, do not suffer from its presence, but in Greece and Italy it was a funeral plant, and poison to cattle. The Hindu calls it the horse-killer; but he so appreciates its charm that he decorates his temples with it, and of its lovely clusters he makes wreaths for the brows of his dead when they go to the burning ghat.

OLIVE

The olive is significant of security and peace, because it was with the olive-branch that the dove returned to the ark, and it is of record in holy writ because it figures in the parable of

MYTHS AND LEGENDS OF FLOWERS

Jotham. Its oil has been in use for thousands of years, and was the base of those perfumed ointments sold for so large a price in Rome and Athens. It kept alight the lamps in the Tabernacle. It anointed the heads of priests and kings. When peace was sought between warring nations, the messengers bore olive-branches, as did the Athenian who sought the Delphic oracle, or waved them in the temples of Artemis to avert the plague. Young saplings that rise about the parent stem afford our common simile of olive branches, as applied to offspring. It is Minerva's tree- the olive. She bade it rise from the earth when Neptune caused a salt spring to open on the Akropolis. For in the contest between Athena and Poseidon for possession of the city that afterward took her name, the deities declared that whichever of the twain bestowed upon it the gift best worth men's acceptance should command the city's worship. Poseidon came out of his element to create the horse; but Athena created the olive, and every gourmet owes a silent thanks to her as he nibbles its fruit or pours its oil upon his salad. And so the city went to Athena, not Poseidon. The commoners of the city believed its destinies in-wrought with that of the olive, so the lamps of their Parthenon were lighted with its oil; and as the favor it enjoyed in Athens led to its being planted roundabout, it came into use to mark comers and boundaries of estates. The general reverence led Solon to promulgate a law for its planting, as the symbol of freedom, hope, mercy, prayer, purity, and order. In neighboring Italy this sanctity continues to our day, for a branch of olive hung above a door will keep out devils and wizards. In the Temple at Jerusalem, the doors, posts, and cherubim were of its wood; and the importance of the tree is suggested in the name of Mount of Olives, and Gethsemane, the latter word meaning "olive-oil press."

When Adam felt his end approaching he sent Seth, his son, to the gates of paradise for the promised oil of mercy. Although four hundred and thirty-two years had passed since the exile, the path made by Adam through the fields and woods was as plain as if marked but the day before, for no grass might grow where feet accursed of God had trodden. Seth walked on and on till at last he saw a tree of wondrous size and beauty, standing in an open place where four great rivers sprang from a single fountain. Although it bore not a leaf, the tree was of commanding height and grace. A serpent twined about its trunk (here we see a likeness to Yggdrasil), and in its topmost branches sat a child in shining vestments: the child appointed by heaven to give the oil of mercy when the time for pardon should have come. As Seth looked upon these things and basked in the loveliness of the landscape, an angel advanced from the tree, bringing three seeds from the forbidden fruit, which were to be placed in Adam's mouth when he was buried. So when Adam died, Seth did as the angel commanded, and lo, from the seeds sprang three several trees : a cypress, a cedar, and an olive. When Moses started on his wanderings through the wilderness, he took these saplings to the Valley of Consolation, the tears and blood of the consecrated keeping them alive in the forty years of marching up and down through the little state. One of them was the burning bush in which Moses saw the Lord. When, at last, the saplings that had rooted in the mouth of Adam were planted, they grew, within thirty years, into a single tree, beneath which David wept for his sins. Solomon, more philosophic and practical, saw its chief beauty in use, and, like any modern investigator, hewed it down to see what manner of timber it would make. It seemed to be sound, but, strangely enough, no amount of shaping and trimming could make it fit its place as a beam for the Temple in Jerusalem, and, finding it blessed or cursed with some uncanny quality that kept it from the use of men, Solomon preserved it as a sacred relic in the grounds of the Tabernacle itself. Here one day a woman of the Romans, one Maximilia, carelessly leaned against it, then sprang away in fright, crying, "Jesus Christ, thou son of God, help me!" for flame had leaped from it and ignited her robes. At the call the fire ceased, but the Jews, who had seen and heard, said she was a witch. "To say that Jehovah had a son is blasphemy," said they. "We will hunt this woman from the city." And they did so. Years afterward the incident came to mind again, for this was the first speaking of the words, "Jesus Christ." Finally, the timber was thrown into a marsh, where the queen of Sheba crossed it, to dry ground, when she visited Jerusalem. As her feet rested there a vision arose before her, and she saw Christ suspended on a cross at the hill-top, undergoing shameful death. And so it came to pass, for after a time the log floated to the surface of the morass again, and on the night of the betrayal it was lifted out and shaped into the cross, some say by the hand of Christ Himself. The pale color of the olive leaves is due to their still reflecting the glory that shone on them when the Sufferer was transfigured on Olivet.

THE ONION AND ITS KIND

That fragrant lily we call the onion has long been esteemed, not merely for its culinary uses, but as medicine, and it also figures in verse and tale as a symbol. The leek was a food of the poor in the orient, therefore it came to mean humility, though it also became the emblem of Wales, because it had the Cymric colors, green and white. Garlic, another relative of the onion, is given to dogs, cocks, and ganders in Bohemia, to make them fearless and strong. Onions are endowed with magic properties, and if hung in rooms where people congregate the vegetable draws to itself the diseases that might otherwise afflict them. In the onion the Egyptians symbolized the universe, since in their cosmogony the various spheres of hell, earth, and heaven were concentric, like its layers.

The onion is sacred to St. Thomas, and at Christmas becomes a rival to the mistletoe. At the old holiday sports, a merry fellow who represented the saint would dance into the firelight when the Yule log blazed, and give to the girls in the company an onion which they were to cut into quarters, each whispering to it the name of the young man from whom she awaited an offer of marriage, waving it over her head, and reciting this spell: Good Saint Thomas do me right, and send my true love come tonight, That I may see him in the face, and him in my kind arms embrace. The damsel will be in her bed by the stroke of twelve, and if the fates are kind she will have a comforting vision of the wedding.

ORANGE

Certain poets would have us believe that the golden apples of the Hesperides were no apples, but mere oranges- too common, surely, to justify the heroics of Hercules, for that much tried man, in his picking of the fruit, involved himself in a journey to Mount Atlas, and a battle with the fearsome dragon that guarded them, yet his labors brought no gain, for, as the fruit would not keep, except under the eyes of Hesperus's daughters, Minerva carried it back; so Aegle, Arethusa, and Erythia regained their golden apples, as the Rhine maidens regained the stolen Rhine gold. They would even have us believe- these poets- that when the crafty Hippomenes outfooted the swift Atalanta it was only oranges that he cast over his shoulder. Because Jupiter gave the orange to Juno when he married her, orange-blossoms are still worn by brides, though the flower's waxy whiteness and luscious perfume entitle it to popularity for its own sake.

ORCHID

Beautiful as is the orchid, there was nothing beautiful in its origin, for the first Orchis was the son of a nymph and a satyr, hence a fellow of unbounded passion. At a festival of Bacchus, being warm with drink, he attacked a priestess, whereupon the whole congregation fell upon him and rent him limb from limb. His father prayed the gods to put him together again; but the gods refused, tempering their severity, however, by saying that whereas the deceased had been a nuisance in his life, he should be a satisfaction in his death, so they changed him to the flower

MYTHS AND LEGENDS OF FLOWERS

that bears his name. Even the flower was alleged to retain temper, and to eat its root was to suffer momentary conversion into the satyr state.

PALM

The palm supplies rude tribes with food and shelter, oil and fuel. From its dates the Babylonians made wine. It stands in the desert as a mark of cooling water wells, and lines the shore with graceful plumes. In Egypt the admiration for its shapeliness expressed itself in capitals of temple and palace columns, which are conventionalized from its tufts of leaves. In the dawn of history the tree signified riches, generation, victory, and light; hence the Greeks sanctified it to Apollo and venerated it as immortal.

The date palm is held in respect among the Tamaquas of Mexico as the founder of the human race after the flood. In the east it was Mahomet who created the palm, causing it to spring from the earth at his command. Typifying Judea, it was the seal of that nation on the coins of the Roman rulers, for to the Jews it was a token of triumph, to be carried in procession, and waved before conquerors; a reminder, too, of the pleasant wells of the promised land, and the successful wars they waged to reach them. Palestine, indeed, is said to take its name from the palm, and its Hebrew name, tamar, was given to women, signifying their grace and uprightness. We still keep Palm Sunday in memory of the day when Christ entered Jerusalem and the people waved and strewed palms before Him- an incident now denoted in the wearing of crossed fragments of palm in hats. Before that time the Jews had their own palm festival, when they retired from the city for a week to live in tents and cabins of palm branches, passing a season of merry-making and family reunions, for it memorialized the final success after forty years of camp life.

MYTHS AND LEGENDS OF FLOWERS

To sufferers for religion, the angels brought palm branches before their souls fled through the smoke, and so the tree came to be called a token of martyrdom. On All Souls' Day, palms are thrown into the fire, and as they rise in smoke they are seized in proof of victory by the souls that day released from purgatory. In the traditions of some countries the palm was the forbidden tree of paradise, and in the coat of arms of South Carolina we read a suggestion of this myth, for we find there a palm circled by a serpent. In the northern lands fragments of palm were precious, for not only would they subdue water devils, but with a leaf of it one might cast down the Wild Huntsman himself. In superstitious uses, it prevents sunstroke, if the person seeking its protection has burnt it as a sacrifice during an eclipse; it averts lightning if a cross of its leaves be laid on the table while the storm is raging; it cures fever if bits of the leaf are swallowed; it drives away mice when placed near granaries; and if one would be rid of fleas he puts a palm leaf behind the Virgin's picture on Easter morning, at the first stroke of the resurrection bell, saying, "Depart, all animals without bones." For one year the fleas will stay away; which is a great comfort.

It was a palm that St. Christopher used as a staff when, in his pre-Christian character of Offero, he bore the weak and small across the raging river and so carried Christ Himself. As the giant stood marveling that so great a weight could be expressed in so small a body, Christ bade him thrust his staff into the ground, where it would blossom in token of the importance of his service. This he did, and it burst into flower and fruit, for it was a date tree. And the dark mind was enlightened. He understood that it was no man child of a common sort he had carried through the river, and he knelt and worshiped, taking the name, Christofero, or Christ-bearer; and, having lived and died in the odor of sanctity, he was gathered to the saints. Another saint is Clara, founder of the order of Poor Clares, who renounced the world on Palm Sunday, receiving from St. Francis of Assisi the palm branch which in those days was the mark of sanctity.

In the legends of the holy family, the Virgin commanded the palm to bend its leaves above the little Jesus during the flight into Egypt, in order that the babe might have its shade. At another time when the mother of Christ was hungry and asked her husband to gather dates for her, Joseph demurred, but the infant Jesus ordered the tree to bend so that she could pluck the fruit, and this it did so willingly that He blessed it and chose it as a "symbol of salvation for the dying," promising that when He entered Jerusalem in triumph it should be with a palm in His hand. In her "Legends of the Madonna," Mrs, Jameson tells how the Virgin was comforted, after the crucifixion, by an angel who appeared, crying, "Hail, Mary, blessed of God! I bring a palm that has grown in paradise. Let it be carried before your bier on your death, for in three days you shall join your son." The angel then took his flight, leaving the branch on the ground, where it shone and sparkled gloriously. And when the friends and disciples were come from the mount of sorrow, Mary gave the palm to John and asked him to bear it at her burial. That night, amid the sound of singing and a gush of strange perfume through the house, the Virgin died with angels about her bed and such a blaze of light arising from her body that those who prepared it for burial were nearly blinded. And the palm was carried to her tomb, where another miracle occurred, for she was rapt to heaven in the flesh and welcomed by choiring angels and players upon harps beyond number for multitude. Looking into the tomb afterward, it was found to hold no corruption, but to be filled with roses and lilies.

We have a palm in the southwest that is peculiar to that region: the desert fan, or Washington filifera, from whose fibers the Indians make their baskets, ropes, and roofs, and with which they sweeten their meal of mesquite beans. Before the coming of trouble, in the form of the white race, the Cahuilas carried each male child to the mountains, soon after birth, and there allotted to him a particular tree which served him as reminder of the deity. It was his to care for and to worship as a natural altar, and when he died it was killed by burning. The Caribs tell us that when the deluge began to cover the earth, people tried to escape by climbing the cocorite palm, whose top reached heaven. An old woman in the lead became dizzy and frightened when half way up, and so became stone, as did all those who tried to pass her; but all who climbed the komoo palm were saved.

PANSY

Our pansy is a development from the violet, the little spots which show clearly in the white violet having been enlarged through cultivation to the markings that have so queer a suggestion of a face. An old German tale represents that it once had as fine a perfume as the violet, but as it grew wild in the fields the people sought it with such enthusiasm that they heedlessly trampled the grass needed for cattle, and even the vegetables required for their own tables. Seeing the wreck that was wrought by this eagerness, the flower prayed to the Trinity to take away its odor, that it might be no longer sought. This prayer was granted, and it was then that it took the name of trinity. To the monks, it was the flower of trinity, or herb trinity; to the laity, it was three faces in a hood; in heathen days, it was Jove's flower; with Christianity, it became the flower of Saint Valentine; heart's ease is another title; and of the accepted name of pansy- which is our way of saying pensee, a thought- there are quaint spellings, such as pauses, penses, paunces, pancyes, and pawnees, these versions occurring in old poetry. Other odd names for it are ladies' flower, bird's eye, pink of my John, Kit run in the street, flamy, cull me, call me, stepmother, sister in law, the longer the dearer, kiss me quick, kiss me at the garden gate, cuddle me, jump up and kiss me, and kiss me ere I rise.

MYTHS AND LEGENDS OF FLOWERS

PASSION FLOWER

In an old Spanish tradition it was the passion flower that climbed the cross and fastened about the scars in the wood where the nails had been driven through the hands and feet of the Sufferer. The early fathers saw in its bud the eucharist, in its half-open flower the star in the East, and in the full bloom the five wounds, the nails, the hammer, the spear, the pillar of scourging, and the crown of thorns, in its leaves the spear-head and thirty pieces of silver, in its tendrils the cords that bound the Lord. This growth upon the cross was not remembered by the people of Jerusalem, but was revealed to St. Francis of Assisi in one of his starving visions. It had turned in his sight from Lady Poverty, the object of his worship, to the flowering plant. When the Spaniards found the flower growing in the jungles of South America they regarded it as a promise that the natives should be converted, and a curious drawing made by one of the priests shows not only a likeness to the implements of the crucifixion, but the objects themselves in miniature; the column, nails, crown, and cup. In allusion to the habit of the flower in half closing to a bell form, a churchman wrote, "It may be well that in His infinite wisdom it pleased Him to create it thus shut up and protected, as though to indicate that the wonderful mysteries of the cross and of His Passion were to remain hidden from the heathen people of those countries until the time preordained by His Highest Majesty."

Naturally, so marvelous a plant was sought and acclaimed by clerics of all degrees, and by the sick and crippled, and so eager is the eye of faith that after the vine was naturalized in Europe the people long continued to see in it those signs and wonders that we do not. When the Jesuits announced, in 1600, that the objects of the passion were disclosed in the flower, an indignant botanist, an early Huxley, exclaimed, "I dare say God never willed His priests to instruct His people with lies; for they come from the Devil, the author of them."

PAULOWNIA

Centuries ago there stood in the dragon gorge of Honan an imperial paulownia, or kiri, that ruled the forest by reason of its height, its symmetry, and the profusion of its flowers. And so it stood for ages, singing to the wind in its own voice. A wizard wandering that way listened, and at a touch of his wand he changed the tree into a harp, which, however, was to yield its music only to the greatest of musicians. The emperor summoned the masters and ordered them to strike its chords, but always when they did so the notes were harsh. Then Peiwoh came, and, instead of smiting its strings with command, as the others had done, he touched the harp lovingly, asking it to speak in its own voice, and not in the music of men. There was no vanity in the man, hence the kiri sang once more, sounding like the breath of a storm across the woods, recalling the carol of birds, and suggesting the sound of rain, of distant thunder, of waterfalls, of falling timber- all the sounds of the wilderness it knew and loved in its life. The emperor, delighted, asked an explanation of the mastery and mystery. "It is that I encouraged the kiri to choose its own themes," answered Peiwoh. In which allegory the art spirit stands confessed.

PEA

This delicate and nourishing vegetable was a food of hearty old Thor, the thunderer, in whose honor, on Thor's day (Thursday) it is still eaten in Germany, The pea came by an ill reputation, because, when the fires which were kindled on St. John's eve drove away the dragons that had been soaring roundabout, dripping pestilence from their wings, those canny brutes, not daring to descend to the hills where the flames appeared, carried up stores of peas and dropped them into the wells and springs, where, rotting, they raised a doleful stench

MYTHS AND LEGENDS OF FLOWERS

and created miseries in the inwards of the public. Peas are used in divination, and ancient ceremonies testify to a regard that in our day of good cooking should be no less. Scottish and English lads and lassies are rubbed with pea straws by way of consolation when they have been jilted. When an eligible miss in shelling peas discovers nine in a pod, she puts the pod on the lintel and holds her breath, for the first male person who enters thereafter will marry her- if he is not already married, and is not related.

PEACH

A popular folk-tale of Japan recites that an old woman washing clothes at a river was startled by a rolling and splashing in the water, and presently there came to her feet a large, round object of pink color. She drew it with difficulty to the bank, where she discovered that it was a peach, containing food enough to serve her and her husband for several days. On breaking it open, they were amazed to discover, cuddled inside the peach stone, a tiny child. The little fellow was cared for by his foster parents, who gave to him the best training and schooling that their means afforded. When he attained his growth he invaded the Island of Devils, defeated its inhabitants, and seized their treasure, which he poured at the feet of the aged couple in reward for their love and their service in delivering him from the peach.

Collectors of porcelains and other works of Chinese art have observed the peach as a decorative figure, but have not always known that in presenting a vase or dish so ornamented the giver implies a hope of long life for the recipient. For in China the peach is the emblem of longevity, the bowls and plates on which it appears in picture being intended as birthday gifts.

MYTHS AND LEGENDS OF FLOWERS

PEEPUL

The peepul, pippala, or asvattha of India, which botanists insist should be called *ficus religiosa*, is sacred to Buddha, and shades many of his shrines and temples. It is the tree of wisdom, for Buddha sat beneath it in that long trance of acquired merit, when he stripped his memory of earthly things and enlarged his mind to the understanding of heaven. The sacred fires are fed with peepul wood and wood of the acacia sumi, the peepul symbolizing the male principle, the acacia the female, and the flame being created by rubbing sticks of the two. Priests drink the divine soma from vessels of peepul, and they who eat of its fruit when they reach paradise become enlightened, for this fruit is ambrosia, food of gods.

The Hindus, who have almost as much regard for this tree as have the Buddhists, represent Vishnu seated on its leaves; but they share in the preservation of the peepul, or bo, at Anuradhapura, Ceylon, which is held to be a scion of the veritable tree under which Buddha received illumination. In Thibet, the Buddhists declare that the peepul is the bridge whereon all worthy souls pass from earth to heaven.

PEONY

The peony, or paeony, is cited by Pliny as the earliest known of medicinal plants. In his very remarkable natural history we learn that the woodpecker is especially fond of it, and that if he sees you picking the flower, he will fly at you and pick your eyes out. The name of the plant perpetuates that of Apollo in his character of physician, for as Paeon he healed the wounds the gods received in the Trojan war. From that fact, the early doctors of medicine were known as paeoni, and medicinal plants were paeoniae. To this day, it is a practice among the peasantry of Sussex to put strings of beads carved from peony roots about the necks of their children, not merely that they may cut their teeth upon them, but that the beads may avert illness of all sorts, as well as the machinations of evil spirits. Apollo, being the healer and giver of light, heat, and other blessings, was praised in the hymn which took his name, and which we still call the pasan. Thus in nomenclature the peony has a more than aristocratic lineage; it is divine. Yet it was a cause of strife and sorrow even on Olympus, for Aesculapius, having been stirred to jealousy by the success of Paeon- who now appears, not as the disguised Apollo, but as a man- in curing a hurt for Pluto, put his rival to death. Pluto, however, saved his physician from the common fate by changing him into the flower he had employed in his wonder work. In one ancient belief the flower sprang from a moonbeam, and in yet another its origin was not a physician, but a blushing shepherdess, Paeonia, whose charms had stirred the love of Apollo.

In the east, where peonies abound, and where the Japanese cultivate five hundred varieties, rearing them to arboreal dimensions, they tell of a Chinese scholar whose chief recreation was in the care of these flowers. Living so largely in their company and in that of his books, it was natural that he should be startled, though agreeably so, by the visit of a lovely maid, who appeared, unannounced, at his door and asked to be taken into his employ. He cheerfully complied with her request, and his cheer increased as time went on, for he discovered presently that she was not only servant, but companion; she had received an exceptional education, knew court etiquette, wrote like a scholar, and was poet, painter, and friend. The young man introduced her to his acquaintances with pride, and they were astonished no less at her accomplishments than at her grace and beauty. She always obeyed him with gladness, till the fatal day arrived when a visit was expected from a famous moralist; then the scholar summoned her in vain. Uneasy at her absence, he went in search, and on entering a shadowed gallery he saw her gliding before him like a specter.

MYTHS AND LEGENDS OF FLOWERS

Before he could overtake her, she had flattened herself against the wall and sunk into it till she was a mere picture on the surface, though her lips continued to move. "I did not answer when you called me," she confessed, "for I am not a human creature: I am the soul of a peony. It was your love that warmed me into human shape, and it has been a joy to serve you. But now that the priest has come, he will disapprove your love, and I cannot keep my form. I must return to the flowers." In vain the scholar argued and implored; she sank more deeply into the wall; the colors of the picture that she made grew fainter; at length she faded altogether, and there was no trace of her from that day. And the scholar went about in mourning.

PIMPERNEL

Scarlet pimpernel is called "poor man's weather glass," from its habit of closing before rain, and is a fair marker for the hours likewise, since it opens at about seven and closes at two, according to English observers. As it grew on Calvary, it was sovereign against spells, and would even draw splinters from the flesh. This formula, however, is to be said for fifteen days running, twice a day, night and morning, if the splinters have been driven in by witches:

> Herbe pimpernel, I have thee found
> Growing upon Christ Jesus' ground;
> The same gift the Lord Jesus gave unto thee
> When He shed His blood on the tree.
> Arise up, pimpernel, and go with me.
> And God bless me.
> And all that shall wear thee. Amen.

PINE

Becoming jealous, Cybele, mother of the gods, put an end to the flirtations of a shepherd whom she loved by changing

MYTHS AND LEGENDS OF FLOWERS

him into a pine. Having thus estranged him from his proper shape, she passed much time beneath his branches, mourning; wherefore Jove, himself a frequent heart-breaker, had such sympathy for her that, in order to make this memorial seemly at all seasons, he ordained that its foliage should be ever green. The Chinese regard the pine, plum, and bamboo as emblematic of friendship in adversity, because of this quality of enduring cold without losing their summer aspect. We find constancy indicated in a Roman legend of a youth and maid who died of grief because their love was thwarted, the one changing to a pine and the other to a vine, growing together for centuries in a fast embrace. There would seem no reason for the diabolic character that Sulpicius gave to the pine in his life of St. Martin, for its uses, its beneficence, and its beauty justify all good report. The tree takes its name from pinus, a raft, because the wood, being easy to cut, was employed for the boats and floats of primitive men. Hence the Greeks held it sacred to the sea god. That men listened to its musical breathings thousands of years before science marred the poetry of nature is proved in the belief that the pine was the mistress of Boreas, the wind, and Pan, the all-god. It bore children, in the German tradition, and every hole and knot in the trunk is the point from which a wood spirit escaped into the outer world, sometimes growing and becoming as other women, as in Sweden, where a famous beauty of Smaland was accepted as a member of a family. Her history was in some doubt, but she did her part in the house and farm work, and no question of her human quality was raised, unless by strangers, who were astonished by her height and her bright beauty, and who, listening to the lulling tones of her voice, thought them as soft as the murmur in a pine. All went well with the family till a knot in a pine board of the house wall fell out, and a way of escape to the forest was so opened. The woman crept to the place and listened to that music of the outer world, that world of her youth and her dreams, and, longing intensely to return to it, her body shrank and shrank till she was a tiny elf. With a smile and a tear, she looked about her home of years, nodded a good-by, and was gone from that place forever.

Near Ahorn, Coburg, an image of the Virgin was miraculously concealed in a pine trunk, but made itself known to the priest, who caused a church to be erected on the spot; and it was probably the steeple of this same edifice that a witch twisted out of the vertical, involving the place in the scorn of neighbor villages for the slowness of the congregation in putting it straight. Matters were remedied when one of the Ahorn peasants, choosing a pine that was stout enough to endure it, made it proxy for the steeple, and by pulling, hauling, and invoking persuaded the tower to imitate the motions imparted to the pine.

For this tree developed mysterious powers and properties when it was discovered that its cone, cut lengthwise, exhibited the form of a hand- the hand of Christ. When Mary was in flight she stopped beneath a pine, and, concealed from her enemies, rested sweetly in a cool, green chamber filled with balsamy fragrance, the tree, as if to prove the love of the plant world, having lowered its limbs about her. Herod's soldiers passed, and the baby, raising his hand to bless the tree for its shelter, thus marked the fruit of it. These cones are eaten by Indians, and were used as food by the Romans also, who held that they imparted strength. Thieves in Bohemia are said to eat them even yet, believing that the oily nut makes them shot-proof. The pine is also a cure for gout, cataract, and for sundry diseases of live stock. It was esteemed by our Puritan fathers, for when they landed at dismal Plymouth it was the only green thing they saw; hence they took it as a device, stamping it upon their pine tree shillings and other coinage, and imposing it on the state seal of Massachusetts. Other pilgrims came, and lopped away the woods, the forest margin retreating northward, and so Maine came to be known as the Pine Tree State, a haven for the wild things, a place of ponds and streams that disappear when the woods are cut and the uncovered soil converts to dust under the pelt of the sun.

MYTHS AND LEGENDS OF FLOWERS

Folk-tales of many lands contain allusion to the pine. One of them is told in Japan: An aged couple had a dog that, scratching in the earth, uncovered gold. A jealous and mean-hearted neighbor asked the service of the animal, on hearing of this fortune, for he believed that equal luck would fall to him : but instead of revealing buried treasure, the dog uncovered a quantity of filth, so enraging the jealous one that he killed the animal and buried it under a pine. Nourished by the body, the tree grew to a noble size and kept the spirit that was in the dog and that it continued to exercise toward its beloved master, who, having occasion to pound his grain, shaped a piece of its wood into a mortar. So long as he used it, barley appeared to well up from the bottom, and there was never lack of food. The neighbor, hearing of this miracle, asked for the loan of the utensil, and the same ill luck he had earned by envy and ill temper came upon him again: all that the mortar turned out for him was moldy and wormy; so, in a passion, he broke it into pieces. But the old man gathered up the fragments, even though the wicked one had burned them, and proved their magic power by casting them against the trees in winter, or against trees that were dead, thus causing them to burst into leaf and bloom. This new wonder brought the old man into favor with his lord, for whom he restored many trees, and who rewarded him with gifts of money and silks, to the renewed anguish of his neighbor. The bad one, thinking to commend himself equally to the nobleman, gathered ashes from the pine and tried to create blossoms, but their virtue had passed, or his hands were not the hands to evoke it; moreover, his talent for bungling led him to experiment just as the prince was passing, when the dust blew straight into the eyes of the nobleman. He, thinking himself insulted by a rude or careless fellow, caused the envious one to be whipped.

Pines are often represented in Japanese art, and one of them, a sacred tree at Lake Biwa, near Tokyo, has a roof to protect it from the elements. It is ninety feet high, has a circumference of thirty-seven, and throws its three hundred and

MYTHS AND LEGENDS OF FLOWERS

eighty branches to an extreme of two hundred and eighty-eight feet. These limbs sag so heavily that they require support, and the visitor has sometimes to stoop in passing through their green aisles.

PLANTAIN

We have two varieties of this weed: one with rounded leaves, bearing a single spike of insignificant blossoms that, when in bud, we give to caged birds; the other with a long, ribbed, sharper leaf and taller spear of flowers. The first we call bird plantain; the second English plantain, though it is as thoroughly domesticated here as the house sparrow which we still call English. Across the water this latter variety is known as ribwort, and also as kemp- a word derived from the Danish kaempe, or soldier, which use of the word seems to have come from a sport of children in knocking the heads from these stalks with others of the same size, held in the hand, turn and turn about. Other names that signify its uses in this contest are fighting cocks, soldiers, devil's heads, hard heads, and French-and-English.

Because the bird plantain came from Europe with the early settlers, the American Indians call it "the white man's foot." This round-leaved plantain is way-bread in parts of England, but not because it is prized as food. It loves the places where men walk, and will inhabit there by preference. Once in seven years it becomes a bird and begins its search for cuckoos on the wing, that it may serve them. Its fondness for cultivated ground evidently gave rise to the Indian name, and the sight of birds rising from it after feeding was occasion for the fanciful belief.

POMEGRANATE

Pomegranate, a symbol of hope in Christian art, is thought by some scholars of antiquity to be the tree of life that

MYTHS AND LEGENDS OF FLOWERS

flourished in Eden. In Turkey, when a bride throws its fruit to the earth, the seeds that fall out will indicate the number of her children, the significance of which practice was emphasized by the old masters, who show St. Catharine holding a pomegranate, as tokening the fruitage of the faith. Yet this was a fruit of hell in early myth, because through eating it Proserpine was forced to return to that dismal region and spend a half of every year. Demeter, or Ceres, goddess of the earth, and mother of Proserpine, or Persephone, left Olympus in anger when her daughter was given by Zeus to Pluto, god of hell, for wife. Ceres came to earth to live among men, blessing all who were kind to her and cursing all who were not. So often did she visit penalties on the multitude that Zeus, realizing his over-haste, determined to restore more pleasant relations between earth and heaven, and summoned Pluto to give up Proserpine. Not daring to disobey, Pluto released her, but just as she was leaving he urged that she eat a pomegranate he had given to her, and in yielding to his desire she gave him the continued hold that doomed her to forego the light and warmth in the winter months. This conditional release did much for the human race, however, because Ceres was now so happy in her daughter's company that she was kind once more.

This legend has been variously interpreted as a season myth, illustrating the release of the earth from winter darkness; as a moon myth, denoting the retirement and emergence of the heavenly lamp; as a symbol of immortality and resurrection; and as a token of nature's fertility, Proserpine being the seed that is dropped into the darkness of the soil, only to emerge again, brighter than before. But the pomegranate signified the power of the world of darkness, therein becoming a type of all fruits that germinate below the earth, and send their seed back to it in the given season. This faith or symbolism of the Greeks doubtless traveled to the east, for we discover it in the Chinese idea that the pomegranate signifies fertility. Women who wish children offer this fruit to the goddess of mercy, and the porcelains designed for

MYTHS AND LEGENDS OF FLOWERS

her temples are decorated with its pictures.

The original pomegranate was claimed by Bacchus, for it had been a nymph of his affection whom he changed into the tree, and whose blossom he shaped like a crown in order to fulfill the prophecy of a soothsayer that she should wear one. Pomegranates that sprang from the graves of King Eteocles and of Menoeceus, a suicide, proved their human relationship by exuding blood.

POPLAR

Philologists variously account for the name poplar: that it means populus, because the Roman populace gathered about it for public meetings; that it comes from papeln, meaning to babble, for its leaves are always chattering. The groves of Academus were of poplar, and the tree was sacred to Hercules because when bitten by a snake he found a remedy for the poison in poplar leaves. The Pillars of Hercules, that long marked the seaward bound of the Roman empire, were erected to commemorate that event. Another Greek myth says that when Hercules had brought the oxen of Geryon from their places, and had killed the giant Cacus, he wrenched a bough from a near-by poplar, such as grew thickly on Mount Aventinus, and crowned himself in token of his victory. His next labor led him into hell, where the smoke and fire blackened the upper side of the leaves, while the under sides were kept cool by the sweat of his brow, and since that time the poplar leaf has been silver-lined.

The tree is also related, mythologically, to Phaeton, who tried to drive the sun chariot of his father, Apollo, and who, unable to control his horses, swerved up and down and from side to side of the course, now burning and blistering the fields, anon drying up the Nile, and lastly killing so many of humankind that Zeus, hearing the cry of the people, unseated the incapable driver with a thunderbolt that hurled him headlong into the river Eridanus. Here the Heliades, his sisters, came to bewail him, and as their tears fell into the water they changed to golden drops which we now call amber; and after a little the mourners took on the form of the trees that had given the precious gum: the poplar. It would seem that spoons are no recent invention, for Jupiter suffered a loss of some, and, having reason to believe that they had fallen into or been hidden in a tree, he bade Ganymede seek them through the wood. The messenger first asked of the oak. Stirring with wrath, the big tree answered, "What know I of spoons? I have leaves of emerald and a thousand silver cups. I am king of trees, and no thief." Ganymede asked pardon and moved on to the birch. "I have silver of my own," she answered. "I am sheathed in it. I have no need of other."

Again the gods' cup-bearer begged forgiveness and resumed his search. The beach scattered its prickly nut-sheaths over him; the elm swung down its branches till they threatened to crush his head; the fir was shaken as by a storm, and hurled cones at him in a volley. So the questioner came to the poplar. "Why should I be charged with keeping the goods of Zeus?" it asked. "See, there is nothing concealed upon me." And forthwith it tossed up its limbs- for they grew low then- intending to show that nothing was hidden beneath them; but the spoons had not been securely stowed, and as the wooden arms lifted, down fell the plunder in a tinkling shower and lay on the earth as white as the leaves, which now showed a deathly pallor on their under side. Ganjonede picked up the stolen silver and hastened back to Olympus, leaving the poplar trembling with apprehension. For its theft and its falsehood, Zeus condemned it to hold up its arms forever.

All over the world we find a religious expression of the idea that success or salvation is to be gained only through pain. The early Christian traditions extended the pain beyond the victim, making it shared by inanimate nature; by the flowers; and especially by the poplar, for out of its wood the cross was made, according to one version, and for that reason it has never ceased to shudder for the part it played in the great tragedy. Some say that Christ Himself had to fashion the cross from poplar trunks, for which reason the Latins hold it sacred, and not a few of the French Canadians refuse to cut "popple" in our lumber camps. Its trembling began at the moment when the sacred blood was poured upon its wood. But another reason for this motion is that it marks its wrath when Judas chose to hang himself upon it after his treachery had become known. It is also said that when Joseph and Mary were flying from the cruelties of Herod they passed through a grove of poplars. All other trees had bent as the holy family went by, but the poplar held itself aloof and would not move its head. The infant Jesus gave one look at the stubborn tree, whereon, struck with remorse, it began to tremble, and has never ceased to do so.

POPPY

Everyone knows this brilliant flower that sparkles amid the grain-fields of the old world, where it is regarded as the blossom of a weed and of evil omen, for its color hints at blood. It became the symbol of death when the son of Tarquinius Superbus asked him what should be done with the people of a conquered city. Tarquin made no verbal reply, but, going into the garden, he slashed off the heads of the largest poppies, therein commending the massacre of the best and most influential citizens. When Persephone was stolen by Pluto, her mother, Ceres, began a search for her that led through all Sicily, climbing Aetna to light torches that she might keep on her journey through the night. Unable to restore her child, the gods caused poppies to spring about her feet, and, curious as to their meaning, she knelt to look at them closely. She inhaled their bitter, drowsy breath, and put the seeds into her mouth, and presently the plant bestowed upon her that rest which her weary body needed. Poppies were offered to the dead, therefore, with a fine symbolism, since they signify sleep. The Saxon name for the plant, popig, is said to have reference to the mixing of its seeds with pap administered to children in order to make them sleep: and as opium is yielded by the flower, we have the origin of those soothing syrups that are still administered to the helpless. Growing, as it did, in corn, it was dedicated to Ceres by the ancients, who painted her picture with wheat ears and poppies in her hair; but it also belonged to *Venus Genetrix*, because the number of its seeds instanced fertility. One of its queer names, "cracking rose," recalls a practice of striking a poppy petal between the hands in order to ascertain whether or no a lover is faithful. If it breaks, it signifies that he is not true, but if it holds together and makes a considerable report, it is a cause for rejoicing.

It is said that after the battle of Neerwinden the fields were covered with scarlet poppies, which the people looked upon as the spilled blood of twenty thousand soldiers, and a sign of heaven's anger at the evil deeds of men. In the east, too, where the flower has the name of little dawn, the plains and vales that armed hosts have struggled to possess are still splashed with these flowers, "blooming in barbaric splendor, gloating on the gore of soldiers slain." And if the Neerwinden story seems too modern for acceptance as folk-lore, we have a still newer instance, arising from our wars with the Indians in the west. After the massacre of Custer and his men by the Sioux the Indians alleged the appearance on the battle-field of a new flower which they called Custer's heart. It had long, hard leaves, curved like a cavalry saber, and so sharp as to cut the hand that tried to tear them from the ground. The plant sprang from the blood of the slain fighters on that day in 1876.

The red poppy is not native to America, but the lovely escholzia is- the representative of the species which has been chosen as the State flower of California, where it lights the mountains as if revealing the gold hid in their ledges. The yellow poppy, or corn poppy, of Europe is a shore plant, and recalls in its other name, *glauciere jaune*, Glaucus, son of Neptune and a sea nymph, who elected to live on land. Still, he was fond of fishing, and, having made a good catch on a certain occasion, he was astonished to see the fish wriggle into the herbage and eat of it voraciously, with the result that they obtained strength to leap back into the sea. Determined to know the virtue of this diet, Glaucus bent and nibbled at a few of the grasses and poppies, whereupon he felt himself so impetuously drawn to the ocean that he leaped in and never came back to the shore. Among the gorgeous new strains that gardeners have created in the poppy family sundry show a cross shape of the pistil, which recalls the old Christian tradition that holy blood stains the flower; but an English legend causes the poppy to appear from the blood of a dragon slain by the holy maid Margaret.

PRIMROSE

Our evening primrose, *cenothera lamarckiana*, now domesticated in Europe, has modified the theory of evolution by showing that, in its own case, at all events, the mutations which are starting points for new species are sudden appearances; not, of need, monstrosities, but, say, the development of smooth leaves from serrate, low stalks from high; and experiment proves these mutations to be steadfast in the progeny. These facts are known as the result of studies by Professor Hugo de Vries, of Amsterdam, who did not artificially fertilize the plants, as professional growers do, but merely planted the seed and watched for results. In fifteen thousand specimens he found ten aberrants, and after four generations he discovered seven different types, the seven numbering three hundred and thirty-four mutants. A less recent interest in the primrose, and of another type, was created by Lord Beaconsfield, when he adopted it as his flower, just as Napoleon took the violet for his own; hence "Primrose Day" is a new feast in the calendar, and one about which myths are as likely to grow in future as we

MYTHS AND LEGENDS OF FLOWERS

know them to have originated in the past from events of equal unimportance. Among the little ushers of the spring, the primrose keeps its popularity in cities where, indeed, the flowers peddled in the shops are one of the few signs of the advancing season. It is no rose, to be sure, any more than is the evening primrose, but is so named through a twisting of the Italian *fiore de prima vera* (first flower of spring). Early Englishmen came nearer to the Italian name in their primerole. Though accounted as one of the most harmless of plants, we are told that the pretty variety, *primula obonica*, sold so largely from American greenhouses, utters a poisonous exhalation, causing headache, and rash on the hands and face. How it may be with others I do not know, but this variety affects me no more than does any other, when it is kept indoors, on tables and windowsills. Wherever English people are, the primrose is especially prized. Hulme tells of one exhibited in Melbourne, Australia, to no less than three thousand people, including rough miners and bushmen, who had heard of its arrival from their old home. They would have taken it amiss had they been accused of sentiment. It has been deeply sentimental in its origin, for it was a human creature once: Paralisos, son of Flora and Priapus. Having died of heartbreak for loss of his sweetheart, he was changed by the gods into this rustic and cheerful blossom.

PUMPKIN

A sage in India, whose name was Iaia, was so rapt in things not of this earth that when his only son fell ill and died, he could not, for his life, imagine what to do. After some days, conceiving that it would be well to remove the body, he enclosed it in the largest pumpkin he could find and carried it to the foot of a mountain, not far away. Happening to visit this region later, he opened the pumpkin, and was startled when a volley of fish was discharged from the vegetable, also a few whales. Although these creatures fell to the ground, so much water ran from the pumpkin that they were able to wriggle away in the current. In

MYTHS AND LEGENDS OF FLOWERS

some astonishment, the wise one reported this phenomenon to the people on the plains, and four brothers hurried to the hills to catch the fish for food. Iaia pursued, for he was fearful lest they harm the pumpkin, but they reached it first, and lifted it, but, seeing him on the road, dropped it again, breaking it in half a dozen places. From each of these fissures flowed a river that swelled and swelled til the earth was covered with water, and most of it never dried away, but is what we call the ocean, which is a strange version of the universal deluge legend. Possibly this momentary importance of the pumpkin is denoted in the respect that is still paid to it by the Chinese, who call it the emperor of the garden and a symbol of fruitfulness, health, and gain.

RADISH

If you will wear a crown of blue flowering radish, called in Germany hederich, you can go about your employments in peace, for no witch or wizard will be able to spoil your day by the cast of a spell or the glare of an evil eye. Here in prosy America the radish seems never to have had its due as a symbol or a poem; it is merely a hors d'oeuvre, to be nibbled between the entree and the roast. But in imaginative Germany it has inspired legends, one of the oldest being that of Rubezahl, who is the soul of a radish, a harsh, peppery, odious creature. He steals a princess and shuts her in his castle, so she can not avoid listening to his protestations of love. She begs him to solace her loneliness with other company, so he touches a number of radishes, which instantly take on human form, but which can keep it only so long as a radish can keep its leaves. When these companions fade, she begs others; so, to show his power, Rubezahl changes another radish to a bee, and the princess, whispering her plight into its ear, sends it off to seek her human lover in the great world. The bee does not return. Another radish becomes a cricket, and that also is pushed out of window with a message to her lover. It never returns. Still pestered by the attentions of Rubezahl, the princess beseeches him to count the radishes he has left with her,

MYTHS AND LEGENDS OF FLOWERS

and he begins to do so, whereupon the girl, seizing his wand, changes one of the radishes into a horse and gallops off on it to meet her lover.

RAGWEED

If ever you are in that wild part of Cornwall where Castle Peak lords it over the moors, a new experience awaits you, if you dare to stay out late. Choose some night when a harsh wind is blowing, and clouds are scurrying across the moon; then you shall see gray, misty figures stealing over the heath. They are witches, gathering ragweed. When they have picked a bunch of strong stems the hags bestride them and off they go, flying faster than the clouds and mixing with them as the ride goes forward to Castle Peak. If you follow, you shall see them gathered at its top, dancing, mingling in obscene worship, or brewing poisons and compounding spells that are to bring death, illness, poverty, wreck, and devastation to their neighbors. Clutch your rosary tight, that night, and wear your crown of radish flowers, for if you are seen spying on this company it will go hard with you.

RESURRECTION PLANT

Now and then will be found in city shops, or in the packs of those who hawk merchandise through the town, a dried plant which is offered for sale as the "resurrection plant." It covers the space of a hand, and, placed in water, its unfolded leaves relax and discover a certain symmetry. Often, too, the wetting restores a semblance of life. This *anastatica hierochuntica*, or holy resurrection flower, is also called the rose of Jericho, *rosa hyrici*, Mary's hand, and our lady's rose; yet it is not a rose, and in nowise resembles one. It grows in the desert, where it is said that the winds frequently uproot it, since it can have no deep hold on the sand. It requires faith to accept the further allegation that wherever it chances to stop it sends down a root and continues its interrupted growth till the next high wind. The early Christian

MYTHS AND LEGENDS OF FLOWERS

church dedicated the plant to the Virgin, and in the east and in parts of Europe it is prized by women who believe that they shall become mothers of many. Wherever the holy family paused in its flight to Egypt this plant sprang from the earth, the first rising from the plain of Jericho to greet the infant Savior.

ROSE

Loved by the world and loving it, the rose is the type of beauty. It is grown and worn in all but Arctic lands and the equatorial belt. Its essence, the fragrant attar, carries to the earth's ends a memory of its sweetness. It has been the symbol of faction, the symbol of peace, the emblem of prospering nations. Its part in history is still told in rites and tributes, for in London the custom holds of laying the city sword on a bed of rose-leaves on Michaelmas day- a memory of the Wars of the Roses. The rose figures from the earliest times in the art, the poetry, the traditions, of the people, and has its place in the legends of the saints. It is with a rose of gold that the Pope requites service to the faith. It is a rosary by which piety still numbers its prayers and aves. The rose blooms in precious stones, among the treasures of kings and princes of the church; it flowers on storied windows; it glorifies tapestries and vestments, silks and canvases, even as it blows in gardens. From the earliest speech, it has figured in poetry and song. It comes from China, Japan, Persia, Damascus, Caucasus, Provence, Iceland; it borrows the name of Sharon; we have the Austrian briar and the double yellow of Constantinople; we pluck the banksia of Scotland and the harsh plant of the Dead Sea border; we have our own lovely roses that will not leave America, for they say that the blooms of Virginia die if they are transplanted.

We find our flower conventionalized in objects of art and even on the reverse of our coins, for Edward III. struck the rose nobles in 1334; Edward IV., "the Rose of Rouen," continued to mint them, while on this side of the sea we had our Rosa

MYTHS AND LEGENDS OF FLOWERS

Americana in pennies and ha'pence before the Revolution. In Hindu mythology Vishnu was floating on the water, to allay the burn of noon, when a lotus beside him began to open its petals. When it had completely unfolded, Brahma was discovered within, cradled in its silk. The two gods discoursed on the relative merits of the flowers. Brahma, rising from the lotus, pointed to it as the supreme expression of natural beauty, but Vishnu said, "In my paradise is a blossom a thousandfold more lovely and sweet than yours. It excels all other flowers in perfume, and its whiteness is that of the moon." Brahma derided this claim, adding, "If you prove to me that you speak truth, I will resign my place in the trinity, and you shall be chief god." As Vishnu's paradise was far from India, the two gods called to them the serpent of infinity, and on his back they traveled out into space till Vishnu's palace revealed itself.

The serpent stopped before its gates, which swung open when Vishnu had sounded a note on his conch. Brahma refused all refreshment, so eager was he to see whether his companion could fulfill his boast, and the two passed through a corridor of mother-of-pearl to a court where was a tree that bore a single rose. This was an immense flower, white as the snows of the Himalayas, and a perfume breathed from it like the incense of an altar, only far sweeter. "The fairest thing in heaven or earth," said Vishnu. But a still fairer was to appear, for the rose opened its petals widely, and Lakshmi stepped forth. "I am sent to be your wife," she said submissively. "Because you were faithful to the rose, the rose is faithful to you." Vishnu took her in his arms, and Brahma, bowing toward the ground, exclaimed, "It is as you have said. Vishnu shall be chief god henceforth, for in his paradise is the rose, and that is supreme above all flowers."

The humanization of the rose in Lakshmi suggests the Romanian legend of the rose-bush: that having achieved the utmost of beauty whereof a plant was capable, it surpassed itself in one huge bud, which, opening, gave birth to a handsome prince. The young man grew and took his part in the affairs of men, but the juices of the rose still mingled in his blood, and he yearned for the tranquility of his infancy. The knowledge that he might serve men through beauty, whereas in war and rapine he lived only for harm, eventually led him back to the scene of his birth. Trandafir (that was his name) stood in the wood alone and said to the trees, "I am of you. Where is the great rosebush that bore me?" And the trees answered that it was dead. Then he asked of the birds, but all declared they could not remember it- all but one; the nightingale. "The rose-tree is gone," he sang, "and I am come to chant a dirge over the spot where it stood. It was a noble tree, and it had a prince for a flower."

"I am that prince," answered Trandafir. "I am weary of the human life. I wish to go back to the life of fragrance and serenity; the life that menaces no other life, and leaves the world better when it is ended." Then said the nightingale, "May it be as you wish, O prince. I will stay till I have sung your soul back into a rose." With a sigh of content, the prince cast himself upon the earth in the spot where he had been born, and at nightfall the bird began to sing, softly, then louder and more sweetly. The music mingled with the prince's dreams and cast out all memory of the world of men. He sank into the moss more deeply; roots began to extend themselves from his limbs and penetrate the mold in all directions; his eyes closed to the earth, lifting only to the sky; and at dawn, behold, a rose-tree, which was Trandafir.

We live in a bleak, material age, yet we can be thankful that so much of its ancient romance lingers in our flower. Can you be a Saxon peasant long enough, in your imagination, to conceive the sincerity of his belief that when a little child dies those who are watching at the window can see the shadowy form of Death steal from the house, enter the garden, and there pick a flower? Or, can you regard with more than adult lenity for the conceits of the children of our race, that belief of the Scandinavians that the rose was under protection of fairies and

MYTHS AND LEGENDS OF FLOWERS

dwarfs, whose king was Laurin, lord of the rose garden? This enclosure had four gates, and should one intrude after the gates were closed, woe was his portion, while the daring thief who plucked a flower was to lose a hand or foot. The medicinal use of roses goes as far back as the known history of the plant. Milto, a maid who gave a daily offering of flowers to Venus, was not forgotten by that goddess in a time of need, for when her beauty was threatened by a tumor on the chin, Venus appeared to her in a dream and bade her apply roses from her altar to the swelling. The cure was so effective that when King Cyrus saw her he was smitten by her beauty and obtained her as a wife. According to Pliny, the rose, in his day, formed not only a part of perfumes and ointments, but of physic, entering into "emplastres and collyries or eye-salves." He gives thirty two remedies compounded of its leaves and petals, and we have his prescription for making rose wine. It was alleged that the drinking of rose wine and sleeping on pillows of rose-leaves allayed nervousness, as all fragrance is likely to do, but we are also told how Heliogabalus, having sickened from bathing in rose wine, eating overmuch of rose salads and conserves, and lolling on rose-couches, was restored to health with a "rose draft," thereby discovering homoeopathy to a waiting world.

They had, in the old days, rose water, rose ointment, rose conserve, sugar of roses, roses kept in wax, rose essence to burn on coals, rose sauce, rose cream, rose tinctures, pastels, pastes, syrups, lozenges, and cordials. The flower was served at table, either as cress and parsley are used today, as a garnish, or as a salad, for the leaves were sprinkled on meats, and the juice expressed to savor certain dishes- a proceeding that "gave no harm, but gave a commendable taste thereto." Gourmets used quince preserves flavored with rose as a quip to their meat; there was rose vinegar, made of sour wine in which flowers had been macerated; there were rose souffles for the ladies, if any were too delicate to drink the rose liqueur, and at this day rose fritters are served by the Chinese on their new year. Science has tried to make of this flower something other than the rose, but always with indifferent success. It is almost a fixed principle in botany that blossoms showing two of the primary colors will not enlarge into the third. Thus, asters are red and blue, but never yellow; chrysanthemums are red and yellow, but never blue; pansies are never red; lilies are never blue; so with carnations; and the blue rose has been sought, yet never realized, in spite of occasional rumors from London and Persia. Yellow may be changed by the expert horticulturist into red or white, as in some strains of the chrysanthemum, or pink into yellow, as in certain carnations; blue, also, will pass into purple and red, but not into yellow; and as there is a red and a yellow rose, there will be no blue one. Indeed, one or two floriculturists assert that there is no true white rose; that all which are so called disclose a tinge of pink or yellow near the base of the petal. A grower in Portland, Oregon, who has succeeded so well with the variety known as the Marchioness of Londonderry as to produce a bloom seven inches in diameter, calls attention to this quality, for he discovers that if placed beside snow, milky quartz, or any other object of absolute white, his pet blossom shows a tinge of yellow.

Artificial treatment has increased the varieties of this flower. The Greeks knew four of them, and they still grow in the Morea, but the Crusaders brought other species from the east, the damasks of Damascus being carried by them in 1100 a.d., to Provence, whence they flourished exceedingly, as they did in all the western lands. We are told of one in Caserta, Italy, that clambered to the top of a poplar sixty feet high, and of one in Toulouse with a stem eleven inches thick, that bore sixty thousand flowers in a summer. Five centuries after its introduction to France the rose had taken on a score of forms; in 1800 there were forty-six; and now their name is legion. Taking, not the legend maker's, but the botanist's, ascription, the flower was born in Persia, and it is believed to have been introduced into Europe by Alexander the Great. The rose is brother, sister, and cousin to a score of valued herbs and trees; to the apple, pear, raspberry, strawberry, blackberry, to the luscious sweetbriar that we sniff in the Rocky Mountains on a summer morning, and leave unpicked, wildest, shyest, happiest of the family; yet valued most are the stately creatures of the garden, a noble company- the Persian, golden, imperial; the white, for brides, for children at their christenings, for maids at their funerals; pink for youth and modesty; crimson for fullness of life, for splendor, for wreaths of conquerors. Mystic, beautiful, with our faces against theirs, we drink the breath of the earth that has turned to spirit; inhaling their fragrance, we taste the air of paradise.

One of the prettiest survivals of old-world custom is the crowning of the rose queens. She of Salency, near Paris, has a titular descent from the fifth century, the first to hold the office being the sister of St. Medard, Bishop of Noyon. That girl succeeds to the title who is judged to be the kindliest, prettiest, and most modest. She must also have a respectable parentage, for the rose queen of Salency is practically vouched for by the lord of the district, her name is proclaimed from the pulpit on the Sunday after his choice, and all who knew of any impediment to her acceptance of the honor are bidden to make it public. On the 8th of June, the Bosiere, in white, attended by twelve girls in white and blue, twelve boys, and her relatives, goes to the castle, where the Seigneur receives them and leads the procession to the church. Vespers being sung, the crown of flowers is blessed and placed on the recipient's head, while a purse of five dollars is put into her hand, and the Te Deum is sung after another march through the village. The names of all the Bosieres are carved in the chapel of St. Medard, but a few have been effaced, because the girls fell from grace afterward. The coronation seems to have been associated with a practice in rural France of giving to daughters a rose crown as a marriage portion, except where there were no sons to inherit the more stable property.

At Toulouse the love of the French for roses was also shown in the award of one of these flowers for the best poem offered at a public reading. Mary Queen of Scots sent to the poet Ronsard (who had been baptized in rose-water) a silver rose worth two thousand five hundred dollars for his festal poem. Indeed, such was the esteem of the rose in Europe that in the middle ages it had a Sunday of its own; for then it had become the Virgin's flower, Venus having left the earth, reluctant, in the train of the bright gods of Greece. Hose Sunday perpetuated the tradition that after the Virgin ascended to heaven roses and lilies were found to have filled her tomb. And it is odd that we should find the revival of the observance in our matter-of-fact United States, for here Rose Sunday is celebrated every year. It is worthy of note that the ceremonies attendant on it are most faithfully followed in the Universalist Church, which is as far removed as possible from the Church of Rome. It is a pretty observance, when babes are brought for christening. As each child receives its name, it takes from the pastor's hand the "gift of the rose, a symbol of the unfolding of the beautiful life." Though not a moral tale, "The Golden Ass" contains a certain symbolism in that the rose becomes the means of salvation. Here Apuleius relates the transformation of a young man into a beast, thereby indicating the effect of passion in degrading the human subject and leading him to folly. To secure his redemption, he is to eat a rose, and his trials, difficulties, and sufferings while seeking this remedy, form the substance of the story. At last the rose is discovered in the hand of a priest of Isis, the goddess having revealed herself in a dream, that the youth might know where to find it. On eating the rose, he regains his human shape and becomes a priest himself.

It may be no occult relation which the rose has to religious history and practice. The use of the rosary is one of the oldest of these applications, for although adapted to the uses of the Roman church by St. Dominick, beads were used for "telling" prayers by the Mahometans, also by Egyptian anchorites, Chinese Confucians, and Hindu and Japanese Buddhists, long before the birth of the dominant religion of

MYTHS AND LEGENDS OF FLOWERS

Europe and America. Such beads were often carved into a rude likeness to roses, and were sometimes made of rose-petals pressed into spheres. The fifteen large beads of the chain represent pater-nosters, and the one hundred and fifty small ones stand for Ave Marias. Buddhists use a chain of one hundred and eight beads, for they have one hundred and eight sins. The word bead, or bede, by the by, means prayer. This rosary, or rosenkrantz, is prefigured in pictures, statuary, and decorations as a wreath or garland of roses, sometimes placed on the head, as a mark of respect, sometimes worn in token of a festival spirit and social gaiety. Just when the flowers were given over for their conventional representations we do not know, although in the thirteenth century London had mechanics known as paternosters, whose work was the turning, piercing, and mounting of beads for devotional purposes. These men lived and worked in Paternoster Lane, close to St. Paul's. Yet the prayer beads were older than the paternosters, for Lady Godiva, she of the famous ride through Coventry, bequeathed her circlet of gems, by which she had often "told" her prayers, to the monastery she had founded.

The Christian legend of the rosary is this: A young man who, in his free days, had twined a wreath of roses every morning to crown a statue of the Virgin, became a monk, and the tasks put upon him in the convent often left him no time for this pleasant practice. He asked an aged brother what he would advise as a substitute for the offering, explaining that even as he had suffered the prick of thorns in gathering the flowers, for the Virgin's sake, so his conscience rankled now. He was told to say his Aves in great number every evening, for prayers were as acceptable as flowers in heaven. Once in a dark wood where he had stopped to pray, a band of robbers overheard him, for, quite unknown to himself, he had paused near their camp. When the fervent tones of prayer reached their ears, they stole softly through the brush and stood watching him from the shadows. As he prayed a light slowly issued from the earth and enveloped him as a luminous mist; it hovered about his head; it increased and took on form, that of an august and beautiful woman. This shape he did not see, any more than he had seen the bandits; but the woman, bending down, placed her hand at his lips and drew from them fifty splendid roses, for his words had taken form as flowers, and binding them into a shining chaplet she placed them on his down-bent head. The robbers, startled and impressed, joined their prayers to his, asking forgiveness for their evil life and promising to amend it forthwith. Indeed, they presently became inmates of the same monastery as the man who had been the unconscious instrument in their conversion.

Roses are often pictured on the brows and in the hands of saints who suffered martyrdom for the church, and it is recorded of St. Vincent that the bed on which he died was formed of them. He had borne serenely the tortures whereto he had been condemned, so Diocletian's proconsul resolved on other measures. "Release him," he commanded, "and let us see what effect luxury will have on his stubborn nature. Let his friends come to him, give him wine and food in plenty and of good quality. If he keeps his stern views of duty and doctrine after that, we may try the torture again." So the saint was taken from the rack, and as a first indication of his new and worldly life he was laid on the couch of flowers; but though he had made no outcry he was too far spent with suffering to know or care on what manner of bed they placed him, and so, on petals red as the blood he had lost, he sighed away his life. The rose is the "attribute" of St. Rosa of Viterbo, famous for charity and austerity in the thirteenth century, and of St. Rosalia of Palermo. The latter, whose statue stands before the cave on Monte Pellegrino, where she lived- high above the world, alone, at almost constant prayer- began her life as a recluse at the age of sixteen and died in her hiding place, unknown to her former friends. When her body was found it was uncorrupted, although she had been dead for days, and on her head was a crown of roses of such size and splendor that they could have come only from the gardens of heaven.

MYTHS AND LEGENDS OF FLOWERS

In the annual feast of the Madonna of the Snows, which is celebrated in the Borghese chapel, showers of white rose-leaves are thrown from holes in the ceiling, "like a leafy mist between the priests and worshipers." This is to commemorate the appearance of the Virgin in a fall of snow on Mount Esquilin. The early Christians held our flower in esteem, Clement of Alexandria maintaining that it should be used only in religious functions, for Christ had worn a crown of thorns, and the rose, by wearing thorns also, commended itself to holy purposes. It is a curious circumstance that in a few instances the flower became an expression of a wrong action or a rejected faith. During a session of the Christian synod at Nismes in 1284 every Jew in town was forced to wear a rose on his breast, in token of a holiday spirit he did not feel, while in Germany it had to be worn as a punishment for immoral conduct, indicated in its red color and its thorn. More pleasing was the custom in the Engadine, which entitled a man accused of crime, but acquitted on the same day- impossible expedition in the law!- to receive a white rose as a token of innocence from the hand of the prettiest girl in the village.

Ceremonial regard goes back for many centuries, for the Romans looked on the secular use of flowers that had been dedicated to the gods not merely as in bad taste, but as sacrilegious; indeed, the banker Lucius Fulvius was sent to prison for sixteen years by the senate for appearing in public with a garland of sacred roses on his head, while P. Munatius was put into chains for stripping the roses from a statue of Marsyas. These acts were regarded as a member of the Roman church would view the stealing of flowers that had been placed on the altar as a decoration for the mass. Gerarde- he of the Great Herball- declares that the rose "doth preserve the chiefest and most principal place among all floures whatsoever, being not only esteemed for his bountie, vertues and his fragrant smell, but also because it is the honour and ornament of our English scepter." For of course its significance in Britain is derived from the wars of the roses, which began in 1450 with the plucking of white and red roses in the Temple garden, London, as badges for the rival houses of York and Lancaster.

These flowers- worn in the caps of the contestants, or pictured in broideries and illuminations on clothing, shields, and armor- marked the factions in a civic struggle that lasted for thirty years and cost the lives of one hundred thousand men. When the war ended, with the marriage of Henry YIL, of the Lancastrian branch, to Elizabeth, Duchess of York, a rose appeared in a monastery garden in Wilts that bore both red and white petals. Until then the bush had borne roses of red on some of its branches and of white on others. In one legend the rose was created by Cybele and nourished by the nectar of the gods. In another it had its origin in the carelessness of Cupid, for the little god, hurrying to a council of the deities on Olympus with a vase of nectar, was heedless of his footing, and, stumbling, spilled the precious liquor on the earth. It bubbled up again in roses.

The rose had Zephyr for a lover, and would open only at his caress. Cupid, having kissed it, was stung on the lip by a bee concealed in its cup, and his mother, to punish the insect, captured so many bees that the youngster beaded them along his bow string from end to end, while Venus, still moved by anger, planted their stings along the stem of the flower by which the boy had got his hurt. Yet another Greek tradition relates that the rose grew red with shame when it saw that it had pricked the foot of Venus as she chased Adonis. With its "divine oil" she had covered Hector's body after his death, and so preserved it. For this was the flower of Venus; hence it was given to the diners at banquets as a reminder that love affairs, told when spirits were high and tongues adventurous, were not to be babbled over the cups, or under other circumstances and in other places. Hence arose the use of the rose as a symbol of secrecy, and in time the giving of flowers simplified and conventionalized into the hanging of one blossom over the table, whence the term, "under the rose." There is an authority who says that the phrase "under the rose," as implying secrecy, dates from 477 B.C., when the Spartans and Athenians were intriguing with Xerxes for giving Greece into the hands of that emperor. The meeting was held in a bower of roses near the temple of Minerva. As the plotting was carried on with extreme caution, it became a custom to allude to that and similar meetings as held "under the rose," and for some time after, the long-locked Athenians would wear roses in their hair when they wished it to be known that they addressed a friend or friends in confidence. In one of their early legends, the Greeks represent the first rose as a maid of intellect, pride, and beauty, whose hand had been sought by kings. In the Homeric days men seem to have made love by platoons. Rhodanthe bade them earn her favor by feats of arms, then, to be rid of them, she entered a temple of Apollo and Diana, hoping to find concealment there. But her lovers were unexpectedly prompt, for they attacked the temple itself. Rhodanthe, hurrying into their presence with a cry of protest, appeared in such a glow of anger that her beauty was heightened, and the lovers cried anew, "Let her be a god and replace Diana!" Swept from her feet by the host and lifted to the pedestal which the effigy of the moon goddess had occupied till that moment, Rhodanthe assumed an air so unconsciously commanding that Apollo, looking from his chariot, and fierce at this insult to his sister, shot his sun arrows at her till she wilted like a plant. Her feet rooted to the stone, her arms shrank and crooked and took on leaves, and presently her charm had transformed to roses. The only relic of her pride was the thorn.

Among the Romans were sybarites who slept on beds stuffed with rose petals, and we hear of one afflicted youth who could not sleep because a petal had been crumpled. Veres traveled in a litter canopied with a net of these flowers, so that their odor was never out of his nostrils. In the rose feasts of Nero, that luxurious tyrant is pictured as necklaced and crowned with flowers, lying on pillows stuffed with petals, which were also strewn over the floor, while fountains flung up rose-water. He spent one hundred and fifty thousand dollars for roses at a single supper. Wine served at his banquets was flavored with rose, and among the desserts was usually a rose pudding. Before and after the feasts his guests were free to bathe in marble lined pools, and the water was perfumed with roses. Imagine Rome on a feast day, when the shrines and triumphal arches were garlanded with roses, when chariots were gay with them, when senators and generals did not disdain to carry bouquets of them in their hands, for they had been given as tokens of admiration by the populace.

"People were not content unless roses swam in the Falernian wine," according to one authority, for their petals lent their fragrance to the drink. At the Bale regattas and water parties, the Lucrine Sea was strewn with flowers. It follows that rose culture was an important industry, and that the output on some of the rose farms exceeded anything of which we have knowledge in America. Cleopatra, at her banquet to Antony, carpeted her hall to the depth of an ell with roses. Heliogabalus bathed and even swam in rose wine. Such was the attention given to the cultivation of the rose in gardens that Horace laments the want of room for useful vegetables. There were traders who dealt in nothing but these flowers, and gardeners who made a specialty of grafting, pruning, budding, fertilizing, and smoking them. Children were accustomed to plant a rose on the day when their parents returned from a long journey, and the soldier would plant one when he returned from war. It was usual for Romans of wealth and station to provide in their wills for the planting of flowers about their tombs, and we read of one who left a certain sum for the planting of three myrtles and three roses above his ashes on each anniversary of his birth. These ashes of the dead, after incineration, were sprinkled with wine, incense, and rose-leaves before they were poured into the urn, and on the Rose Feast (May 23) the urns were decorated by surviving relatives. According to Tacitus, the whole battlefield of

MYTHS AND LEGENDS OF FLOWERS

Bedriacrun was strewn with laurels and roses, and this annual feast ended with a banquet at which each participant received roses, which he placed on the tombs of those he most revered. At all the banquets of the rich these blooms were freely employed, the triclina being stuffed with them, others being scattered over the floor, and the participants sprinkled with sweet waters. We caravans dispatched with roses from Milan to the Emperor Carinus in the year 281, and of fleets laden with them sailing from Alexandria and Carthage. Portraits, statues, and tombs were festooned with these flowers, they were flung before returning troops in the triumphs, and tossed into the chariots of the generals. So common was the practice of strewing roses over graves that the cemetery is still called "the rose garden" in parts of Switzerland, and the flower is sculptured on the tombs of girls in Turkey, where it is believed that the rose came from Mahomet. The tradition is that when he made his journey from heaven the sweat that fell from his forehead bloomed from the earth as white roses.

Flowers are of ancient use in funerals, and lend themselves as easily to them as to weddings and christenings, softening grief and cold by their bright color and glad odor. Not only were they so used by the Greeks and Romans, but savages strewed them on the biers of their dead. In Wessex and Cornwall a wreath, denoting purity, was carried before a girl's body to the grave, by some maid of her age, then hung over the seat she had occupied in church- white roses. The red rose, per contra, was for life- love- the blood of broken hearts, or hearts that throbbed with happiness, and when an English girl died during her engagement she was buried with red roses on her breast. St. Denis, guardian saint of France, was bewitched in a strange and lonely land. He had no food but vegetables and fruit, for not a creature could he slay, and his horse was his only company. Wandering, he knew not whither, he found, after a time, a tree bearing purple berries, and, being hungry and thirsty, he fed upon them eagerly. It was not a meal to increase one's bulk, but, after a little, his head grew so heavy that he was forced to drop upon all fours, and, coming shortly to a spring, where he bent to drink, he tried to cry out, being so moved by astonishment; but only a snort came from his lips. The fruit had completed his enchantment. His helmet and armor had fallen off, showing his body covered with hair, horns branched from his forehead, his eyes were large, round, and frightened: he was a deer. Galloping back to the tree from which he had eaten, he fell on the earth and groaned in hopelessness. Then, to his surprise and comfort, he heard an answering complaint. "I am Eglantine, the king's daughter," spoke the tree, "punished for my too great pride. For seven years I must wear this shape, and for as long a time you must keep the form of a hart. But there will grow in this desert a purple rose, and if you eat of it your human form will return to you, and you will have power to free me. Then you must cut this tree and put me at liberty."

Nothing more said the tree, though the transformed knight waited and listened, and almost daily returned to visit and to lie beneath its branches. At the end of the seven years, which he counted with great impatience, keeping company with his horse, a deep sleep came over him, but his horse did not share it. The steed rambled away to a mountain where many roses bloomed, and among them was a bush of purple flowers. A branch of this the faithful creature picked and carried to its master. St. Denis, waking and seeing the flowers beside him, was filled with joy, and he eagerly devoured the blossoms, which caused him to lapse into another sleep. In the morning he arose as a man, and, with many tokens of gratitude to his horse, he found and resumed his armor and rode away to the tree where Eglantine awaited deliverance. With one tremendous blow of his sword he severed the trunk, and it fell to the earth in a fire and cloud of smoke. As the air cleared, he saw standing before him a beautiful girl with downcast eyes. "I do not know whether you are angel, fairy, or woman," he said, "but I am right glad to set you free and would continue to serve you, if I might." The maiden asked only that he would take her to her father's palace, where she was doubtless mourned as dead. Her vanity was gone; her lesson had been learned. And as she had some memory of the way, they crossed the wilderness in safety, and so into the unenchanted and beautiful world for which they had grieved so long. In time they reached the palace, where great welcome was given to them and St. Denis received high honor. Even the horse was cared for with lavish hospitality. The rose of salvation was then named Eglantine, in memory of the princess.

In Persia they commemorate with a feast of roses an incident in the life of Zoroaster, or Zarathustra. The infant sage was taken from his people by the king, whose astrologers had warned him that the babe would be a menace to him, and was placed on a pile of burning logs. The little Zoroaster did not even wake, for the brands became flowers- a bed of roses. Those flames were first caught up by priests and have been transmitted as a holy fire, which has been kept alive to this day, and give rise to the name of fire-worshiper as applied to those who accept the Zoroastrian doctrine. It is in Persia, too, that the bulbul, or nightingale, begins to sing when the roses blow, for so the bird tells his love for the flower, and at dawn, overcome by weariness and by the perfume, he falls to the earth beneath the bush. When Allah made the rose queen of flowers, instead of the white and sleepy lotus, the impassioned nightingale, flying toward the perfume, thrust one of the thorns against his breast, and so spilling his blood over the petals, changed them to red; and even now the Persian tells you that he presses against a thorn that he may be kept awake all night to worship and to sing. And as he sings, the rose, responsive, bursts from bud to bloom.

From this land of Persia we have the attar, or oil of rose. It is told how the favorite sultana of Jehangir prepared the bath for her lord by throwing rose-leaves into the water. A little shining fluid came to the surface, and, fearing that this might irritate his majesty, she had the pool skimmed clear of it. Such a fragrance arose from the oil that the idea of preserving it was at once suggested. Avicenna, the Arabian doctor, conceived the idea of extracting this substance by distillation, and even now in some Persian houses the guest will receive an asperge of it as he enters. Avicenna's discovery was made in 1187. Naturally, the rose figures in oriental poetry, and the Gulistan (place of roses) is an expression of the national spirit, of love, of music and of all delights. It was reserved for two western poets, however, to tell the Romance of the Rose, for this was begun in the thirteenth century by Guillaume di Lorris and continued by Jean de Meung in the fourteenth. In this we read- if we have patients to follow a matter of twenty thousand verses- how Dame Idleness takes the poet to the Palace of Pleasure and gives him into the charge of Love, Sweet-Looks, Courtesy, Youth, Joy, and Competence, who lead him to a bank of roses. He chooses one, but at the moment Love with an arrow stretches him helpless on the earth. Coming to his senses, he determines to regain the flower, and in a symbolic narrative that suggests "Pilgrim's Progress," now aided, now deterred, by Welcome, Shyness, Fear, Slander, Reason, Pity, Jealousy, and Kindness, he finds the object of his search.

Our gracious flower sprang in the footsteps of the just, bloomed on their graves in the belief of the faithful, and was ever regarded as sanction and proof of their virtue. It embodied the spirit of goodness, and even in our day the Cuban poet Cazals planted on his mother's grave a rose which he insisted was kept alive by his mother's spirit, and spoke to him in the wind, just as Paganini, who had held his violin to the lips of his dying mother, heard her voice in the instrument whenever he played it afterward. One of the legends of the crucifixion names the rose brier, or dog rose, as the plant chosen for the crown of thorns. It was by the dog rose that Satan tried to climb back to heaven, and this is one of many "trees" on which Judas was hanged. As drops of the Savior's blood fell on the earth, roses sprang from the spot and blossomed. And in Bethlehem was the Field of Flowers, to which a girl was taken to be burned on a wrongful charge of crime. She prayed for a miracle to let her innocence be known. In answer to her prayer the flames died and the fagots burst into leaf, their last embers expanding into crimson roses, while the unburnt wood and ashes became roses of white. A similar tale is told by the Ghebers, of Abraham, when he was thrown into fire at Nimrod's order, adding that he was not even wakened by the flames, but slept among the flowers till morning. The relation of this story to that of Zoroaster is plain. Another sun legend, this from Romania, is of a princess bathing in the sea, who, being seen by Apollo, so filled his heart with love that for three days he forgot to urge on the horses of the sun, remaining stationary in the sky, watching for her reappearance and delighting in her memory while she slept. As a consequence of his neglect to move forward and bring night to the world's relief, the heat was so great that the girl was fain to leave her house and bathe for coolness the oftener. When he had descended to declare his love, his fervent kisses filled her with such confusion that she hung her head and blushed, and that attitude and color of modesty have pertained to her ever since, for she is the rose.

St. Francis of Assisi, being tempted by the devil to leave the monastic life and go back to the ease, comfort, and cleanliness he had left, was so tormented by these suggestions that he left his cell, went into the bleak hills, and rolled in the snow. Now, there were at that place many rose-bushes, and as it was the deep of the year, without life on earth, they were as stalks and fagots. His poor rag of a gown was no protection, and the thorns cruelly tore his flesh. Yet he bowed himself repeatedly against them, thinking on the thorns of the Crucified One and suffering willingly. He went out with the feeling, unexpressed to himself, that his cell would be a more tolerable place for the contrast with the sharp weather, and he would go back to it, narrow, hard, comfortless, as it was, with a sense of gladness. By physical pain, his thoughts would be at least diverted from the images of luxury and satisfied desire. Nature pitied his plight, however, and heaven sorrowed for his tempting, for straightway the sun shone bright, a warm wind breathed across the land, and lo! the blood of Francis, that dripped from the thorns, burst into flower as roses. The saint gathered many and placed them on the earth: a gift to Christ and Mary. His offering was accepted, for angels came, and, gathering the flowers, arose with them to the sky, their fragrant petals showering about the praying figure.

Mythologists may relate this legend to the older one, lately quoted, that red roses grew from thorns that had pricked the feet of Venus, and so were crimsoned as she ran through the wood seeking Adonis; that yellow roses were smitten to that color by the setting sun on the day he died, while white roses sprang from her tears. The tale that the red rose was originally white, but blushed with joy when Eve kissed it in Eden, is doubtless of later origin than the Venus myth. There is, however, a Talmudic legend, as ancient as the Greek, that tells how the rose was painted red: At midnight before the vernal equinox, when Cain and Abel were to make their offerings to the Lord, a vision came to their mother, Eve. She saw a little lamb bleeding its life away on Abel's altar, and the white roses he had planted about it were suddenly full blown and red. Voices cried about her, as in despair, but they died away and only a wonderful music was heard instead. Then, as the shadows lifted from her eyes, a vast plain unfolded, more beautiful than the paradise she had left, and grazing there were flocks watched by a shepherd whose robe of white was so fine and shining that the eye was dazzled by it. He wore a wreath of roses which Eve recognized as having lately grown about the altar, and he struck the strings of a lute, waking entrancing harmony.

Day broke, and, dismissing the vision as an idle dream, Eve watched her sons as they went forth to make sacrifice to the deity. She heard the cries of the little creatures of the flocks as they were put to death, and was glad that her children were willing to do this thing in the belief that suffering was agreeable to the author of life and love. At evening her sons were still afield, and as darkness came she went to seek them. Her dream returned to her, and she was disturbed. The fires on the two altars had burned out, and the bodies of the lambs were charred and broken. From a cave hard by sounded roarings of despair: she knew the voice for Cain's. And before his younger brother's altar lay the most pitiful sacrifice of all: the body of Abel, cold and rigid; and his blood had bespattered all the roses he had planted. Eve sank upon the body of her son, and again the vision of the night returned; she saw the shining one again, and it was Abel who shepherded in the new paradise. He wore the roses, but they were beautiful and fragrant, and, striking the harp in a triumphant measure, he sang, "Look up and see the stars shining promise through your tears. Those cars of light shall carry us to fields more blooming than Eden. There sighs and moans change to hymns of rapture, and there the rose that has been stained with innocent blood blooms in splendor."

Then Eve was comforted, and, gathering the roses he had planted, she bound them about his cold brow as she had see him wear them in the vision, and buried him before the altar, just as the rose of a new day unfolded in the east.

This is the legend of St. Dorothea, of Cappadocia. For her faith she was arrested and taken before the governor, Sapricius, who threatened her with grievous injuries unless she renounced Christ. She answered only, "Do your worst. I shall feel no pain, so long as I am ready to die for Him." "To whom do you refer?" asked the ruler. "He is Christ of whom I speak, the Son of God." "Where is He?" "Over all the earth and in all the heaven. It is from heaven that He summons us- heaven, where the lilies always bloom, the roses are in flower, the fields are always green, and the water of life springs forth continually."

A mocking lawyer, named Theophilus, cried at this, "I should like to see those roses. I beg you, send me some."

Dorothea answered simply, "I will." The governor, persuaded that it was necessary for the political safety of his province to suppress this dangerous band of Christians, ordered the girl to the block, and after her head had been struck off, Theophilus told his companions, with laughter, how he had obtained the promise of roses from heaven. While he jeered there appeared beside him a figure of the saint, tall, fair, exceeding white, and in her hand she bore a bunch of roses of wondrous size and color, which exhaled such fragrance that all the room was filled with it. They shed light as well as perfume, and the mocker fell back in astonishment, remorse weighing at his eyes and plucking at his heart. Dorothea bade him take the flowers, which he did, and, convinced that the faith she had upheld was true, he chose it and made public confession of his choice before the same stern officer who had ordered her to be slain. Like her, he went forth to receive the baptism of blood, bearing the heavenly roses to the grave.

Still better known than these traditions is the story of Elizabeth of Hungary. There are variants on this theme, the commoner representing her husband as a coarse tyrant; but such he was not. The cruel one was a plotting cleric, who had forced himself into the household as confessor, and used his place to gain money and power. Princess Elizabeth, suspecting guile of no man, was constant in her charities, and no doubt was as constantly imposed upon. On the day of the miracle Elizabeth was carrying food to a sick person when her husband came galloping through the wood and stopped before her. Noting that she carried a burden in a fold of her dress, he dismounted and reached toward it. "You should not tire yourself in these works," he said. "Give me the parcel, and I will carry it for you. Happily those whom you bless with your charities are better able than you to walk these rough paths and carry bread and wine." Half bashfully, half playfully, Elizabeth held her burden closer to her breast, and the husband also in mingled sport and earnest tried to wrest it from her. The wrapping fell away, and lo! the warmth of her heart had changed the bread and meat to white and red roses of amazing size and of such fragrance that the winter air seemed changed to summer. Standing apart from her in astonishment, the husband saw the lifted countenance of the saint shining with a soft, strange light, and in a low voice and on his knees he begged one flower, which he put into his breast. Then he rode away with downcast eyes, for he knew that, much as he loved his wife, and much as she loved him, heaven was between them.

Famous among rose-trees is that of Hildesheim in Hanover, which is believed to be more than a thousand years old. Ludwig the Pious assembled his knights and his dogs one autumn morning in the year 814 and prepared for a day of happiness. He armed himself and his people with instruments for stabbing and cutting and set off to waste the innocent life of the forest that surrounded his castle. In haste to begin the killing, the company could hardly restrain its impatience while a priest invoked God's blessing on the knives and spears, and on the dogs that would presently tear the flesh from victims of the sport. So soon as the Amen was pronounced, the troop galloped away with shouts and laughter, leaving untasted the holy bread and wine, used in the communion, on the ground where the priest had put them. Next day a rose bush was found shadowing the sacrament. It had sprung up as soon as the king was gone, and increased miraculously, and there the king ordered a chapel to be built.

The golden rose is a decoration bestowed by the Popes on members of royal, noble, or distinguished families, soldiers, literary men, or, it may be, on congregations or even cities, that at the end of a year are proved to have done much for the Church. The practice of bestowing this costly gift began in the twelfth century, and it was a substitute for tokens of varied character, for we are told that one of the Popes sent a golden shirt to a king who had been zealous for the faith. The rose is blessed on the fourth Sunday in Lent, but if nobody appears worthy to receive it, it is put away in a cabinet of the Vatican, to be brought out and, if possible, awarded, next year. The first of these roses was a simple image of a flower, shaped with skill, but without decoration. As time went on it increased in size, a stem was added, then leaves, then the petals were doubled, then they were dewed with rubies and diamonds, and finally it evolved into a small bush bearing two or three flowers and set in a pot bearing the papal name and arms. One of these offerings, sent to a queen of France, weighed eight pounds and represented a value of one thousand eight hundred dollars in metal. Of late the stones and pearls that ornamented the branches have been omitted, and in recent days not even pure metal is used, for the token is of silver gilt, of small intrinsic value. There attaches to it an omen of ill fortune, that makes even devoted members of the Church unwilling to receive it, although American women to whom it has been given seem to be immune from evil consequences of the acceptance. Countess O'Leary, Marquise de Mermville, and the wife of General Sherman are these Americans. But among the women of its history, it is true that many were doomed to early or painful death, poverty, dethronement, or other misfortune. Joanna of Sicily, the first rose queen, was strangled; the Queen of Naples, Empress Josephine, Princess Isabella of Brazil, the Queen of the Belgians, the Queen of Portugal, the Queen Regent of Spain, ex-Empress Eugenie, the Empress of Austria, Bloody Mary (daughter of Henry VIII., who himself received three of these roses), all suffered desertion, exile, political opposition, or assassination.

Some early legends of the rose have been here set down, but the Orient has others, for it was in the east that the first moss rose grew. It had been like others until an angel slept beneath it. Waking, he thanked the bush for its shade and perfume and asked if he could grant any favor to it. "Yes," replied the bush. "You have praised my beauty. I would wear one other grace, to prove that I can hear sweet words, yet retain modesty." The angel touched it, and its stems and buds were clothed and softened. To our day it has kept this delicate covering.

MYTHS AND LEGENDS OF FLOWERS

Other myths of the Orient equal this for age, for they say that the rose disappeared from paradise when our parents fell, into knowledge. Long afterward there lived a Jewish maid, one Zillah, whose charms had spoiled the sleep of a young man, Hammel. His love she rejected; hence, wrathful and embittered, he charged her so explicitly with lapses from virtue that the people demanded her death. She was tried, in the old harsh manner of a day when a man's word weighed more than a woman's oath, was found guilty and condemned to the stake. When Zillah was bound upon the fagots and the torch applied to them, the flames leaped forth like lightning, and pierced Hamil's guilty breast; he toppled into the fire and was burned to a cinder at his victim's feet- feet that were unscorched. As the wood sank beneath the girl's weight, it was seen to lose its glow and take on a more tender hue than flame, while the smoke ceased to roll, and she breathed a ravishing sweetness in its stead. For the coals were roses- red where the brands had suddenly cooled to flowers; white where the wood had been unburned. Standing on this cushion of bloom, unscathed and with heightened beauty, Zillah needed no words to proclaim her innocence. The priests were saddened as they thought how nearly they had debased their sacred office to abet the crime of Hammel.

It is in a cold country, Russia, namely, where we would not look for a love of flowers, that we find an odd survival from that love. Until lately, and maybe even yet, a sentry; paced a beat at Tsar-skoe-selo, the imperial domain, nineteen miles from St. Petersburg. He never knew why, nor did the officers who stationed him, except that, "it was orders;" but it is because Empress Catherine a century ago commanded a soldier to guard a bush that had budded in a sheltered place in the garden, that no careless courtier or visitor might injure it. The roses ripened, were picked for the empress's table, but nobody remembered the sentry, and as orders had been issued to maintain this beat, the guard detail included the bush. The roses faded, yet the sentry tramped on. What was a mere soldier? Winter came, yet still he paced, back and forth, in the arctic weather. The bush died. Catherine died. Sentries died, and others kept the earth worn smooth. And still the sentries pace, watching the ghost, the memory, of a flower.

It is of another sort of soldier they tell in France, the General La Hoche. He, with other accused aristocrats, was immured in the Conciergerie. One morning there came to him from some unknown friend a splendid bouquet of roses. The haggard prisoners cried in delight at the sight and begged for them when he appeared at the leanly furnished table where they took their meals. Beginning with the women, fair daughters of misfortune whose pretty heads were so soon to be shorn away by the guillotine, he distributed the trophies, and it seemed as if the flowers brought light and hope into the gloomy place. The babble was almost cheerful. But while all tongues were wagging, the door grated on its hinges and an officer in black appeared, followed by a file of soldiers. He carried a paper holding a list of those who were to die. "Citizen," said a young woman to La Hoche, "I shall wear your rose to the scaffold."

"And we also," cried the others. And when the tumbrels passed through the street the ruffians of the pavement looked in wonder, for every man held a rose to his lips, and every woman wore a rose in her bosom, a rose pale as death, or red as the blood that was shortly to be spilled in the name of justice, liberty and love.

ROSEMARY

This plant, which is not a rose and is not dedicated to Mary, takes its name from the Latin, *ros marinum*, or sea dew, for it is fond of the water. The Romans made decorative as well as ceremonial use of rosemary, crowning with it the guests at banquets, employing it in funeral rites, wreathing it on their household gods, and purifying their flocks with its smoke. They

MYTHS AND LEGENDS OF FLOWERS

believed that the odor of the plant tended to preserve the bodies of the dead, and the lasting green of its leaves made it an emblem of eternity, for both which reasons they planted it near tombs.

In northern England, a relic of this custom is seen in the bearing of rosemary in funeral processions, the sprays being cast on the coffin in the grave. As a plant of remembrance, it formed a part of bridal wreaths. When Christmas was the heartiest of holidays, rosemary decked the hall of feasting, the roast, the boar's head, and the wassail bowl, this service in possible memory of the rosemary's opening to hide the Virgin and her child from Herod's soldiers- a legend it shares with the juniper and other trees. And because Mary spread the linen of her babe on a rosemary, it flowers in memory of him on the day of the passion. In Sicily it is a heathen plant, for fairies nestle under it, disguised as snakes, which circumstance has not prevented its extensive cultivation, even in monastery gardens, where it was prized for its medicinal qualities.

Mixed with rue, sage, marjoram, fennel, quince, and a few other matters- pity that the recipe could not have been preserved!- it kept one young so long as he wished to be. If a maid is curious as to her future, she may obtain information by dipping a spray of rosemary into a mixture of wine, rum, gin, vinegar, and water in a vessel of ground glass. She is to observe this rite on the eve of St, Magdalene, in an upper room, in company with two other maids, and each must be less than twenty-one years old. Having fastened the sprigs in their bosoms and taken three sips of the tonic- sips are quite enough- all three go to rest in the same bed without speaking. The dreams that follow will be prophetic.

RUE

Rue, herb of grace and memory, stands for repentance also, and we have made the word into a verb, the villain of melodrama assuring the heroine that she will rue the day when she refused to place herself in his power, as she invariably doesn't. It drives away the plague if you merely smell of it; it keeps maids from going wrong in affairs of love, if only they will pause to eat it when tempted; it makes eyes keener and wits more eager; it heals the bites of snakes, scorpions, wasps, and bees. For internal poisons, it seems to have been no less effective than for snake bites; at least, Mithridates, whose subjects were continually trying to poison him, felt a need to accustom his stomach to innutritions material in the faith that if he could not live on it, he could at least keep a-dying for an unconscionable while. And this antidote, which he would take after meals or before a glass, consisted of twenty rue leaves, two figs, two walnuts, twenty berries of juniper, and a pinch of salt.

If all this be not enough, you may, with rue, keep off epilepsy, dizziness, insanity, dumbness, inflammation of the eyes, and the evil eye. Boil gun-flints with rue and vervain, and the shot will reach your victim, human or defenseless. Lastly, carry a bundle of rue, broom, maiden-hair, agrimony, and ground ivy, and you may know every woman for a witch who is one, no matter how plain or otherwise she appears to you.

SAGE

It has been claimed that when the Virgin had begun her flight into Egypt she sought refuge from the hunters of Herod in a sage, which she blessed, whereupon the plant put forth a blush of fragrance in all its leaves. A later tale, which may have its roots in a sun or season myth of pre-Christian time, represents the sage as a nymph living in a hollow oak beside a pool where jonquils sprang, dulling her shyer beauty. But she had no jealousy. She looked into the water mirror and saw her own face there, without pride, and she looked on the blossoms of the wood and loved them. Long she lived there in peace and happiness, and did not know the human face. But the silence of the wood was disturbed by a call of horns and baying of hounds, and the king rode that way, hunting. As he came to the foot of the oak, where Sageflower stood, her modest beauty charmed him. It was death for her to love a mortal, yet so deep was the affection which the sight of the young king stirred in her breast that she made no attempt to check it. He had only to tell her of his love to receive her confession. "The fine days are gone," she said, "but solitude is still beautiful. Let us remain here alone together. It lightens my heart to be with you. You ask my love; I give you my life." The king did not understand, and he folded her passionately in his arms. Sageflower returned his caress, but her arms relaxed, her head drooped. The king placed her on the bank and hurried to dip water from the pool to revive her. But the heat of love had been more than the fragile Sageflower could endure. She had faded out of life. And the king went away, mourning. Which is a poetic way of saying that the flower loves the sun and fades in the heat after fertilization. Sage is a plant of wide range. Its ghostly tufts dot our Western deserts, and it also flourishes in our gardens, where it is picked for the stuffing of geese and turkeys. An ornate variety is the salvia, whose plumes are very flames of scarlet. In the middle ages, when plants were much more remarkable than now, the common sage prolonged life, heightened spirits, kept off toads, enabled girls to see their future husbands, mitigated sorrow, and averted chills.

SAINT FOIN

Saint foin- *onobrychis sativa*- memorized a saint of the name of Foin, in popular fancy in England; but the name is French and signifies holy hay. When the Holy Family arrived at Bethlehem and could obtain no room in the inn, a place was found in the stable, and the only bed that offered even there was the stone manger. So Joseph went about the fields gathering wisps of hay and stubble, which he spread as softly as he might, that his wife should suffer as little as possible; and most of this hay was the plant of rose-colored blooms that we now call lucerne, or cock's head clover. The frosts had killed it, so that it was wholly dry, and on that rude but fragrant couch the little Jesus slept peacefully. When the wise men came, and He was lifted, that they might worship, behold, the saint foin had come to life again, and a circle of blossoms marked where His head had lain. So the Italians will deck their mangers with such plants as show green at Christmas, or with moss, as a substitute for the holy hay that was pressed by the infant Savior.

ST. JOHNS WORT

Hypericum perforatum is supposed to show its red spots on the 29th of August, the day on which St. John was beheaded: hence its name of St. Johns wort; but it also wears the names of devil's flight, and devil chaser, because if hung in windows on the anniversary of St. John's birth, the 24th of June, it will keep away ghosts, devils, imps, and thunderbolts. Should you be tramping about the fields of the Isle of Wight, however, you must beware of trampling on this herb, for if you do a fairy horse will rise from its root, squarely under you, so that you shall find yourself mounted for a ride. All through the night the steed will carry you, up hill, down dale, and just at dawn will sink into the earth, wherever he happens to be, leaving you with the prospect of a weary walk to breakfast. Taken internally, the plant cures melancholy, "if it is gathered on a Friday in the hour of Jupiter, and worn away about the neck"; and if hung on the wall of a bedroom it enables a young and hopeful maid to dream of her future husband.

SAL

Shorea robusta, known to India as the sal, is a sacred tree, for the mother of Buddha held a branch of it when that founder of a faith was born, as if in token that it should serve him for protection in his life; and when that life was about to end, Prince Buddha lay in the shelter of two sals at Kucinigara

MYTHS AND LEGENDS OF FLOWERS

and took food at the hands of an artisan who dwelt in the grove of sals hard by. At the instant when the wife of Brahma was announcing that Buddha had entered paradise, the thunder rolled, the earth shook. But the life went out in beauty, for the sal trees bending above him burst into bloom, although it was not the flowering season, and while soft music sounded from the heavens, the trees showered their blossoms over him, covering the form of the perfect one with color and perfume. Tree marriage is a custom among the lower castes in India, the girl being mated to a sal, or even to a bunch of blossoms, if she can not find a man to marry her. There is a superstition that if a girl weds a tree and afterward a man, the dangers of a second marriage will all be imposed upon the tree, and it must thenceforth suffer the illnesses and injuries that might be visited on the bride; but another reason for the ceremony is that in wedding a tree the wife acquires something of its strength and fertility.

SAXIFRAGE

Burnet saxifrage (*pimpinella saxifrage*) is indeed a plant of magic value, for if a woman eats it, at least, in Italy, her beauty will increase. If a soldier will steep his sword in the blood of moles and the juice of pimpinella before going into battle, the blade will bite harder and do more mischief. Yet in a tale of Hungary it is as powerful to cure as it is to hurt, for King Chaba, having fought a terrible battle against his brother, that left him with fifteen thousand wounded soldiers on his hands, healed every one of their cuts with the juice of this little plant.

SHEPHERD'S PURSE

Our common little peppergrass, or shepherd's purse, was once known as pickpocket and pickpurse, because it sowed itself eagerly and so robbed the farmer of the fertility of his land. Among its other titles are St. Jameswort, poor man's pharmacetty, toywort, caseweed, and, in Ireland, clappedepouch. This last has reference to the likeness of its seed pouches to the leather wallets carried by licensed beggars and lepers, who would stand at the crossways by days together with a bell, wooden clapper, and pouch, summoning the public to give money or be vilified. Peppergrass is a name confined to New England, and betokens the smart of its flower stalks in the mouth when they are chewed.

SILK COTTON

In the West Indies grows a tree with huge roots that extend half way up the trunk in buttress-like extensions, and rounded masses of foliage in whose shade the native vendors doze while waiting to sell their wares. Yet the white man would pass under it with a shudder, could he believe, as the Negroes do, that the tree is inhabited by cloudy forms and that death lurked in its trunk. Obeah, or voodoo, is a form of magic which in parts of the Antilles is unfortunately real. One may express such contempt as he will of the spells and incantations by which the obeah man seeks to injure the enemy of his client- for these conjurers sell their influence, like lawyers- but subtle murder has been done by these malignants, especially through the use of vegetable poisons. Where possible, they will obtain underclothing of the intended victim, steep it in the poison, and he dies a mysterious and lingering death. Diseases, too, have been disseminated through the use of infected clothing and articles of household use.

Yet discovery and conviction of the conjurer are difficult, for he is held in such dread by the natives that they dare not confess what they know of him. His employers are not always so ignorant as his protectors; at least, one who was hanged in Jamaica involved several planters and white people of consequence in his confession. Now, this obeah man is in league with spirits, good and evil, such as the duppies, rolling calves, the mial people, the fan-eyed, and Anansi- a devil absurdly Englished as Aunt Nancy. And among the evils these creatures do is to steal the shadow of a man or woman, and thereby cause a decline in health, a wasting in substance, that has but one end- death. When a shadow is stolen it roosts in the silk cotton tree, invisible for much of the time, but a tree may be so filled with stolen shadows that in quiet weather they can be heard whispering and rustling among the leaves. A negro will rarely put an ax to the tree, for fear of these larvae, and also because the deaths that live in the trunk will enter his soul through his nostrils if he tries to destroy it. To the end of pacifying the deaths, and the shadows, and the duppies, a sort of worship, as of the Druids, is ordained. When an obeah man has charmed away a shadow, the unhappy one who misses that adjunct hies him at once to an angel man, or shadow-catcher, to pray it out of the keeping of the ceiba, or silk cotton. A high price is charged for the job, for the angel men who guarantee success are few and are highly important persons.

The Caribs and Indians of Guiana have a tradition, which folk-lorists may relate to Yggdrasil of the Norsemen, in that God created a wonderful tree that yielded all vegetables good for men- the banana, maize, cassava, potatoes, yams, and all fruits besides. At the command of a voice in the skies, men set themselves to cut down this giant. It took them ten months to destroy it, and it fell with a mighty crash. Then, at the command of the voice, the people took leaves and cuttings, planted them in mellow lands, and they sprang, not like the parent tree, but as bananas, yams, maize, mangoes, and coconuts. And this mythical tree seems to relate to the silk cotton, in that the ceiba was the seat of the Mighty One. Its branches lifted to the clouds, and when he scattered twigs and bark these fragments changed to living creatures; so were men made, as well as birds, beasts, fish, and reptiles. But not so came the white race; it was only the withered and useless leaves, that fell upon the waters and drifted to distant places, that fermented into the tribe of spoilers and slayers, all to be drowned when the time came, in the great deluge that poured from the Haytien gourd.

SNOWDROP

When the first winter lay white upon the earth. Eve sorely missed the beautiful things of the fields. An angel who pitied her seized a flake of the driving snow and, breathing on it, bade it live, for her delight. It fell to the earth a flower, which Eve caught to her breast with gladness, for not only did it break the spell of winter, but it carried assurance of divine mercy. Hence the flower means consolation and promise. In another legend Kerma, finding her lover dead, plucked a snowdrop and placed it on his wounds. It did not rouse him, but at the touch his flesh changed to snowdrops, hence the flower is also an emblem of death. Even now in rural England the flower is in ill repute, and it is unlucky to carry the first spray of the season into the house, while it is downright indelicate for a person to give it to one of another sex, since it implies a wish to see the recipient dead. This *galanthus nivalis* is variously known in England, France, Italy, and Switzerland as virgin flower, snow piercer, winter gallant, firstling, blackbird flower, little snow bell, little white bell, baby bell, spring whiteness, and white violet.

SPEEDWELL

The legend of St. Veronica, associated with the veronica, or speedwell, is mentioned in the early Christian legends. The plant has other attributes, however, than that of suggesting the picture of Christ on the handkerchief wherewith the saint wiped the blood and sweat from His face as He went to His death. Its "True blue," as well as the story of Veronica, has caused it to be chosen as the emblem of woman's fidelity. Long ago it was valued for its medicinal qualities and for them it attained the distinction implied in its German name of ehrenpreis, or, honor prize. It was a shepherd who discovered its worth as a curative,

MYTHS AND LEGENDS OF FLOWERS

for he saw a deer, wounded by a wolf's bite, rub itself against an oak, then lie in a speedwell patch. The stag remained in its nook for a week, eating of the speedwell from time to time, and when it came forth the wound was cured. Now, the king of that country had been smitten with a leprosy and was lying on his bed, so ill he doubted if he should ever again rise from it. To him the shepherd made his way with a dish filled with new-gathered flowers of the speedwell, and related what he had seen. The monarch applied them to his bleeding skin and also drank a decoction brew from the plant. As a result, he left his bed, sound in health and full of thanks for the blessings that the Lord had showered upon the earth.

SPRINGWORT

Springwort, or blasting root, to be found on St. John's night among the ferns, is hard to lay hands upon, because it has the magical quality of seeming to dodge about. Once it had the power to open locks, hidden doors, and entrances to forgotten caves, like the "sesame" of All Baba, and if a horse treads on it the springwort will surely pull his shoes off. This variety of euphorbia may be had in this manner: In the nesting season track a woodpecker to his hole, and plug it while he is foraging. As soon as he finds the place occluded, he will hurry away for springwort, which, by its magic, will cause the plug to be ejected, so the watcher, who is standing below, may pick up the weed the bird has dropped.

This belief is older than Pliny, who declares that an electric force in the plant draws out the obstruction. Later peoples have believed springwort to be a product of water and lightning, and that birds carrying it above either a fire or a vessel of water must let it fall. In Suabia it is burned on a mountain top, as a lightning averter.

MYTHS AND LEGENDS OF FLOWERS

SPRUCE

From strips of spruce, the Haida Indians, of British Columbia, make not only remarkable mats, but hats and baskets, so finely woven that when swollen with moisture they hold water like bags of skin or jars of pottery. They are rudely and quaintly decorated with figures that symbolize tribal myths and history. A legend relates that two girls, being treated cruelly by their stepmother, decided to leave their home. They were found by a man who took them to his lodge and married them. After some years, they felt a longing to revisit the scenes of their childhood, but this meant a journey of some difficulty and distance. Their good totem spirit bade them weave two baskets apiece from spruce strips, small enough to fit over the end of the thumb. These they were to fill with dried meat and deer tallow. Now, these little baskets, holding less than a mouthful apiece, were as the baskets that contained the loaves and fishes, for though the two girls ate all they wished, the supply never diminished. When they arrived at the parental lodge, the baskets suddenly swelled to the proportion they would have reached had they contained the food actually used on the trip, and the strength of many people was needed to carry them into the house.

The old stepmother was still there, and, being easily persuaded to eat of the contents of the baskets, gorged to that degree that she could no longer breathe, and so died, in a rapture of sufficiency, and her stepdaughters were avenged.

STRAMONIUM

The vexatious "jimson weed" is so called from its abundance in Jamestown, Virginia, when the English settlers, thinking its seed might have food properties, ate of it, cutting strange antics as a consequence. This plant, which in dignified botanies is *datura stramonium*, is valued by the Indians of the southwest for medicinal properties unlike those discovered by the faculty in cities of the whites, the Zunis using it both as a narcotic and anodyne, applying it externally to cuts and bruises. The powdered root and flower is the common form of the medicine, and when the rain priests go out at night to beg the birds to sing for showers, they carry a little of this powder in their mouths, believing that the birds will cease to fear them when they do so. When one asks the spirits of the dead to pray for the rains, he chews a piece of the root, but he must obtain this from the rain priests, or from the Little Fire Brotherhood, to whom it is sacred. A priest may also give it to one who has lost property by theft, to the end that the victim may see the image of the robber in a vision and accuse him to his face next day.

The Zuni legend of the plant is that it is the descendant of two children, a boy and a girl, who displeased the gods by wandering about their place of council and telling their mother of the strange things they saw. Their curiosity and gossip led the gods to change them into plants, on eating whereof the people continue to tell of what they see.

STRAWBERRY

Strawberries, of which Swift said that God could doubtless have made a better beery, but doubtless He never did, were sacred to Friga, and when the new religion spread over the darkened north the Virgin inherited from her heathen predecessor the right to this fruit. Indeed, it was considered that the Virgin acquired such fondness for it as to demand all of it that grew, and if a mother presented herself at heaven's gate with the stain of strawberries on her lips the Mother of the Merciful One would cast her down to everlasting torment for trespass on her fields. One reason for this belief is that infants ascended to heaven disguised as strawberries; hence the people of the earth never knew when they were committing cannibalism by eating them, and the safer way was to avoid. As John the Baptist was contemporary with the Virgin, however, he lived fearlessly on this berry, and to denote admiration for the preacher, Don John, of Portugal, adopted it as his device, as did sundry of the English nobility, for strawberry leaves are shown in gold on various of their coronets.

SUGAR

Sugar, whose sap sparkles in snowy crystals on the tables of the world, is somewhat of a luxury in the regions of its growth. Solemn Orientals may be seen chewing it as they ride and walk, and the boy, who discloses various attributes of his species, whether you find him in Greenland or Jamaica, not infrequently contrives to possess himself of a couple of feet of the cane, and sucks it as cleaner children mouth sticks of candy in lands of supposedly better fortune. The Hindu planter bums the cane that may be left after harvest, as a sacrifice to Nagbele, spirit of the plant, but one reason for his so doing is that it may bear no flowers at the end of the season, for to have flowers of sugar bloom on one's land is not merely bad form, but bad luck, as it signifies that a funeral must presently occur in the planter's family.

SUNFLOWER

Various plants have been known as sunflower, and the chrysanthemum, the dandelion, and the elecampane- a bouquet of which fair Helen carried when she was to elope with Paris- suggest the day god as truly as the honest, coarse, assertive sunflower of our farms. The supposition that the *helianthus annuus* is called by a more familiar name because it turns its face to the sun is common; but the clumsy blossom and the stiff neck on which it stands, are not readily moved. Being an American plant, it could not have been the sunflower of which Ovid tells, hence we are to imagine that when Clytie, dying of grief at her desertion by the sun god, was turned into a flower, it was a more modest one. Being such an obvious symbol of the globe of light, our big sunflower was much esteemed in Peru by the sun worshipers.

Their priestesses, in the sun temples, wore copies of these flowers in gold, to the great joy of the Spaniards, who immediately possessed themselves of these shocking evidences of unauthorized religion, and put the objectors to the sword.

TAMARISK

Osiris and Isis came to the earth to persuade mankind to better living, and their services so endeared them to the people that the jealousy of dark and bitter Typhon was aroused, and he plotted to put his brother Osiris to death. Typhon invited a multitude to join him in sports, and during the merry-making he challenged such as might to lie in a chest made from precious wood, promising to bestow it as a gift on him who should fit it most nearly. He had previously taken the measure of Osiris, so of course the sun god fitted it, but no sooner was he lying at his length than Typhon clapped down the lid, bound it fast, and flung the chest into the Nile. Isis lamented her husband's absence, and searched for him everywhere. The casket had gone ashore at Byblos and become entangled in a tamarisk, which the warmth from the body of the god caused to grow with wondrous speed and to such a height that it was the marvel of the nation. In its ascent it enclosed the coffin. The king of Phoenicia, fearing that some subject might use the tree for base purposes, cut it down for a column of his palace, and when Isis discovered the casket hidden in its core, she hurled a thunderbolt against the pillar to split it. She then concealed the body of her lord, but Typhon stole to the place at night and cut it into fourteen pieces, which he flung into the river. Isis recovered all these fragments but one, and this the goddess eked out with a piece of sycamore, that she might complete the image of her husband when she buried it in Philae, where a great temple was built to his memory.

MYTHS AND LEGENDS OF FLOWERS

It is said that the manna which fell upon the ground and relieved the hunger of Israel in the wilderness came from the tamarisk, and a manna still made at Mount Sinai consists of a sticky, sweet sap of the *tamarix gallica*.

THISTLE

In a Greek story, Earth made the thistle in a moment of grief, that she might express her love for Daphnis, shepherd and musician, poet and hunter, when he had passed beyond the knowing of it; but it was associated in the north with Thor, the thunderer, who protected it and those who wore it, and who called the spiny thing a lightning plant. From the inexhaustible mine of German folk-lore is extracted a tale of the humble weed: A merchant who was passing through a lonely country, and who must have neglected to wear his thistle on that day, was met by a peasant who, noting the tokens of prosperity in the stranger's costume and belongings, was filled with envy and bitterness. Seeing the road empty, save of themselves, he fell upon the merchant and put him to death. The victim, dying, fixed his eyes on the murderer and solemnly declared, "The thistle will betray you." Whatever this warning meant, the peasant showed contempt for it by gathering up the merchant's gold and making off. Still, as every one knows, riches bring discontent, and the peasant lost his spirits, became suspicious, fearful; he hesitated to spend the money he had stolen, yet he dreaded its loss at the hands of other thieves. His neighbors especially noticed his dislike for thistles, for he would avoid them in walking through the fields. They asked the why of it, and he answered, "dare not say, and the thistle can not say." "But what have thistles to do with you?" they insisted. And in the end, half-demented by remorse and dread, he confessed the crime and was hanged. On the scene of the murder, in Mecklenburg, a thistle grows where the merchant fell, and it is seen that its buds and branches resemble human heads, arms, and hands. Cereus, or torch thistle, is the lamp borne by Ceres, while the carline thistle perpetuates

MYTHS AND LEGENDS OF FLOWERS

the name of Carolus Magnus, or Charlemagne, who, perturbed by an outbreak of plague during the prosecution of a war, and fearing that the loss of his soldiers by disease might force him to abandon his enterprise, prayed earnestly for help. An angel who descended from heaven in answer told him to shoot his crossbow and note where the arrow fell, for there he would find an herb to stay the epidemic. The bolt fell upon a thistle, which, boiled and administered to the invalids, cured them speedily. It was this belief in its efficacy as a drug that gave to one species the name of blessed thistle, holy thistle, and our lady's thistle. This plant was the badge of the Order of the Thistle, founded in honor of the Virgin in France in the fourteenth century. Another order of the same name is held to be the oldest company of nobility in the world, having been created by Archius, King of Scots, after his victory over Athelstan in the tenth century; but this assertion is denied by those British historians who claim the creation of the knights for James II. of England. The choice of the thistle as a Scottish national symbol dates back to the Danish wars. A marauding Danish army, thinking to surprise a camp at night, advanced barefooted on its foes, but a soldier, stepping on a thistle, could not forbear from uttering a howl of pain. At this the Scottish camp bestirred itself and defeated the invaders, hence "the guardian thistle" became seal of the kingdom, with the fitting motto. *Nemo me impune lacessit.*

For all this, the thistle is not cultivated assiduously; indeed, legislatures have fulminated against it, and it is usually treated as an enemy to be rooted out of the soil wherever found; yet the ass thrives on it, and the question is put to doubters of its nutritive value, "Did you ever see a dead donkey?" Moreover, a man who was lost in the Yellowstone country, years ago, supported life for some weeks on thistle roots. An old writer commends it as a vegetable and pot plant- its thorns being removed- and declares that it "changes the blood" as the season changes. If it lives up to the further claim that it cures ague, jaundice, and, in wine, "expels superfluous melancholy out of the body and makes a man as merry as a cricket," we may have our thistle patches in the future, as well as our beet and turnip gardens.

TULIP

In a folk-tale of Devon, the pixies, having no other cradles for their children, put them at night into the blown tulips, to be cradled by the winds. A woman who had gone into her garden with a lantern and found the tiny babes asleep in the flowers was so delighted that she planted more tulips at once, and soon there were cradles enough for all the fairy people round about, and she would steal out in the moonlight to watch the wee creatures folded away in the satin cups and swinging in the perfumed breeze. The fairies, watchful, but seeing that she wished them well, rewarded her goodness by causing the tulips to take on bright colors and smell sweet, like the rose. And they blessed the woman and her cottage so that she had luck and happiness so long as she lived. When the woman died, a worldling occupied her cottage: a hard, moneymaking man, one of whose first acts was to destroy the garden as of no use, and plant parsley where the flowers had bloomed. This roused the ire of the little people, and every night when it fell dark they would troop out of the wood and dance on the vegetables and tear and hack at their roots and throw dust into their blossoms, so that nothing thrived on that land for years, and the parsley leaves grew fringed and ragged as you see them now. But the grave where the woman was buried they kept green and fair.

At the head nodded a cluster of beautiful tulips, gorgeous in color, sweet of smell, and these bloomed long after all other flowers had faded. In time other men without eyes for beauty came into the region, so the woods disappeared, the grave was beaten flat by passing feet, the flowers were rudely broken, and the fairies withdrew to the fastnesses of the hills. From that time the tulips lost size and splendor and fragrance though they keep

MYTHS AND LEGENDS OF FLOWERS

enough of beauty to endear them to every gardener. Turkey has made the tulip the subject of an annual festival; and, indeed, the sight of a great tulip garden, glowing like stained glass, is worth going far to see. In the spring we wait impatiently that uprush of color from the earth which is denoted in the tulip, and when the snows are gone and earth and sky soften with the first rains, we bethink us of the season-myth of Isis, hurrying to the help of Horus as he lay wounded on the battle-field. It was a bleak and wintry plain where the god had fallen, fertilizing its yet unbreathing life with his blood, but as she knelt beside him and vented her tears, each drop arose from the earth again, a flower; for, behold, the spring was come.

The Persian swain gives a tulip- it is the Persian thulihan (turban) that named it- to his beloved to signify that his love flames like its color, and his heart is charred to a coal by its ferocity, just as the flower's base shows black. Gerarde observes the plant more reverently, for he maintains that it is the "lily of the field" that toils nor spins, the others declare for the *lilium syriacum* as the object of the apostrophe. That was a curious chapter in the history of popular rages which is disclosed in the "tulip mania" of Holland in the seventeenth century.

Rare strains were sold for nearly as much, during that excitement, as we have since paid for new varieties of chrysanthemums- and in our twentieth century men have paid ten thousand dollars for a fresh form of the Japanese flower, and seventy-five thousand dollars for the privilege of owning the first of a handsome variety of carnation. Some indication of the extravagance of growers and speculators may be found in Dumas's tale of "The Black Tulip," which is not absolutely a work of fancy. Government finally stopped speculation in tulips after the bulb of the Viceroy had been sold for four thousand three hundred and three guilders.

MYTHS AND LEGENDS OF FLOWERS

VALERIAN

Valeriana jatamansi is the spikenard which ranks with saffron, myrrh, and frankincense as a perfume. The precious ointments of the east contained this substance; it was poured upon the feet of Christ by the Magdalen; its smoke has long ascended before the altars of the Roman church bearing with it the prayers of the worshipers; hence its use is ancient, but sometimes secular, for Chaucer, who calls it the setewale- "as swete as is the rote of licoris or any setewale"- was used to it as a seasoning for broths. The odor of valerian is inviting not only to men, but to some animals, for cats and rats enjoy rolling in it and chewing its roots and leaves. In a Hindu legend a man who is compelled by an emergency to leave his house, directly after his marriage, plants a spikenard in his garden and shows it to his bride, telling her that he will be safe so long as it is in health. Years pass before he can return, and, wishing to test the woman's constancy, when he reaches his home he puts on the rags of a beggar and enters his garden. Yes; the 'nard is there, a flourishing tree, giving off fragrance and yielding beauty to the eye; but more beautiful than all is his wife as she kneels before it, trimming and watching its branches and occasionally pearling its leaves with a tear. He throws off his disguise and the wedded life begins in happy reality.

VIOLET

One would suppose that the violet would be welcome anywhere, but a fear of it still lingers among English rustics, for whom it had its funerary uses, like rue and rosemary; but while those plants are thrown into the grave "for remembrance," the violet guarded the mourners against poisonous exhalations from the cemetery.

Violet perfume is expressed for toilet uses, tons of its

MYTHS AND LEGENDS OF FLOWERS

blooms are thrown about in the Italian carnivals, in winter it sells for fanciful prices, whole conservatories being devoted to its cultivation near the cities, and it is turned into confections for rich demoiselles. The violet, like the rose, has been used as a food, not merely to color and garnish puddings, broths and other dishes, but as a salad, mixed- think of it!- with lettuce and onions! A dish known in England as vyolette consisted of the flowers, boiled, pressed, and brayed with additions of milk, rice flower, and honey. These employments, however, have never lessened the sentimental regard for the blossom, for to this day in parts of Germany it is a custom to decorate bride-beds and cradles with it, a practice extending back to the Celts and the Greeks. In a myth of the latter people the violet sprang for Io, a priestess of Juno's temple, with whom Jupiter was almost caught in one of his flirtations. Not having time to conceal her, he changed her into a white heifer; but grass not being good enough for so delicate a creature, the god created the violet as her special food. So the Greeks named it ion, and the nymphs of Ionia- which bore that name because it abounded in violets- consecrated the flowers to Jupiter. From Ionia to the mainland was but a step, hence the Athenians made the flower the symbol of their city. Even in that day its mortuary service had begun, for when a Greek was buried his body was concealed with violets, and they were also placed about his grave, or tomb, so that the dread receptacle was carpeted with color and fragrance. A violet of gold was a prize in the Provencal singing tourneys, for the half superstitious fondness for the flower and its ceremonial use had passed easily into Christian lands. Though raised for Io, it in some way became sacred to Venus and its perfume was held to be not only soothing, but stimulating to the ardor of affection. We have only the poet Herrick's authority, however, for believing that it was Venus who made the violet blue. She had been disputing with her son Cupid as to which was more beautiful, herself or a bevy of girls, and Cupid, a disobedient scamp, with no fear of his mother before his eyes, declared for the girls. This sent Venus into such a rage that she beat her rivals till they

MYTHS AND LEGENDS OF FLOWERS

turned blue and dwindled into violets.

The old gods having died, the violet passed to the Virgin, and in some countries it is usual to place it, in wreaths, upon her altar, though roses and lilies are commoner. Among the flowers on which the shadow of the cross fell on the day of the crucifixion was the violet, and, like others in that shadow, it drooped in sorrow, thereby tokening its consecration to Christian service. Its color is suggested in the purple of church mourning and the wearing of amethyst jewels by persons in orphanage or widowhood. Mahometans regard it almost with reverence, because it was a favorite of the Prophet. Napoleon was known as Corporal Violet because this was his favorite flower, and when sent to Elba he declared that he would return when the violets bloomed. During the exile his adherents might recognize one another by the little blossom. And the emperor was true to his promise, so there was a wonderful display of violets when he reentered the Tuileries. It was much worn during his reign, and came to be so well known as his emblem that on the restoration of the Bourbons it was treasonable to wear it in public or even to carry it in bouquets. Even the Republic forbade its representation, as it forbade the exhibition of the royal bees.

When the Bonapartes returned to power the violet again became popular, and when Napoleon the Little led Eugenie to the altar the sturdy women of the markets offered a huge cluster of violets to her. Till then she had been all smiles, but when the purple mass appeared she turned pale, her figure lost its queenly dignity, and tears sprang to her eyes. The women whispered, "It is the funeral flower; the token of ill luck." And when Eugenie had become an exile in England and wore mourning for her son, killed by savages in Africa, they said, "The flowers foretold it." And purple, being a funeral color, it was fitting that her husband, the emperor, should be carried to his tomb under a pall of woven violets, as he was.

MYTHS AND LEGENDS OF FLOWERS

Of late the violet has been mentioned in reports of the medical faculty, claims having been made for its uses in the alleviation and even cure of cancer. Infusions and poultices of the leaves are alleged to be of benefit, these reviving a practice of the time of James I., for in his day the herbalist Culpepper wrote, "It is a fine and pleasing plant of Venus, of a mild nature and no way hurtful. It is used to cool any heat or distemperature of the body, either inwardly or outwardly, as in inflammation of the eyes, in imposthumes and hot swellings, to drink the decoction of the leaves and flowers made with water or wine, or to apply them as poultices to the affected parts."

Our eastern tribes of red men have a legend that a Hercules who had killed a giant heron that preyed on his people invaded the fastnesses of the witches in the mountains, brought away the medicine roots that cured the plague, and defeated a hostile tribe, saw in the camp of the heathen people a girl so fair that his rest was broken from that hour. He stole from his own lodge, night after night, to run through woods and over hills, to guide his canoe across ponds and rivers, that he might be near his loved one and breathe the same air with her. He recited her perfections to the stars and sang his love in terms of such music that the birds listened and their warbling was sweeter when they had heard. After he had waited for several moons to meet the girl, his patience was rewarded, for she wandered into the wood one day, and springing from his concealment, he seized and ran with her toward his own village. Her people, who followed all the night, and at dawn came up with the pair, were the more furious when they saw that the girl had already plighted troth to her captor, for she had wound the braids of her hair about his neck, in token that they were married. No time was given for explanations; the tribe fell upon both the abductor and the maid and killed them on the spot, leaving the bodies on the earth as they marched gloomily back to their camp. When the sun shone warm in spring a shy new flower appeared amid the winter wreckage that the winds had showered over the dead lovers- it

MYTHS AND LEGENDS OF FLOWERS

was the violet; and to the red man this signifies courage, love, and devotion, for the birds carried its seed to every land, as if they were carrying tokens of these qualities for the delight of men and maids. And on the little petals may be seen the strands of the Indian girl's hair, which she had bound as a tender chain about her lover's neck. And the red men know the plant as "heads entangled."

VINES

Once a year, when the moon is bright, the spirit of Charlemagne arises, clothed in the shadows of his ancient state, and wanders beside the Rhine, enjoying the green of the vines and the fragrance of the grapes he planted there. Then he crosses the stream on a bridge of mist and light, and if, on reaching the center, he is seen to lift his hand in blessing, a rare vintage will follow. For in his day, as in ours, the vine was one of the glories of the Fatherland, as it is of other countries that produce the cheering juice. It has become the symbol of refuge and shelter, and we still speak of the vine and fig-tree as typifying home. In Italy some relic of its ancient use as sanctuary appears to be denoted in the play of children, who make it "goal," where they are safe from the touch of the boy who must tag his playmates.

In days old and new it crowned the revel and bespoke the joys of the cup that cheers and also inebriates. For as the pawnbroker is known by the sign of the three gilt balls, adapted from the Lombard coat of arms, and as the barber perpetuates on his pole a representation of the bandaged arm that betokened his former trade of blood letting, so the bush, till recent years denoting that drink was for sale beneath it- though we have the Shakesperean assurance that good wine needs no bush- was but a fragment of the vine that yielded the grapes. When we speak of the vine we commonly mean that which produces grapes: the "life-giving tree" whose leaves crowned Bacchus, and whose spirit filled his sinful old skin. Saturn gave it to Crete, Osiris gave it to Egypt, while Geryon carried it to Spain. The spies that Israel sent into Palestine returned with a bunch of grapes so heavy that it took two of them to carry it. In Persia a woman who had intended to poison herself drank some juice of the grape that had become fermented, and astonished herself and her family by her playfulness and mirth, also by her long sleep and headache. She had made a discovery, and before the frightfulness of her example was realized the fame of the spoiled grape juice had gone abroad.

Vines of all kinds ask for human liking and forbearance. Their grace, their dependence on other objects for support, the beauty of their leafage and efflorescence, have caused them to appear often in literary figures, and the ivy and oak, as representing woman and man, are a common enough item in toasts and other preconcerted eloquence. Every vine, unless it might be poison ivy, and that is less harmful than is popularly supposed, may be said to express the gentler qualities. Hymen's altar was decked with ivy, in token of the clinging love of woman; and if you wear a wreath of it, you are empowered to distinguish between good women and bad, for you will learn to know witches when you see them. You may also eat its berries as a medicine against plague. The cultivation of the ivy may date as far back as the Arthurian reign; at least, when Isolde died, lamenting her Tristan, King Mark, in his anger, buried them apart; but an ivy that grew from Tristan's breast soon met another that grew from Isolde's grave, and the vines twined together, declaring the loves of the unfortunates. Seeing this, the king recognized their love as natural, if not righteous, and buried them together in his church.

What is known as ground ivy, or periwinkle, yellow bugle, gill-by-the-ground, haymaid's cat's foot, ale hoof, and tun hoof, was a substitute for hops in ale, but that was probably before the time of Henry VIII. who amended for his morals, as well as he could, by introducing into England turkeys, mackerel, beer, and hops, the latter in Russia typifying joy and plenty, and so serving as a crown for brides. But the hop surely was never so powerful a medicine as the ivy, for all parts of the latter were once used by the faculty; stem, root, leaf, bark, and gum. If cooked in wine, its extract was sovereign against burns and sores, and Bacchus, the wise god, taught his worshipers to crown themselves with its leaves when they drank deep, and so prevent a frenzy. It was a common belief, when ivy was a crown for poets and conquerors, that it was a proper head-dress for topers likewise, for it preserved them against the self-sought effects of alcohol. Because of these worldly associations, the church long refused to allow the plant to be brought indoors, even as a holiday decoration for its altars, but it has become an outward decoration for more churches than houses, and at Christmas takes its place with other green things, signifying neither the ambition of the soldier, the afflatus of the poet, nor the drunkard's base content, but enduring life. That toleration of the heathen vine had become established so early as the twelfth century, this legend of Florence will signify: In that time there stood beside a convent in the city a tall tree clothed with ivy, such as covered also the walls of the retreat. The brethren preserved a tradition that if the ivy fell from the tree it would also perish from the walls, and if the walls were once uncovered the place itself was in danger. A fearful plague broke out in Florence. Appeals for help came from every hand.

As the monastery was rich and populous, the citizens flocked to it in numbers, beseeching aid, but the abbot told them, sternly, that the affairs of monks were affairs of heaven, not of men; hence he begged them to be gone, for he could give no succor. Indeed, the rules of his order forbade the inmates to go forth into the world; they could not relieve the sick, minister to the dying, nor bury the dead. A family entered the monastery grounds, nevertheless, a day or two later, and begged for refuge. The gate-keeper answered, "The brethren are at prayer and cannot be interrupted. But you may take the shelter of the trees."

MYTHS AND LEGENDS OF FLOWERS

Half ill, wholly disheartened, the fugitives plodded wearily into the garden and flung themselves upon the earth in the shade of the ivy, hoping that food and medicine might presently be served. They found a certain rest in the silence, and coolness, the color of the flowers was sweet in their nostrils, the chanting of the monks was pleasant in their ears; but hour after hour went by, and still there came no help. The fever was beginning to work. Toward sundown the eldest of the family, divining that there was to be no shelter for him or his loved ones that night, arose and solemnly cursed the monastery and its inmates, while his youngest child, in petulance, hacked at the ivy on the tree till it was severed from its root. When at last the monks had finished their services for the day and come into the garden for the air and to lighten their eyes with the sunset, the people who had asked their shelter were at the last gasp; the swift plague had done its work. Next day the ivy was dead on the tree, and its leaves were falling over the earth, brown and withered. Gathering his monks about him, the abbot offered new prayers for the salvation of the monastery, realizing for the first time that one might be as selfish in his search for heaven as in the search for wealth and power and pleasure. He urged them to amend for their mistake, and to that end he set aside the rule of close confinement and bade them go abroad and give service where they might. They did so willingly, but it was too late. Already the plague was sweeping through the town, and now it appeared among the brethren themselves. As the ivy on the convent grew sere and dropped its leaves, so the souls of men who had lived for tranquil years behind this mask of green cast off their bodies and sought the light. No hand replanted the ivy: the doom foretold had come, and today the buildings are in ruin.

WALLFLOWER

Troubadours and knights often affected the wallflower, carrying it in their caps during their enterprises up and down the world, to express constancy to the feminine ideal. It doubtless

MYTHS AND LEGENDS OF FLOWERS

came to type that virtue because of its clinging to the wall where it had been set ; also because of its indomitable flowering the whole summer long. The *cheiranthus cheiri*- Chaucerized as cherisaunce, and likewise known as heart's ease, wall violet, winter gilliflower, blood-drops-of-Christ, and bloody warrior- had its legendary origin in a castle on the Tweed, whose lord had a fair young daughter, who fell in love with the laird of a neighbor clan, desperately hated by her father. Their secret was discovered, with the result that the maid was confined to the castle. But the Romeo in the case loved his Juliet with a fervor that dared all things, so in the disguise of a minstrel he obtained entrance, and, sitting in apparent carelessness beneath the window where he knew she was listening, he strummed his lute and sang a tale which he knew would translate itself readily to her ear. When she heard a moor-cock call in the night, she was to slip from her room to the rampart. He would contrive to throw to her a rope which she was to fasten to a battlement and let herself down into his arms. The call was sounded, the maid crept out upon the platform, and caught the rope that was thrown to her, but she fastened it improperly and so fell to the cruel stones and died. The powers of white magic that prevailed about the place took belated pity and changed her body to the wallflower, so a new form of beauty appeared where one more prized had been.

WALNUT

The Greeks, who knew it as the Persian tree and royal tree, dedicated the walnut to Diana, and her feasts were held beneath it; yet, like the Romans, they gave to it other than a chaste significance when they strewed its nuts at weddings, to denote fecundity. In later times, yokels have used the nuts in telling fortunes, for spirits, commonly of evil, lurk in its branches and exert an influence! over its fruit, and over those who use it. There was a walnut in old Rome that was so filled o' nights with mischievous imps that they became a public scandal, and some centuries ago it was found necessary to cut it down and build the Church of Santa Maria del Popolo on its site. It is a common belief that its leaves and husks are so astringent as to be harmful to other vegetation, especially to grass and herbage on which they fall in autumn, wherefore the tree came to an ill renown, as poisonous. The use of the juices of its nut husks to stain the face, impart a gypsy complexion, or serve as other disguise, should give the lie to this assertion, but in England it is common to find hostility to the walnut among farmers, who declare that the black walnut will not only prevent the growth of plants and grass beneath it, but will blight all the apples round about.

In some countries the peasantry will assemble about the tree and heartily cudgel it, though if you ask why they do this thing they tell you that it is to make it yield more plentifully. In Russia they have a dreadful saying: "A dog, and a wife and a walnut tree; the more you beat them, the better they be." Possibly it is the nut of the whipped tree that used to be found effective in averting thunderbolts, fevers, and spells, and it has a most precious property in that, if dropped under a chair in which a witch is seated, she will find it impossible to rise. The Lithuanian legend of the deluge will in part explain these virtues, for in that the deity was eating nuts while the waters overwhelmed the earth, and the righteous, climbing into the shells as they fell upon the surface of the sea, found in each an ark, and so escaped the death that was dealt to the wicked. The walnut is a melancholy tree, for in parts of the old world, as you walk beneath it of an evening, you may hear the servants of the devil whispering, snickering, and gibbering in its branches. A famously bad tree of this type was the walnut of Benevento, for the unchristianized of its neighborhood worshiped it and performed unhallowed rites in the darkness which was made by the spread of its branches. They jogged on in their wickedness and content till the time came to let understanding into their heads, and this ungrateful task fell to the Emperor Constantius. There was a great deal of dissatisfaction when he camped before their walls and announced that he was to be a missionary to them, nor did it appear to mend matters when one of their own people, a Saint Barbatus, upbraided them and assured them that the siege, with all the horrors that it promised, was the result of their own slowness in accepting the true religion. Still, if that was all that lay in the way of preventing farther hostilities, they would reform at once; so they were baptized, voted him bishop, and the first use he made of his new authority was in cutting down the walnut. As it fell, a serpent was seen to glide beneath its roots, and, having his suspicions of the reptile, the saint sprinkled holy water on it, whereupon the disguise fell off, and the Evil One was discovered. Having confessed himself, he vanished. So entirely was the curse removed from the walnut that when Saint Agatha crossed the Mediterranean from Catania to Gallipolis a nut shell sufficed for the journey, and she continues to make it in this little bark, every year.

WATER-LILY

In the German fable, the water nymphs hide from the eyes of men by taking the shape of water lilies, resuming the forms of women when the strangers have passed, while the evil nix, or water sprite, lurks beneath the round leaves of the plant and will do a mischief, if he can, to any who try to gather his "sea roses." The Teutons have long employed the lily in ornament and in their heraldry. Seven "swan flower" leaves decorated the Frisian arms, and King Herwic bore a banner of blue embroidered with the same device. This flower, rising through pure water and unfolding to the sun in petals of snow, has been fitly chosen to represent chastity, and the Wallachians, who know it as a scentless flower- it is the American nymphea only that is perfumed- make it the judge of all other blooms, for they hold that every flower has a soul. If those others have used their odors generously and well, they are admitted to St. Peter's gate to bloom thenceforth in paradise; if not, they wither and disappear. In the east the water flower is carried before the dead on the way to burial, as typing the virtues that made the deceased beloved; yet in the folk-lore of the plant it is averse to love, being too pure, no doubt, and a couple of thousand years ago by carrying a water lily one could break the effect of a love potion secretly administered by some too enamored maid or swain. Although the man who renamed the Lake of the Clustered Stars escaped hanging, for all that he called it Tupper's Lake, that sheet of water is as beautiful under one name as the other. Here, on its hilly shore, abode the Saranacs, of whom Wayotah (Blazing Sun) was the chief, and Oseetah (The Bird) the fairest maid. Oseetah loved the tall and sinewy leader; she delighted in his tales of war and his boasting; but her parents had promised her to a younger and less warlike man, and it was her parents, rather than her inclinations, that she felt bound to obey. Wayotah laid strong siege to her heart, but although she marked her flights with tears, she still avoided him until, on his return from a successful campaign against the Tahawi, he followed her across the lake in his canoe. She eluded him when he sought to embrace her; she was silent when he asked her to sing; then, when grown more eager, he advanced toward her with outheld arms, she ran up on a rock projecting over the water and, looking back at him with a glance that made confession of her love, yet raised her hand to warn him back. Wayotah was not to be warned. He was close beside her and smiled as he sought to grasp her hands; but before her intent had been divined, she plunged into the lake and the waters closed above her. The young chief leaped in to the rescue, yet, strangely, nothing could he see of her; she had disappeared as the rain-drop vanishes in the stream. After long waiting and long search, he returns to his village and tells his people of this happening, whereon there is long lamenting, and the girl's parents are sore stricken. Next day a hunter comes running to the village with amazement in his eyes. "Flowers are growing in the water!" he cries; and the people hurry to see. Their fleet of canoes is speeded toward the Island of Elms, and there it is as the messenger has said; the lake is white and gold with bloom, and the air deliciously perfumed. "This was not so yesterday," exclaim the men. "Tell us what this means," demand the women, of their prophet. He answers, "This bed of flowers is Oseetah, changed in death to these forms of life. Her heart was as pure as these petals; her love burned like the gold they enclose. Watch, and you will discover that the flower unfolds in the warmth of the sun, and when it sets its life will be darkened, and it will close and sleep on the surface of the lake." Then Wayotah went into the forest and sat with head bowed toward the earth.

WILLOW

People who have been brought up under the kindly influences of old china will remember the plates and cups of willow pattern that decorated their sideboards; but it is likely that many of them have never heard the tradition attaching to the picture. The tale is this: Koong Shee, winsome daughter of a mandarin, loved Chang, her father's secretary. When this attachment was discovered, the stern parent forbade the marriage and imprisoned the girl in the house shown at the left of the plate, with a lake before it. From the window she could see the water and the willow that overhung the bridge, and she wrote despairing poems telling how she longed to be free that she might see the peach tree bloom. Chang smuggled comfort to her in messages enclosed in shells of coconuts that were sent for her refection, and she committed to the lake a shell with a tiny sail; a sail of ivory on which was written, "Do not wise farmers gather the fruits they fear may be stolen?" Chang, wandering by the shore, disconsolate, saw the shell dancing over the water, lifted it out, read the message, and took heart. The meaning was plain; if Chang wanted his bride he must take her. And he did. Disguised as a traveling priest, he gained admission to the pavilion where the fair one was kept, and, gathering her jewels and other consolations, the two fled hastily, crossing the bridge where the willow rioted in defiance of all the natural laws. Before they had crossed the bridge the old mandarin was after them with a whip, and if you look closely you will see the escaping pair, Chang

MYTHS AND LEGENDS OF FLOWERS

with the jewel box, Koong Shee with a distaff, and the parent with the lash, crossing the bridge in sedate procession. Being young, nimble, and eager, the lovers were presently out of reach, and, taking the boat, which is pictured as crossing the lake in the middle distance, found safety in the pagoda-like house on the farther shore, and there they lived in peace till the rich old codger who had expected to become the husband of the girl discovered their retreat, and set fire to their home, burning them to death. The plate farther illustrates what happened, for you will observe that just above the willow are two doves in full flight. They are the spirits of the lovers continuing in another form the endearments that jealousy interrupted in their human shape.

Willow figures in a Japanese tale or allegory as the humble companion of a tall and luxuriant bamboo. It was when the world was young and new plants were coming into it every little while, some of them to be pleasantly greeted by the early comers, others snubbed, somewhat as quiet mortals have been snubbed by those more aggressively conscious of superiority. And so, when an unknown plant, a timid, pleading sort of thing, came out of the ground between the bamboo and the willow, the bamboo tossed her plumes and turned away, muttering that there were too many upstarts. The willow, old, gnarly, but more kind, whispered through its leaves to the little plant, bidding it take courage, for the sun was shining and the rain falling for everything that grew. Still, the liking of the infant was for the bamboo : it stood so tall and proud and shapely. "Let me take hold of you till I can feel my strength," it pleaded. But the bamboo swung itself away, and bade the child plant keep its distance. Again the willow spoke: "Grip your little green fingers into my bark. I shall not mind. You will find in my shadow strength and protection. Lean against me and don't be afraid."

Still looking toward the bamboo, the little plant crept over the grass to the willow, and the old tree seemed to lift it to itself. After a time it was not the willow that sheltered the vine so much as it was the vine that sheltered the willow, for it had grown to its top and was flaunting banners of green as if in gladness at the completion of the ascent. Tree and vine established a loving unity and were fair to look on. And having put out all its leaves, the vine began to bud. Once again the bamboo deigned to look at it. "And what," it asked, "are those unsightly knobs that are growing on that vine? Some disease, belike, that the creature has brought among us and may afflict the entire country." The willow made no answer and whispered the vine to take no notice; so with a rustling sneer the bamboo tossed its head again and contemplated the distance. But when the next sun arose the buds burst and the old willow was decked from crown to foot with glorious color and bathed in perfume. And the owner of the land called his friends to see the wonder, for it was a gift of the gods. His men gazed in admiration. "We must clear a space about it," said the lord, "to see its beauty the better. Keep the willow, but cut this bamboo." "It is a fine and straight bamboo," his laborers objected. "Yes, and so is much of its kind, whereas no man has seen the like of this vine before."

And that was done which had been ordered. And the beauty of pride and the pride of beauty were as naught. It is claimed that the weeping willow took its name, not from the drooping habit of its branches, but from association with those of Israel, who hung their harps upon it and gave themselves to tears because they were troubled. Long before that time, the sisters of Phaeton, wailing his death when he fell from the car of the sun, were changed into willows, and the long green streamers they put forth were as cascades of tears. The tree has been fond of dampness ever since. And on such a grove of willows the sorceress Circe hanged those of her suitors who least pleased her, the others being changed into beasts. The association of the willow with death and the uncanny is denoted also in the custom of planting it in cemeteries- a custom inaugurated by the Chinese, thousands of years ago. Sprays of willow are strewn on coffins in China, for, being of long life, it is a reminder of immortality; and it is often used as a decorative motive in Chinese art. In some countries its branch is a wand of divination and implement of protection against evil spirits; at least, it preserved Orpheus from the fiends when he descended into hell. The willow bears a curse, inasmuch as it is one of the several trees on which Judas hanged himself, being planted by the devil in order to lure people to suicide by the peculiar restful swinging of its branches. It begets snakes, while its ashes drives them away. It is a meeting place and abiding place of witches, for if a witch embarks deliberately on her career of evil, her first step is to a willow, where, sitting on its root, she solemnly forswears God and all holy things; then, writing her name in her own blood on the book that the devil offers, she consigns herself to eternal torment. So, if you shall be tramping a desolate country alone between the middle of the night and the break of day, and shall hear a voice luring or laughing from a thicket of willows, beware, for it is Kundry, the witch of "Parsifal," who is there. She is that Herodias who asked the head of John the Baptist, and who, as Christ went to his death, laughed at Him. Christ turned one reproving look upon her, then bade her go into the world and wander till his return, forbidding her the solace of tears when she was weary of her fate- a form of the legend of the Wandering Jew.

Apart from tales and superstitions that associate the willow with tragedies and mishaps, is the English faith that it had virtues on Palm Sunday when used as a substitute for the palm; for its branches on that day became valuable for healing and the aversion of spells. It had of old a purifying agency. The *agnus castus*, a variety of willow, yielded beds for maids in the festivals of Ceres, where they might sleep and retain their innocence, its repute coming down to later times when it became the piper mona-Chorum, because its odor expelled impure thoughts. Hence monks made girdles of its withes, declaring that "it withstandeth all uncleanness or desire to the flesh." In our country the weeping willow is an exotic, the first one coming to us through the agency of Alexander Pope, the English poet, who stripped it, a tough green withe, from a box of fruit sent from Smyrna to his friend Lady Suffolk. "Perhaps," said he, "this will produce something that we have not in England." Pope set the twig into the earth on Thames bank, at his villa in Twickenham, and a young British officer tweaked a small limb from it long after, intending to plant it in our soil. He came with the king's troops to the Colonies, and, never doubting the success of the royal arms, had decided to settle in America on the conclusion of the war and end his years on the big estates he expected to receive from the beaten enemy. When the war ended he gave the twig, which he had preserved in a wrapping of oiled silk, to John Parke Custis, son of Mrs. Washington, who planted it on the Abingdon estate, in Virginia, where it rooted and flourished, and from that ancestor have come all the weeping willows in America. The willow at Twickenham was chopped down by the Briton who bought the property, because travelers came in such shoals to worship under it and cut souvenirs and ask questions, that they interfered with his privacy.

Another willow that has multiplied itself from cuttings, and grows by proxy in many lands, is that on St. Helena's island, beneath which Napoleon often sat and thought on his fallen fortunes. On the night of his death it was uprooted by a storm.

WORMWOOD

Wormwood, absinthium, is the poisonous ingredient in absinthe that causes so many antics in Europe. If it be rubbed over a child's hands before he is twelve weeks old, wormwood will keep moths out of his hair, and he will never suffer from heat or cold. Curiously, this herb was steeped in the wines of the ancients in order to counteract their alcohol, and it likewise defended one against hemlock, shrew mice, and sea dragons. The variety known as mugwort takes the name of artemisia from Artemis, wife of Mausolus, though some say it is Artemis, the

MYTHS AND LEGENDS OF FLOWERS

Greek Diana, and it was therefore used in female disorders, as well as in the secret incantations wherewith one brought the spirits of the dead and the fiends of the netherworld to the surface.

"Eat muggins in May" and escape consumption, poison, tire, bills, beasts, and other disorderly besetments. Made into a cross and put on the roof, mugwort will be blessed by Christ Himself, hence it must not be taken down for a year. A Russian, passing through a wood, fell into a pit of serpents who guarded a shining stone which served them as food if only they licked it, and she, too, was kept alive in this manner. In the spring the snakes bound themselves into a ladder by which she climbed out of their den and so into the world of light and green things. As she was about to leave them, the queen of the snakes granted to her the power of understanding the speech and uses of plants, on condition that she never named the mugwort; but when suddenly asked by a stranger what grew beside the path, she answered, "Tohornobil" (mugwort), and her mystic knowledge forsook her. So one Russian name for it is "herb of forgetfulness."

YEW

The yew attains great size and great age, one in the churchyard of Fortingal, Perthshire, being said to be two thousand five hundred years old. One in Hedsor, Buclas, is twenty-seven feet around, and three thousand two hundred and forty years of age, but the oldest living thing on earth is a yew in Chapultepec, Mexico, one hundred and nineteen feet around and six thousand two hundred and sixty years old. Yew furnished bows in the day when the archer was your only soldier, and the only hunter. This use of it for bows gave to the tree its botanical name, *taxus haccata*, or bow yew. With bows fashioned from its tough wood, Robin Hood and his robbing horde enforced their demands in Sherwood Forest. After swearing fealty to Richard, life was dull for Robin, and he did not sorrow deeply when the king died, leaving him free to resume his career; but times had changed; poaching, theft, and violence were not in their old favor; the pestered community declined to accept them as jokes any longer. So they took to hunting the hunters. Then Maid Marian, wife or mistress of the bandit, died, and life lost its relish for him. Next came an order from the new king, urging that all highwaymen be hunted down, and offering rewards for Robin, who was hurt presently in a fight with the king's men. He bade Little John help him to Kirkley Hall, where his sister, abbess of a convent, kept a room prepared for him, and where he was made as comfortable as possible. But his wounds were beyond surgery. With his horn at his lips, he sounded the three blasts by which he was used to summon his band, and Little John ran in, knowing that the end was near, for the sound was faint. As he entered the room, the dying man asked for his good yew bow and arrows. "Bury me where this arrow falls," he entreated; then, fitting an arrow to the string, he shot. The missile fell at the foot of a yew which might have yielded such a bow as he held in his unconscious grasp. A sigh, and Robin Hood was a memory. The mortal part of him they buried, as he had bidden, under the yew.

That Robin's yew was growing in a graveyard is significant of a practice that extended back to the Ptolemies in Egypt, and was implanted in Greece and Rome where yew fed the cinerary fires, was carried in procession at funerals, and placed in the grave before the body was lowered- this last a ceremony that survives in the Egyptian custom of throwing basil over tombs, in the masonic rite of casting acacia into a grave, and in a growing usage of lining graves with evergreen to soften the asperity of the cold, wet earth. There was a sanitary motive for planting yew in cemeteries, inasmuch as it was believed to drink up the poisonous exhalations from ground infected by the dead- true, in a measure, of all plants. An English legend gives a ghastly significance to this churchyard tree, for it recites that a priest, having fixed the eyes of love on a girl of his congregation, became so enraged at her refusal to elope with him that he killed her and cut off her head. This relic being hung upon a yew limb imparted sanctity to the tree, for it symbolized martyrdom for righteousness's sake, and the people collected pieces of the bark as charms, especially prizing those filaments that might be likened to hair. Hence the name of the town where the tragedy was enacted: Halifax, meaning, holy hair. In Vreton, Brittany, is another holy yew that sprang from St. Thomas's staff, and was so revered that not only did the people refrain from touching it, but birds would not pick its berries. A band of pirates, seeing how stout it was, climbed into it to cut bows and spears, but while at this employ the branches broke and in their fall the skulls of the rogues were cracked beyond repair.

YLANG-YLANG

Like the locust and wistaria, the ylang-ylang of the Philippines bears its flowers in drooping, greenish-yellow clusters, which emit a delightful fragrance. For years the perfumers of Europe and America have used them in their preparations, and until the coal tar products of the synthetic chemist have driven flower juices out of the market, the ylang-ylang will continue to be prized, by all except the Tulisanes. And why not by them? Well, to begin at the beginning, they had incurred the displeasure of Naga, greatest of the many gods that were worshiped in Pauay, and whose likenesses in the groves and temples were of a particular wood, held sacred to his use, a rare wood, hard and handsome. Every town and hamlet had its statue of Naga, and it received worship and offerings each day. Naga was not a handsome god; at least, he had several mouths, one above the other, a disfigurement, or circumstance, that has left its effect on the handles of the native bolos, which are sometimes carved with faces suggesting his. What it was that excited the ire of Naga against the Tulisanes has been forgotten in the night of history. But Naga determined to exterminate them, and, to that end, he blighted their crops so that they should die of hunger; and marked them for accident and pestilence. They could abide it no longer, but came trooping down from the mountains, and took a fearful revenge on Naga by smashing all his images and burning all the trees from which they had been carved.

The other tribes gave battle, and eventually drove the Tulisanes back into the mountains, but the dreadful problem of providing new statues of the god confronted the victors, for unless such figures were erected in the towns the people would forget him, and he would not receive his due of praise. It was resolved to release a captive bird and use as wood for the statues that of the tree on which he should alight. The bird perched on the ylang-ylang. Then, behold, a miracle; the tree, which had never borne fruit nor flower before, now burst into bloom, and each little bird-like flower filled the air with a fragrance such as till then had never been breathed. Naga had sanctified the tree; and from that time all the likenesses that were made of him were carved from its wood. Is it any wonder that the Tulisanes regarded this survival of their enemy in the clouds with discontent?

THE END

Made in United States
Orlando, FL
08 September 2024